GW00818658

MRS DAR
PAGAN ELI

A Celebration of Air, Fire, Water, Earth and Divine Spirit

MRS DARLEY'S
PAGAN ELEMENTS

*A Celebration of Air, Fire, Water,
Earth and Divine Spirit*

Carole Carlton

First edition
Published in Great Britain
By Mirage Publishing 2010

Text Copyright © Carole Carlton 2010

First published in paperback 2010

A CIP catalogue record for this book
Is available from the British Library.

ISBN: 978-1-90257-865-1

Mirage Publishing
PO Box 161
Gateshead
NE8 4WW
Great Britain

Printed and bound in Great Britain by

Book Printing UK
Remus House, Coltsfoot Drive, Woodston, Peterborough, PE2 9JX, UK

Cover © Mirage Publishing
Layout by Artistic Director Sharon Anderson

Papers used in the production of this book are recycled,
thus reducing environmental depletion.

To my precious parents whose love gave me life.

Contents

Introduction: The Elements   9

Chapter 1   Air   17
Chapter 2   Fire   75
Chapter 3   Water   155
Chapter 4   Earth   233
Chapter 5   Ether   303

Other titles   315

Disclaimer

Disclaimer: the entire contents of this book are based upon research conducted by the author, unless otherwise noted. The publisher, the author, the distributors and bookstores present this information for educational purposes only. Any exercises presented here, either physical or mental, are to be practiced with caution. Should you experience any discomfort or trauma from any of the processes involved you are advised to stop. This information is not intended to diagnose or prescribe for medical or psychological conditions or to claim to prevent, treat, mitigate or cure such conditions. The author and the publisher are not making an attempt to recommend specific products as treatment of disease, and neither do they have any financial interest in the sale of the substances described in this book. In presenting this information, no attempt is being made to provide diagnosis, care, treatment or rehabilitation of individuals, or apply medical, mental health or human development principles, to provide diagnosing, treating, operating or prescribing for any human disease, pain, injury, deformity or physical condition. The information contained herein is not intended to replace a one-on-one relationship with a doctor or qualified health care professional. Therefore, the reader should be made aware that this information is not intended as medical advice, but rather a sharing of knowledge and information from the research and experience of the author. The publisher and the author encourage you to make your own health care decisions based upon your research and in partnership with a qualified health care professional. You and only you are responsible if you choose to do anything based on what you read.

Introduction

The Elements

Tread Softly
Sail lightly on the wind my love,
Sail lightly on the wind,
For here the Goddess breathes my love
Sail lightly on the wind.

Dance wildly in the fire my love,
Dance wildly in the fire,
For here the Goddess lives my love
Dance wildly in the fire.

Drink deeply of the lake my love,
Drink deeply of the lake,
For the here the Goddess bathes my love
Drink deeply of the lake.

Tread softly on the earth my love,
Tread softly on the earth,
For there the Goddess sleeps my love
Tread softly on the earth.

The Elements
To have an understanding of the four classical elements
of air, fire, water and earth is to have an appreciation of
what is essential in order to survive on our beautiful
planet. To have an understanding of the mysterious fifth

element of ether or Divine Spirit is to have an appreciation of the sanctity of life.

Mrs Darley's Pagan Elements sets out to explore the classical elements, from their appearance in the natural world to the Deities, elementals and mythical creatures which have become associated with them over millennia.

The elements, however, extend far beyond their physical form and exist symbolically on the subconscious plane as thoughts, intuition, feelings and sensations, all of which are investigated throughout the book.

The element of ether is one of mystery and is not something that can be easily taught or explained, hence the concise nature of the final chapter. Ether has to be considered, intuited, felt and experienced by the individual and this book offers the reader an invitation to explore.

The many and varied aspects of each element are brought to life by the esoteric teachings of the often eccentric and yet delightfully wise Mrs Darley, my once next door neighbour when I lived on the south eastern edge of Bodmin Moor in Cornwall during the early 1990's. She not only opened my eyes to the mysteries of life but encouraged me to look at the world from a different view point.

A selection of Mrs Darley's charming friends, also welcomed me into their lives, each one colouring my world with their knowledge and often leading me beyond the confines of this realm to brush the threshold of the next.

Mrs Darley Tale: The Comet
We sat before the burning brazier, Mrs Darley and I, her face glowing in the firelight as long wisps of stray dark hair floated about her head, bringing a youthful yet

almost ethereal quality to her features.

I noticed, as I looked around, that there was evidence of some earlier activity around the fire. There were several empty glasses and plates stacked on a tray by the steps, whilst a wooden chest was secreted beneath Mrs Darley's chair upon which sat a neatly folded cloth.

My suspicions were aroused and I began to wonder what type of gathering had taken place here earlier in the evening. On one hand I felt relieved that I had perhaps missed what I suspected was a sojourn into the magical realms, for this still made me a little nervous, whilst on the other hand I felt strangely left out.

'A few of us got together this evening, dear,' said Mrs Darley, obviously noticing my eyes scanning the scene, 'we were celebrating and giving thanks for what is a very rare and exciting time.'

'Why is it a rare and exciting time?' I asked.

'Strange events always herald a time of change, of movement, of new beginnings, of discovery and that,' she said pointing towards the sky, 'is a clear message from the universe to mankind, telling us to wake up and become conscious of the needs of our planet, of our fellow man and of ourselves.'

I lifted my eyes towards the black abyss of space and once again was lost in wonder at the beauty of the Hyakutake Comet as it lay across the heavens, for tonight it was almost fluorescent green.

Earlier in the evening I had attended what turned out to be a most peculiar dinner party in Tavistock and on my way back home I stopped the car just outside St Anne's Chapel in order to admire the comet as it lay in an emerald swathe above the Tamar Valley.

'It is beautiful,' I murmured, 'And yet I suppose it's just made up of bits of debris and rocks?'

11

Mrs Darley's Pagan Elements

'Nothing, my dear, ever comprises of just one thing or one element and a comet is no different. You might like to think of a comet as a cosmic iceberg orbiting through space and, as it is warmed by the sun, it gives off various gases and particles of dust, allowing us to see and admire the spectacular tail that follows.'

'That's rather interesting,' I murmured.

'Well, my dear, just like the comet, we each contain a little of the four elements, whether on a physical or subconscious level.'

'Do we?' I asked. 'I understand the concept of the four elements of air, fire, water and earth but I don't really know what you mean by them being present in our subconscious.'

'Ah,' said Mrs Darley. 'Well, my dear, as you are beginning to learn, everything upon this earth is not always as it seems and the elements are no different. In fact most people don't even give them a second thought and yet without each and every one of them life here would not exist in its present form.'

'I agree with that,' I smiled, 'so tell me more.'

'Perhaps another time my dear, it's getting rather late.'

'Please,' I said, 'just for a minute or two?'

Mrs Darley smiled. 'Very well,' she said, 'just until the embers die away.'

I nodded, grateful for just a gem or two of wisdom before I went to bed.

'We will begin then with the element of air. Air is essential to life; it is our very breath, it gives us space in which to move, it is the wind that kisses our cheek, it is Nike; the winged Goddess of Victory, it is the abode of the bird, the bee, the moth and the bat. It carries words of love, songs of joy and the sounds of nature. It brings us light from the sun and the first smell of summer, whilst in the depths of our subconscious it symbolises the realm of thought, inspiration and imaginings. It is purified by the sylph elementals and carries the seeds of our dearest hopes and our wildest dreams.'

'Well,' I said, 'I never realised, in fact, I've never even considered just how important the element of air is and how it affects almost every aspect of daily life. What about fire?'

'Fire is housed within the sun, without which the earth would not be able to sustain life in its present form. It manifests in erupting volcanoes, in lightning strikes and is a necessary requirement for a rainbow to be seen. It is the abode of the elemental salamander and brings us the comfort of the domestic fire and the flicker of the candle flame, bringing both warmth and light into our lives. We are warm blooded creatures and need fuel with which to produce energy and heat to survive, too little and we become weak and cold, too much and we can experience skin eruptions and fever. Inwardly and symbolically, fire manifests as anger, passion, determination and intuition, encouraging us to blaze our own trail and set the world alight with the essence of who we are.'

'Hence the saying, "having a fire within your belly", I presume?' I asked, beginning to have some understanding of how the symbolic aspects of the elements lived in our subconscious.

'Exactly,' Mrs Darley replied. 'Now water, meanwhile, is in us and around us. We physically comprise of up to seventy percent water, whilst two thirds of the earth's surface is covered in this miraculous substance. We cannot live more than a few days without it and yet most of us do not avail ourselves of this magical liquid. Water heals and purifies, cleanses and

13

soothes. Cared for by the elemental ondines, our oceans and rivers house a myriad of fish and molluscs, plants and mammals, from the microscopic to the largest in the world. Beautiful clouds form from the oceanic waters and the falling rains quench our thirst. In our inner world water symbolises our emotions, whether calm and peaceful or turbulent and chaotic. This element enables us to feel on many levels, from empathising with others, to experiencing the wonder of love and the bitter depths of despair.'

'And earth?' I prompted.

'And earth,' continued Mrs Darley, 'is our home. It is our Mother, our provider. It offers us deeply wooded forests, sheltered mountain caves, rolling hills, fields of corn and a plethora of animals and plants. It is the food on our table and the touch of someone's hand. The earth is always in a constant state of flux beneath our feet, confirming that nothing stays still and that the only constant is change. The earth element is the abode of the gnome and reminds us that we are flesh and blood and should not live our lives in a constant state of otherworldliness but should enjoy the pleasures of the senses of sight and smell, of hearing, taste and touch and in doing so, give thanks to the Divine essence for allowing us this experience.'

I sat in silence for a moment or two after she had finished speaking.

'Of course,' she whispered, drawing close as though we were conspirators, 'there is the fifth element'.

'Which is?' I asked.

'Which is for you to discover,' she said. 'Come, it's late and us earthly creatures will benefit from a good night's sleep.'

I looked up at Hyakutake, giving a moment's thanks

for bringing about this fascinating conversation and knew, deep inside, that I was about to embark on the third phase of my training.

I am
I am the sun,
I am the earth,
I am the life,
I am the birth.

I am the whisper,
I am the dream,
I am the ripple,
I am the stream.

I am the river,
I am the pool,
I am the wise man,
I am the fool.

I am the ocean,
I am the rain,
I am the seed,
I am the grain.

I am the wind,
I am desire,
I am the flame,
I am the fire.

I am the voice,
I am the breath,
I am the end,
I am the death.

Chapter 1

Air

Air
Sweet intoxication of a honey bee's gathering,
Peaceful promises beneath the shadow of the dove.
Love filled words, fired on the arrow of Eros,
Impossible dreams borne upon Ariel's wings.

Angelic lips speak the language of miracles,
Imprisoned souls glimpse the gates of heaven.
Silhouetted crones sweep ebony skies
Releasing still winds and lifting the sail.

Butterfly thoughts flit through muddled minds,
Seizing inspiration from the mouths of the Gods.
The sanctity of life, bestowed upon the first breath,
The freedom to fly, granted with the last.

Introduction
Air is an enigma, intangible, invisible, undetectable by
sight, touch or smell and yet we can see its effects in the
bending of the trees, feel its breath upon our cheek and
smell the sweet scent of summer blooms in the hot, heavy
air of a sultry evening.

Air is vital to life on earth, from flora and fauna to
creatures of land and sea. It is our breath, our life and the
space through which we move.

The skies are a superhighway for creatures of all

shapes and sizes, from the tiniest wren to the majestic eagle, from the humble gnat to the busiest bee. Our butterflies and moths, dragonflies and bats flit effortlessly through the air whilst earthbound creatures such as ourselves can only stand and admire their ability to fly effortlessly towards freedom. Or is it freedom?

Each year over fifty million creatures fly to British shores in order to breed and feed before returning to their winter homes but can this actually be classified as freedom, or is it simply an inbuilt program demanding that they too follow the life patterns of their kind?

Regardless of whether it is freedom or patterning, flight is certainly a phenomenon that has captured the imagination of mankind since the beginning of time and, over millennia, a myriad of flying devices have been invented in order for man to take to the air. Objects such as kites and gliders, balloons and planes, enable us to dance, glide, float and fly through the skies, whisking us away from the mundane and slicing through time and space in order that we might be set down in far flung locations.

Since earliest times mankind has sought to harness the power of the wind to enhance his life. He has built wind farms to provide power, created magnificent sailing ships with which to cross the world's oceans and built beautiful windmills to mill the grain.

Air carries the waves of sound and light, bringing uplifting music and inspiring words to our ears. Air carries to our senses the gift of aromatic molecules and brings a myriad of exquisite aromas into our world.

The element of air however extends far beyond its physical form and also exists symbolically on the sub conscious plane as thoughts, inventions, communication and inspiration and, like the wind is changeable, moveable and beholding to no other element.

It is one of the four elements upon which we depend in order to live; from the moment we take our first breath to the second we breathe our last.

Mrs Darley Tale: The Realm of Thought

'That's quite nonsensical, dear!' said the unmistakable voice of Mrs Darley, her words carrying a note of exasperation as they sailed through the open door into my garden.

I looked up, curious as to the cause of this rather passionate outburst, but with no further disturbance apart from the distant murmur of normal conversation, I returned to my own musings and the blank note book that lay before me on the picnic table.

'You look deep in thought.' Mrs Darley's words made me jump and I dropped the pen that I had been idly twiddling between my fingers.

'Mmmm,' I said looking up, 'I was just thinking how to word a letter to a client in order to hopefully avoid what could be a potentially difficult situation.'

'Ah,' said Mrs Darley, 'you'll be needing this then,' and promptly placed a loganberry fool and a glass of homemade elderflower cordial on the table beside me.

'That looks delicious,' I said, pushing my note pad aside.

'Brain food, dear,' she smiled, 'the words will come all the easier when you've eaten.'

'I hope so,' I sighed. 'Mind you I might leave it 'til later and do my week's paperwork first.'

'More left brain work?' asked Mrs Darley.

'I don't know, is it?'

She nodded, 'everything you do is left brain oriented; admin, figures, form filling, the lap top, in fact you do very little to engage the creative side.'

'I don't have time!' I protested, 'and besides, I'm not very good at the creative arts'.

'Rubbish! she said, 'on both counts! A) You can always make time to do anything, it's just that you choose to fill every moment with work, work and more work and B) Everyone has a creative side, but some people,' she said pointedly, 'choose to bury it and only let the logical brain have a say, therefore becoming totally imbalanced.'

'Oh dear,' I smiled, 'you make me sound quite dull and boring.'

She looked at me and arched her eyebrow.

'So I am dull and boring?' I laughed.

'You have the potential not to be,' she said, getting her point over with a modicum of diplomacy. 'I often think you've forgotten who you really are. You hide behind a mask of smiles and tact, never an opinion of your own, never a controversial word with which to rile someone, always aiming for perfection, just to prevent anyone from saying a bad word about you. You stay within your comfort zone of work and the tasks that surround it, for fear of trying anything new, just in case you fail, just in case you're made to look a fool, but remember my dear, the fool, is the person who fails to try. And yet, very occasionally, perhaps when you're caught unawares or when you allow your mask of perfection to slip, I see a glimpse of the real you through the words that you speak or through a flicker of emotion that fleetingly dances across your face.'

I looked up at her, shielding my eyes from the sun. 'You always have a way of making me look at myself in a new light and not one that I'm always keen to see.'

'Ah well, better our light shines brighter because we

are brave enough to make changes rather than living in the half light of self-denial and obscurity. Phyllis and I do it all the time.'

'Do you?' I asked, somewhat surprised at this candid admission.

Mrs Darley laughed.

'Of course! We all need someone who can see us as we truly are, without bias, without a wish to hurt, yet who will nudge us gently back into the waters of life when we might otherwise flounder on the rocks.

Now then, the right hand side of that brain of yours is crying out for the chance to express itself, so what is it that you intend to do?'

I shook my head, 'I don't know!'

'That's not an answer, or at least not one I'm going to accept. Come on, what were you good at as a child, before you sold your soul to the logical world?'

I laughed, 'Well, I always liked writing I suppose, poems, stories, that sort of thing.'

'Now that wasn't so difficult was it? Did you ever do anything with this love of writing?'

I felt the colour beginning to flood into my cheeks and avoided her gaze, 'I had a few poems published in an anthology when I was fourteen and came second in a short story competition during my twenties.'

'So why the embarrassment?' she asked. 'Why the constant need to hide your light under the biblical bushel?'

I shrugged and was saved from answering by the arrival of Phyllis at the gate.

'Ah there you are,' she said to Mrs Darley, 'I've found a word, that I think sounds so much better than the so-called "nonsensical" one I used earlier.'

'Good!' replied Mrs Darley, 'By the way, I've found a

new member for you to take along to your writers' group next Monday.'

'Who?' asked Phyllis.

Mrs Darley looked at me pointedly.

'I think it must be me,' I said.

The Natural World

The Atmosphere

The atmosphere is amongst the most precious of earth's possessions, for without its protective nature the earth would be unable to sustain life.

It comprises of several distinct layers, which although quite uniform in their chemical make-up, decrease in density with increasing altitude as does the resulting air pressure exerted on the earth. The majority of the atmosphere lies at the lowest levels, with ninety-nine percent of it contained within eighteen miles of the earth's surface.

The atmosphere comprises of ninety-eight percent of dry air, made up as follows:

- 78.09% nitrogen.
- 20.95% oxygen.
- 00.93% argon.
- 00.03% neon, helium, methane, hydrogen, krypton, xenon, nitrous oxide, ozone, radon and carbon dioxide.

The two latter gases not only fluctuate in volume but are also the ones that give scientists most concern, as they feel that both are detrimental to the climate. Add to this the world's toxic cocktail of industry gases such as ammonia, nitrogen dioxide, hydrogen sulphide and sulphur dioxide and the effects can be devastating to the delicate balance of life on earth.

The remaining two percent of the atmosphere comprises of water which is present in three different forms:

1. Water vapour.
2. Liquid water.
3. Ice crystals.

Although only two percent of the earth's water is found in the atmosphere, it nevertheless plays a very important roll, for it lets in incoming light waves and ultraviolet waves but traps outgoing infrared rays, therefore keeping the average temperature of earth at a constant fourteen degrees centigrade.

Water also stores energy from the sun as latent heat and it is the release of this latent energy through temperature changes that causes the formation of huge storm clouds.

The final components of the atmosphere are aerosols. These are microscopic solid particles of dust, volcanic ash, pollen, sand, sea salt and smoke and, despite their size; they too play both a detrimental and beneficial role in the overall effects of the atmosphere.

Some of the particles are released when it rains and can therefore contribute to the effects of acid rain, whilst many aerosols reflect sunlight back towards space thereby reducing the effects of global warming.

The atmosphere comprises of five distinct layers: the Troposphere, Stratosphere, Mesosphere, Thermosphere and the Exosphere. The exosphere has very few atmospheric molecules which can escape into space.

Mrs Darley's Pagan Elements

The Troposphere

This is the lowest layer and extends to approximately five miles high at the poles and ten miles high at the equator. It is the layer where the weather forms and in the higher reaches of the troposphere, the temperature drops dramatically as does the air pressure, which is why mountaineers have to carry an oxygen supply and the cabins of aircraft are pressurised.

The Stratosphere

In 1898, the pioneer of the weather balloon, Leon Teisserenc de Bort, discovered that at around six miles up in the atmosphere, the temperature not only stopped falling but even rose a little, a fact which led to the discovery of the second layer of the atmosphere known as the stratosphere. The stratosphere is eighteen miles thick but contrary to the troposphere, the temperature increases with altitude. This increase in temperature is due to the presence of ozone which lies around sixteen miles above the earth's surface.

Ozone is a highly reactive and toxic gas which comprises of a rare form of oxygen, in that is has three atoms of oxygen (O_3) as opposed to two atoms of oxygen which we normally breathe (O_2). Ozone however, still remains vital to life on earth in so much as it screens out shortwave, ultraviolet solar radiation, which causes sun burn whilst also absorbing radiation and re-emitting it as heat, therefore explaining the rise in temperature in the stratosphere.

Ozone remained stable for thousands of years until the 1920's, when scientists synthesised CFC's (chlorofluorocarbons) or non-flammable gases used in solvents, industrial cleaners, propellants in aerosols and coolants in refrigeration units and were unaware at that point how these revolutionary inventions would impact upon the ozone. In 1983 scientists with the British Antarctic Survey discovered an 'ozone hole' over the South Pole, a fact which subsequently led to worldwide debate and the signing of protocols to phase out the use of CFC's.

The Mesosphere
This layer is to be found approximately thirty miles above the earth's surface and for the first five miles the temperature remains constant, however from here to a height of around fifty miles the temperature falls with altitude, to around minus eighty degrees centigrade, a sharp contrast to the temperatures found in the final layer.

The Thermosphere
The thermosphere stretches from approximately fifty miles above the earth's surface to a height of 350 miles and here the temperature rapidly increases with height, reaching up to 700 degrees centigrade in the outer regions due to the absorption of ultraviolet radiation. Eventually the outer layer of the thermosphere known as the thermopause extends out into the exosphere or interplanetary space where space shuttles and weather satellites orbit at approximately 620 miles and 22,300 miles respectively.

The Exosphere
This final layer extends from the top of the thermosphere to 6,200 miles above the earth. The upper boundary of the exosphere reaches about halfway to the moon, 120,000 miles. This is a transitional zone between earth's atmosphere and interplanetary space. In this region of the atmosphere, hydrogen and helium are the prime

components and are only present at extremely low densities.

The Wind

In times past, the wind was both feared and respected as a Divine force that could both give and take away from mankind and its nature was often determined by the direction from which it came.

The ancient Greeks associated wind directions with different gods and honoured one at each of the four cardinal points. The north wind was called Boreas, the east wind, Apeliotes, the west wind Zephryos and the south wind, Notos.

Aristotle meanwhile, added four intermediate directions to his octagonal wind tower, namely; northwest, northeast, southwest and southeast whilst the Romans added a further sixteen points to their wind rose, bringing the total number of wind directions to twenty four.

So revered were the winds that many of them still carry the evocative names once given to them by differing cultures around the world such as the 'Mistral', the 'Bora', the 'Sirocco' and the 'Chinook' and gradually people began to have an understanding that it was possible to predict the weather according to the direction of the wind.

The earth is in constant motion as is the air around us and it is this constant movement that acts as a worldwide air conditioning unit, transporting warmth from the equatorial regions to the areas of higher latitudes and then returning cooler air back to the tropics.

Although it may seem to us that the winds blow from any direction at any time, it has been discovered that in each place, the wind blows more from one direction than another and these are known as prevailing winds. The most well known are the 'Westerly's', the 'Polar Easterlies' and the 'Trade Winds' and it is knowledge of these prevailing winds that dictate the positioning of manmade structures such as airport runways.

Because the air is constantly moving, it looks for ways to escape from areas of high pressure to areas of low pressure and it is this movement of air that causes the wind. The greater the difference of pressure between the two areas, the stronger the wind, therefore both wind speed and wind direction are dictated by the position of areas of high and low pressure.

In 1805, Sir Francis Beaufort devised the Beaufort scale, a system originally meant for sailors to judge the strength of the wind at sea according to certain visible features. It was later modified for use on land by providing easily visible guidelines such as the direction of smoke, the stability of chimney pots and the movement of trees as illustrated in Table 1.1 below.

Force	Description	Events on Land	KM/H	MPH
0	Calm	Smoke rises vertically	Under 1	0 – 1
1	Light Air	Direction of wind shown by smoke, but not wind vane	1 – 5	1 – 3
2	Light Breeze	Wind felt on the face, leaves rustle, wind vane turns to wind	6 – 11	4 – 7
3	Gentle Breeze	Leaves and small twigs in motion, small flags spread	12 - 19	8 -12
4	Moderate Breeze	Wind raises dust and loose paper, small branches move	20 - 29	13 -18
5	Fresh Breeze	Small leafy trees sway, wavelets with crests on inland	30 - 39	19 - 24

		waters		
6	Strong Breeze	Large branches move, whistling in telephone wires, hard to use an umbrella	40 -45	25 - 31
7	Near Gale	Whole trees in motion, difficult to walk against the wind	51 – 61	32 - 38
8	Gale	Twigs break from trees, hard to walk	62 – 74	39 – 46
9	Strong Gale	Slightly structural damage to buildings, chimney pots, roof tiles and TV aerials removed	75 – 87	47 -54
10	Storm	Trees uprooted, considerable damage to buildings, cars overturn	88 -101	55 – 63
11	Violent storm	Widespread damage to all types of building	102 – 119	64 – 74
12	Hurricane	Widespread destruction: only specially constructed buildings survive	120+	75+

Table 1.1

As well as prevailing winds, there are also daily and seasonal winds which cause air movement at specific times of the day or year.

On a daily basis certain winds are generated due to solar heating. The air over the land warms up and cools down faster than over the sea and it is these contrasts that cause land or offshore breezes and sea or onshore breezes.

Some winds however occur at different times of year such as the 'Sirocco' wind, whose effects are even felt in Britain. This hot wind occurs in the spring and blows dry dust filled air from the North African deserts across Europe as far as the UK where it deposits the sand as 'red rain' or 'blood rain'. Scientists estimate that a staggering 3.3 billion tons of dust is carried away each year from these African deserts, some of which is carried high into the atmosphere and eventually comes back to earth as far north as Greenland and the Caribbean.

Hurricanes and Tornadoes

All of the winds discussed so far have been relatively gentle however the really big winds such as hurricanes and tornadoes are created by several factors such as air masses and weather systems.

An air mass is a body of air that covers most of a continent or ocean and acquires certain characteristics from the earth's surface directly beneath it. For example, air over a continental land mass will be drier than air over the ocean and will also be warmer in the summer and drier in the winter.

When different air masses meet, they are unable to simply merge together due to the fact that they are of different temperatures and densities. Cold air, because it is heavier, slides beneath the warm air and lifts it, thereby creating a boundary known as a 'weather front'.

The combination of circulating air around the globe and these air masses cause certain types of pressure systems. Warm air masses cause low pressure systems whilst cold air masses cause high pressure systems. Over the course of the year the distribution of air masses and pressure systems change as the earth spins on its axis and travels around the sun, thereby often having a dramatic effect of the world's weather.

When two differing prevailing winds of varying temperatures and humidity levels clash, they create a state of atmospheric instability, often forming great vortices which isolate themselves and whirl around inside the general circulation system, a phenomenon known as a cyclone which brings bad weather such as clouds, storms and blizzards.

If however, the atmospheric instability is extremely compact and intense, then a tropical cyclone occurs, causing hurricanes and tornadoes. Hurricanes can last from between a few hours up to thirty days, causing raging winds of up to 160 miles per hour, terrifying thunder storms and enormous waves out at sea which unleash their fury once they hit the shore. Once the tropical cyclone hits land the supply of warm moist air dissipates and the storm immediately begins to lose impact, but often not before the coastal resorts have borne the full brunt of nature's force.

Every season the first hurricane is given a name beginning with A with subsequent ones moving through the alphabet. If however a hurricane causes great damage then its name is not repeated. The largest hurricane ever recorded was Hurricane Gilbert in 1988 which formed east of Barbados and passed over Jamaica and the coast of Mexico.

Hurricanes may produce the largest storms on earth but tornadoes are the fiercest, with some wind speeds reaching 300 miles per hour. The word tornado comes from the Spanish 'tornar' meaning 'to turn' and the Catalan word 'tornado' meaning 'thunderstorm'.

A tornado is a violently rotating column of air that extends down from a cloud to the ground and destroys almost everything in its path according to the particular type of spinning air that it contains.

Tornadoes are associated with massive thunder storms and are caused by the clash of warm and cold air currents at high altitudes which lead to both atmospheric instability and severe turbulence. The majority occur most spectacularly in 'Tornado Valley' in North America although most of the world is subject to a less severe form of the same phenomenon. A tornado can last from a few seconds up to an hour and usually has a path of between one and three miles.

Even in Britain we are not immune to the tornado phenomenon as on 21 November 1981, no fewer than 105 tornadoes were recorded moving across the UK.

Air Superstitions

The direction of the wind has always played a part in superstition, as the following examples indicate, whilst winged creatures of the air also bring their own magical lore to the foretelling of events:

- When a birth is imminent, a south wind indicates a girl and a north wind a boy.
- A south wind indicates fine weather.
- Cats clawing the carpet indicate high winds.
- In Ireland pigs are thought to have the ability to see the wind and when they scurry about in their sties or carry straw in their mouths a storm is immanent.
- If caught, falling leaves indicate good luck.
- *If New Years Eve night, wind blows south*
  It betokeneth warmth and growth
  If west, much milk and fish in the sea
  If north, cold and storms there will be
  If east, the trees will bear much fruit
  If north-east, flee it, man and brute!
- An albatross flying around a ship in the mid ocean means that a strong wind will soon blow, bringing storms.
- Bees flying into the house indicate good luck as

31

long as they are allowed to fly out of their own accord.

- A bird flying into the house indicates a message
- Blackbirds nesting by your home portend a year of good luck.
- If the first butterfly you see in the year is white, this foretells of a year of good fortune.
- To carry a feather from a Kingfisher is said to confer protection and good fortune.
- A ladybird brings luck if landing on the hand or clothes, however to maintain the luck it should be allowed to fly away by itself. The deeper the colour and the more spots it has the better the luck.
- The magpie should always be saluted and greeted by wishing him good day and enquiring as to his and his wife's health.
- If a large black moth flies into the house it is thought to be the spirit of a deceased loved one that is visiting.
- Bringing peacock feathers indoors indicates bad luck, whilst to hear the harsh call of a peacock predicts rain.
- If ravens leave the Tower of London, then Britain is said to fall to her enemies, which is why their wings are clipped. To kill a raven is thought to bring extreme bad luck as the bird is thought to carry the spirit of King Arthur.
- Swallows flying low above the house indicate bad weather.
- Placing a swan's feather in your lover's pillow will ensure fidelity.

- Carrying a wren's feather is thought to prevent drowning.
- Swans in flight indicate strong winds.

Air Deities

Gods of the Winds

In Ancient Greece the empire of the winds was shared between the four sons of Eos, Goddess of the dawn and Astraeus, God of the starry sky; Boreas, the north wind, Zephyrus, the west wind, Eurus, the east wind and Notus, the south wind. Only the former two, however were ever attributed with specific qualities.

Boreas was strong, violent and often depicted as a winged old man with a grey shaggy beard, long flowing hair and a billowing cloak. He dwelt in the mountains of Thrace with his brother Zephyrus and was said to have carried off the beautiful Oreithyia from the banks of the Ilissus and had many children by her. In recognition of this event and the fact that Boreas had saved them from their enemy Xerxes, the Athenians built a temple in his honour on the banks of the same river.

Zephyrus was originally portrayed as a savage and baleful wind who delighted in brewing storms at sea, however his reputation gradually softened and eventually he became a sweet scented wind that fanned the blessed lands of Elysium. He took Chloris as his wife and had a son by her whom he named Carpus, meaning fruit. In his honour the Athenians consecrated an altar to him on the road to Eleusis.

The Odyssey however, tells us that the winds made their home in the Aeolian Islands, where they were kept under the guardianship of Aeolus, son of Poseidon. Aeolus was a pious and just deity, popular with the other

33

Gods and was attributed with inventing ship's sails. In recognition of these qualities, Zeus initially appointed him 'guardian of the winds'. Aeolus however, was able to both excite and soothe the winds at will and in recognition of this fact he earned the title of 'father of the winds', although in Roman mythology he was referred to as 'God of the wind'.

In contrast to what may be referred to as 'regular winds', there were the wild stormy winds, whose mission it was to destroy mankind and these were personified by a selection of monsters, born of Typhon, spirit of the hurricane and Echidna who was part nymph and part serpent.

One such monster was the Chimaera who had the head of a lion, the body of a goat and the tail of a dragon. She was said to vomit horrible flames and personified the storm cloud.

Winged Deities

Hermes originated as an ancient Pelasgian deity and was thee son of Zeus and Maia. He was worshipped by many including shepherds, travellers, thieves, liars and harlots. In later times however he undertook the role of a 'psychopompus', or 'conductor of souls' as he was thought to guide the souls of the deceased to the underworld.

Perhaps however he is most well known as the winged messenger of the Gods, although this is a role he shares with the Goddess of the Rainbow, Iris.

Hermes is usually depicted carrying a winged staff or 'caduceus' around which serpents are entwined. He also wears a winged hat or 'petasus' and winged sandals. The wings are symbollic of his speed when delivering Divine messages from Zeus to mankind. These messages, according to Hesiod, are said to manifest within man through inspiration, impressions and imaginings.

His speed and winged attire also made him a favourite amongst athletes and, in his honour, his statue once stood at the entrance to the stadium at Olympia.

Mrs Darley Tale: New Year

'Come on.'

Mrs Darley's voice was almost inaudible above the roar of the waves as she jumped lightly down onto the sand from the last rocky step.

I stood watching her from the safety of the final viewing platform, a few yards above the beach, knowing that it was only a matter of time before I was summoned down to join her. It was New Year's Day and we had come over to the North coast to see the spectacular Atlantic in its full glory and, as always, it never disappointed.

Eventually beckoned by Mrs Darley's wildly waving arms I reluctantly made my way down the remaining steps and onto the dark golden sand, still wet from the high tide.

'Isn't it wonderful?' she shouted, turning towards the sea and holding out her arms to form a five pointed star like Vitruvian man.

I nodded, wrapping my arms tightly around my body and secretly wishing that I was back in the car away from the biting cold of the north wind and the mighty force of the powerful Atlantic.

I watched as the waves thundered into the safety of the awaiting cove in which we stood and quickly moved back towards the cliffs as they broke angrily upon the shore, dowsing us in an iced foam spray.

'Feel it!' she called. 'Feel the vibration of the waves beneath your feet, feel the icy fingers of spray upon your cheek, feel the wind whipping away your fears. Face the elements and feel the power of the Goddess.'

I pulled my head out of my collar and reluctantly turned towards the sea where, very slowly, a feeling of exhilaration began to spread through my cold wet body and I became almost intoxicated.

Mrs Darley stood behind me and I was suddenly aware of her body pressed up against my back whilst her hands gently began to, unfurl my tightly crossed arms, slowly pulling them apart until I too stood like a pentagram, balanced upon the wind.

The Boundary of Air

Since the evolution of man into his Homo sapien form, he has looked skyward, envying the creatures of the air and their incredible ability to fly. Although practically there was little need for man to take to the air, the longing to experience the exhilaration of flight was felt deep within his psyche.

Today condensation trails from aircraft crisscross our skies and airports around the world receive and dispatch hundreds of flights on a daily basis. Air travel is, of course, an accepted part of our modern lives, however it is only in very recent history that man has taken to the skies in such spectacular fashion and for thousands of years previously all he could do was dream. Or was it?

The major achievements in aviation history are well documented. Historians tell us that the Montgolfier brothers were the first to pioneer balloon flight in 1783, whilst Otto Lilienthal from Germany made the first successful glider flight in the later part of the 19th century. In 1903 the famous North American Wright brothers finally made aviation history when they successfully took to the air in a small engine powered plane and remarkable though these achievements were, they were certainly not man's first attempt at flying.

To be accurate about man's first attempt to fly is virtually impossible due the lack of written records, however there are a few myths, legends and historical facts that take us way back into history and may perhaps change our viewpoint about aviation history.

The most famous story, dating back to approximately 1400 BC, concerning early flight was that of Daedalus and Icarus from Greek mythology.

King Minos of Crete had once dared to anger the Greek sea God, Poseidon, who, in revenge, gave Minos' wife Paisiphae a great passion for a bull. Her subsequent union with the bull resulted in the birth of a monster, half bull and half human, known as the Minotaur.

The Minotaur, who fed exclusively on human flesh, needed to be contained and so it was that King Minos ordered the building of a labyrinth. In order to accomplish this task he turned to Daedalus, a man of dubious reputation but known for his ingenuity and cunning. Daedalus made a good job of constructing a complex labyrinth, but upon hearing that King Minos' daughter Ariadne, had fallen for Theseus, the young man who was to enter the labyrinth and attempt to destroy the monster, Daedalus felt sorry for her and gave Ariadne a ball of thread to give to Theseus in order that he might find his way out after destroying the monster.

In response to this act of treachery, King Minos had both Daedalus and his son, Icarus, imprisoned in the labyrinth. During their imprisonment, Daedalus fashioned two pairs of wings from wax, feathers and string, with which father and son made their escape. Icarus however made the fatal mistake of flying too close to the sun, at which point the wax melted and he plunged to his death, although Daedalus managed to escape.

Whether this is fact or fiction is difficult to ascertain, however, Daedalus and his son were certainly not the only ones to risk their lives on a pair of artificial wings.

In 850 BC, King Bladud of New Troy who was, according to legend, a practitioner of magic and necromancy decided, after communication with the spirits, to build a pair of wings which he attached to his arms. He then leapt somewhat unsuccessfully, from the temple of Apollo, falling to his death.

Around the same time the Chinese were also determined to make man air born by introducing the kite, a device upon which many took to the skies. In 1295 upon his return from China, Marco Polo claimed to have seen Chinese sailors hoist drunken crew members into the air on large kites.

At the end of the first millennium AD, man was still trying to get off the ground and the first reasonably reliable account of attempted flight came around 1000 AD from Nisabur in Arabia. Here Al Djawhari, a great Turkish scholar tied two pieces of wood to his arms and climbed to the top of a tall mosque where he announced to the gathering crowd:

'O People! No one has made this discovery before. Now I will fly before your very eyes. The most important thing on earth is to fly to the skies. That I will do now.'

Sadly things did not quite pan out as expected and Al Djawhari too plunged to his death.

Five centuries later, Leonardo da Vinci painted, sculpted and engineered many wonderful masterpieces, among which, was the 'ornithopter', a complex drawing of a machine that sported flapping wings like a bird. It is an unknown fact as to whether Leonardo ever built the ornithopter however, after da Vinci's death, one of his associates Cardanus wrote that Leonardo had tried in vain to get the ornithopter off the ground, a problem that was to plague a few of his contemporaries and mankind for centuries to come.

If only John Williams from Conway in North Wales had been born a century later he may have been fortunate enough to heed the words of Juan Caramuel y Lobkovitz. Lobkovitz was a seventeenth century ecclesiastical writer who offered some rather sensible advice to the early pioneers of flight stating:

God denied to men the faculty of flight so that they might lead a quiet and tranquil life, for if they knew how to fly they would always be in perpetual danger.

Master Williams however was born well before these words were uttered and, like most seven year old boys, John Williams thought that he would like to fly. One day whilst wandering around the walls of Conway he decided to launch himself out towards the sea, hoping that the long coat he was wearing would fill with air and carry him over the waves. Unfortunately the child fell onto the rocks below and was immediately castrated. He did however survive the fall and went on to become Archbishop of York, living to the ripe old age of 78.

In 1770 it was the turn of a rather eccentric French clergyman called Abbe Pierre Desforges, to head for the skies. After spending a year imprisoned in the Bastille because of a treatise he wrote stating that Catholic priests should be allowed to marry, he found time to study the mating habits of swallows whilst in his prison cell. Upon his release he constructed a pair of wings, but did not have the confidence to try them out for himself and so he strapped the wings to a poor unsuspecting peasant and led him up to the top of a nearby belfry. Here, Desforges instructed the peasant to flap his wings and launch himself into the air. The peasant however refused to take part in what he clearly considered to be a suicide attempt and so the Abbe went back to the drawing board.

After two years, Desforges finally unveiled his flying machine which was a six foot long gondola covered by a canopy and attached to wings with a 20ft span. The Abbe managed to secure the help of four peasants to carry the machine to the top of a look out tower near to his church, although this time Desforges was brave enough to try the machine out for himself. Once he was securely fastened in, he instructed the peasants to push him off the tower and promptly crashed, fortunately suffering only a broken arm.

Further Frenchmen attempted to get off the ground including the Marquis de Bacqueville. He awoke one morning in 1742 with a sudden urge to fly from his Parisian mansion located on the quay, across to the other side of the river Seine, a distance of around 500ft. After spending the next few months designing the ultimate flying machine, a great crowd finally gathered on the banks of the Seine to watch the Marquis jump from the terrace of his mansion sporting a large pair of wings. Initially the flight looked quite promising however, as he drifted out across the river he began to lose height and eventually slammed into the deck of a barge, breaking his leg and making a promise to himself never to fly again.

Without all these often ridiculous yet pioneering attempts at flight, man may never have left the ground and yet within the last century not only have we as a species, learned to build machines that can carry us around the world, but we have also constructed rockets that are capable of taking us beyond our own atmosphere into the unexplored territory of space.

These achievements are no doubt a testament to man's scientific and engineering abilities and yet the question of the cost of aviation to our planet and the environment as a whole is one that must be addressed by the government, the aviation industry and air travellers themselves.

Air: a Matter of Life or Death

Creation myths involving the element of air as a primary force are somewhat scarce however the Pelasgian creation myth from ancient Greek literature is one of the oldest stories concerning the origin of the world. In sharp contrast to those of the patriarchal religions, it is matriarchal in nature and illustrates how one Goddess dominates man and also predates her contemporaries.

It is to Robert Graves' work; 'The Greek Myths', that we must turn for a rounded account of the story which survives in fragments from ancient Greek literature.

At the beginning of time, Eurynome was born from Chaos but, as nothing else existed, Eurynome had nowhere to live. Her first task therefore, was to split the waters from the air and live amongst the seas. As she travelled towards the south to begin her task, she felt the pressure of the north wind upon her back and considered this to be a separate entity.

Eurynome caught the north wind between her hands and fashioned a third entity from it, which became Ophion, the serpent. The north wind, along with Ophion, formed a union with Eurynome and planted within her the first seed of new life.

Knowing that she was carrying the seed of creation, Eurynome changed her form into a dove and eventually laid an egg, which she instructed Ophion the serpent to curl itself around seven times until it hatched into two

41

halves. All things were subsequently born from the egg including the sun, moon, planets, the land with all its flora and fauna.

With their task complete, Eurynome and Ophion inhabited Mount Olympus until Ophion made the fatal mistake of trying to claim all the credit for the creation of the universe, at which point Eurynome kicked Ophion out of Mount Olympus, condemning him to imprisonment in the caves below the earth for all time.

In the absence of her consort, she decided to assign each of the powers of the universe to a male and female Titan. Hence Table 1.2 over on the next page clearly illustrates those who became well established in Greek myth.

Titan Couple	Universal Power
Theia and Hyperion	Sun
Phoebe and Atlas	Moon
Metis and Coeus	Mercury
Tethys and Oceanus	Venus
Dione and Crius	Mars
Themis and Eurymedon	Jupiter
Rhea and Cronus	Saturn

Table 1.2

As soon as a baby leaves the protective amniotic waters of the womb and emerges into the world, or from the moment a bird breaks out of its protective shell, the first breath of life is drawn and the element of air becomes an essential requirement of life, every moment of every day until the physical body breathes its last.

The Christian Bible illustrates in its creation story the importance of the first breath in Genesis 2:7:

'The Lord God formed the man from the dust of the ground and breathed into his nostrils the breath of life and man became a living being.'

The breath in the Christian Bible is also attributed with the bestowing of Divine gifts such as the Holy Spirit as illustrated in John 20:22:

And with that he breathed on them and said, 'Receive the Holy Spirit.'

In death too, air plays its part as is evidenced in the North American Indian tribes of the Yuchi, or the '*Tsoyaha*', as they refer to themselves as, meaning 'children of the sun'.

The Yuchi believe that if they cease to practice the sacred ceremonies taught to them by the sun, then the sun will immediately set in the east, there will be darkness all around and the world will end with a violent wind which will sweep across the earth destroying all in its path.

In addition to the wind being the both the creator and destroyer of life, many cultures around the world have also used air as the medium with which to dispose of their dead.

The Australian Aborigines, the Polynesians and certain North American Indian tribes left the bodies of their dead exposed to the air in order to rot on the ground, in a tree or on a high scaffold.

The Parsee people of Northern India still practice this ancient Zoroastrian rite of placing the body of the deceased upon a high scaffold. These scaffolds are referred to as '*dakhmas*', meaning, 'towers of silence', where the body remains until picked clean by the vultures.

For the Parsee Indians, and if you are not born one, it is very difficult to become one, any other method of disposal is looked upon as defiling the natural elements of air, fire, water and earth.

Mrs Darley's Pagan Elements

In Appreciation of the Honeybee

There are hundreds of thousands of winged creatures that inhabit the air from midges and moths, to bats and birds, with each having a vital role to play in the eco system of our precious earth. This brief but heartfelt mention is meant to pay respect to every creature that inhabits our skies; however space dictates that only one can be looked at in detail within this book and that creature is the honeybee.

The honeybee, without doubt, deserves a special mention, for a world without them would have serious implications and, considering their current plight, it is perhaps an ideal time to bring this subject to the attention of everyone who may read this book in order that we can each do at least one thing to help.

Honeybees are truly man's friend, for without them and other species of bees, plant life would be reduced to mainly wind-pollinated grasses and trees which, in turn, would dramatically affect food production worldwide due to the lack of pollinated flowering plants.

The native bee '*apis mellifera*' has been associated with humans for millennia and cave paintings dating back some 8,000 years depict mankind harvesting honey. Later civilizations domesticated bees by providing artificial hives, and subsequent breeding has since produced the docile Western Honeybee now kept purely for honey production.

Honeybees are social insects and create elaborate nests, or hives, that contain up to 20,000 individuals during the summer months, although domestic hives may contain up to 80,000 bees. The bees work together in castes and belong to one of three groups, namely; queens, drones and workers.

Each hive has a large queen who is some twenty

millimetres longer than the worker bees and who has a life span of up to eight years. She also has a multi barbed sting, which can be used many times. Her sole purpose is to breed and, during her active life, she is capable of laying up to 1,500 eggs per day. A few of the developing larvae will be lucky enough to be fed on 'royal jelly', a type of bee super food which causes these larvae to grow bigger and offers them the opportunity to become future queens.

When the queen bee approaches the end of her life, the first of the potential queens to hatch will invariably kill her competitors and then take off with the male bees or drones on what is often referred to as a 'marriage flight'. During the flight she will be fertilised by as many of the drones as she can. She will then return to the hive and, if the old queen is not dead, kill her predecessor and take over the throne as a breeding machine, never leaving the hive again.

The drones are male bees that are unable to sting and only live approximately eight weeks. Their sole function is to mate with the new queen, should one be produced during their life span. At the end of the season, however, they are driven from the hive by the female worker bees in order to die as they are considered to be non essential.

The remaining caste, are the female worker bees, all of which are sterile and make up the largest part of the hive. The young workers are referred to as 'house bees' and undertake the tasks of comb construction, tending the larvae, drones and queen, cleaning, maintaining temperature regulation and generally defending the hive. The older workers are called 'field bees' and these are the bees with which we are familiar, foraging to collect pollen, nectar, water and plant resins both for hive construction and for use in the production of honey.

Workers born early in the season will live approximately six weeks, whilst those born later on will usually live until the following spring.

The workers are quite complex creatures, having a 'corbiculum' on each hind leg which acts as a pollen basket, an extra stomach for storing and transporting nectar or honey and four pairs of glands on the underside of their abdomen which secretes beeswax. They only have one straight barbed sting which, when used, rips out their stomach causing their death.

These fascinating creatures have a very keen sense of smell, a fact which is being exploited by man in order to sniff out substances such as explosives. The bees are trained by rewarding them with a sugar solution each time they react to the foreign substance by sticking out their tongue. Following their training they have been seen to congregate around bombs or landmines, sticking out their tongue and hoping for their reward, without any danger of setting off the device.

Bees in Danger

Bees have had to adapt to the many changes of flora around the British Isles as agricultural practices have changed. The introduction of improved pasture and the elimination of white clover is one major loss of a nectar source, whilst the close trimming or complete removal of hawthorn hedges is thought to be another contributory factor to their decline.

Recently the spread of the 'Varroa Mite' among the bee population has threatened their future. Originally this was a sucking parasite found only in Asia, but they arrived in Britain and North America after the Second World War. The mites not only debilitate the bees by sucking their blood but also carry various infections. One of these infections is American Foulbrood Bacteria (AFB), which infects the larvae causing them to turn dark brown and die.

The most recent cause of death to a hive, is Colony Collapse Disorder (CCD) which has been found throughout North America and in some parts of Europe where a quarter of the bee population has disappeared. Mysteriously most of the bees leave the hive within the course of a week never to return, and any that remain are overcome by viruses and fungal infections. There is no full explanation for this strange phenomenon that threatens the bee but it would appear that those using organic farming methods along with individual bee-keepers have not been affected so badly.

The following remark (often attributed to Albert Einstein) paints a dark picture of a world without bees:

If the bee disappeared off the surface of the globe then man would only have four years of life left. No more bees, no more pollination, no more plants, no more animals, no more man.

Although scientists acknowledge that this scenario is unlikely to happen, it nevertheless illustrates just how important the bee actually is to the world's agricultural economy and it is estimated that a third of the food we eat is pollinated by bees. Fewer bees will mean less pollination, less honey and fewer plants, resulting in a staggering rise in the cost of the food that we eat.

The role of bees in the food chain is so important that in 2007 The National Audit Office worked out the value of honeybees to the UK economy as being two hundred million pounds a year whilst the retail value was closer to one billion pounds.

The only way to continue the work of the honeybee is to employ people to go around manually brushing the insides of plants with pollen, a time consuming and costly way of replacing this valuable insect. Considering that a hive of 50,000 bees pollinate on average 500,000 plants a day, this would certainly not be a practical solution. In China, however, this method is already being employed to pollinate pear trees where insects are extinct although experts there estimate the cost of a piece of fruit to double.

What we can do to help:

- Become a beekeeper or offer a space in your garden for a local beekeeper to keep his bees.
- Plant your garden with bee friendly plants: Allium plants, Mint, Beans, Flowering herbs, Asters, Sunflowers, Hollyhocks, Larkspur, Foxgloves, Willow trees, Lime trees.
- Buy local honey.

Wind
Flowers dance,
Rains squall,
Skirts lift,
Leaves fall.

Seas seethe,
Colts ride,
White waves,
High tide.

Mills turn,
Boughs break,
Wind gives,
Wind takes.

Mythical Creatures of Air

Spirits of the air are usually referred to as sylphs, often described as beautiful winged creatures with human characteristics, save for their hawk like eyes and angular faces. They can range in stature from the tiny creatures which many of us imagine, to the size of a human. They are said to inhabit the high, wild places of earth or dwell within the clouds, where they are thought to live for hundreds of years, never seeming to age.

The wind is their vehicle and, as benevolent creatures towards humankind, they help to purify our atmosphere, neutralising toxic gases and cleaning the air. It is because of their strong connection to the air element and its association with the mind, that sylphs are considered to bring inspiration to man. Those who are active in the creative arts will automatically draw sylphs to them.

Sylphs are considered to be connected to the '*Sidhe*', a powerful supernatural race comparable to the fairies or elves in Irish mythology. The Sidhe were believed to be the ancestors, the spirits of nature or even the Gods and Goddesses themselves.

Paracelsus, the 16th century alchemist was probably the first person to bring the world 'sylph' to the modern world. Considering however that these were turbulent times in which to discuss anything that could be deemed as being outside the rigidity of orthodox Christian belief, Paracelsus found himself on rather uncertain ground following the publication of his work, 'On nymphs, Sylphs, Pygmies, and Salamanders', and was forced to refute accusations of sorcery on more than one occasion.

In his work however, he did not put sylphs forward as fantastical creatures but attempted to fit them into his view of the cosmos by describing them as 'natural beings', a mixture of human, animal and spirit. He was also careful not to say that he had actually seen these beings himself, but rather that they could be sensed and, like humans, had the capability to be both good and bad. He stated:

'They are witty, rich, clever, poor, dumb like we who are from Adam.'

The first mention of sylphs in mainstream western literature comes courtesy of the poem, 'The rape of the Lock', by Alexander Pope in the 18th century. Here Pope satirizes Rosicrucian and alchemical writings by inventing a theory to explain the creature referred to a sylph.

He pretends to have discovered a new alchemy where the sylph becomes the mystically condensed humours of peevish women. In the poem, Belinda, a rather vain young woman is warned by her guardian sylph, Ariel in a dream that some disaster will befall her later that day but that Ariel will do his best to protect her. Belinda however dismisses the warning and after much preening before the mirror goes off to Hampton Court Palace where a group of wealthy socialites are gathering for a party. Among them is the baron, who has already made up his mind as a joke, to steal a lock of the vain Belinda's hair.

After two unsuccessful attempts, the baron is finally successful and is delighted when he holds a lock of Belinda's hair in his hand. Belinda however is furious and, despite being asked by Clarissa, a friend of the Baron to take it all in good part and release her vanity in favour of good humour, Belinda refuses and, in due course, a scuffle breaks out as she tries unsuccessfully to retrieve the lock of hair. The poem ends with the poet consoling Belinda with the suggestion that the hair has not been lost but has perhaps been taken up to heaven and immortalised as a constellation.

The verse below is taken from the First Canto of 'The Rape of the Lock', by Alexander Pope:

Of these am I, who thy Protection claim,
A watchful Sprite, and Ariel is my name.
Late, as I rang'd the crystal Wilds of Air,
In the clear Mirror of thy ruling Star
I saw, alas! some dread Event impend,
Ere to the Main this morning's Sun descend,
But Heav'n reveals not what, or how, or where:
Warn'd by thy Sylph, oh pious Maid beware!
This to disclose is all thy Guardian can.
Beware of all, but most beware of Man!

Angelic Beings

Historically angels have always been viewed as divine messengers, although traditions vary as to whether angels have free will or whether they have ever experienced what it is like to be human.

The word 'angel' derives from the Greek word *'angellos'* meaning 'messenger', although there are many types of angelic beings including:

- Irinim - High Angels or 'watchers'.
- Cherubim - Mighty ones.
- Seraphim - Fiery Ones.
- Chayyot - Holy Creatures.

In Judaism the term *'Malach Elohim'* is used to describe a messenger of God, although the Jewish texts of the Greco-Roman period expand on the subject of angels, by mentioning a hierarchy. The passage in Zechariah 4: 10 is considered to refer to seven levels of angelic beings:

Mrs Darley's Pagan Elements

'These seven are the eyes of the Lord, which range throughout earth.'

As monotheism took over from polytheism in the Jewish tradition, the re-emergence of angels seemed to bridge the gap between Pagan and Jewish beliefs, for although a range of angelic beings appeared with differing responsibilities, they were all considered subordinate to one God.

The early Christians adopted the idea of angels from their Jewish counterparts although the concept of an angel changed somewhat from being merely a messenger of God to sometimes being God himself. Certain angels also received formal identification such as Michael, Uriel, Raphael and Gabriel as illustrated in Revelation 12:7-9:

And there was war in heaven. Michael and his angels fought against the dragon, and the dragon and his angels fought back. But he was not strong enough and they lost their place in heaven. The great dragon was hurled down – that ancient serpent called the devil or Satan, who leads the whole world astray. He was hurled to the earth and his angels with him

By the beginning of the fifth century the powers that held sway in the Christian church agreed that there were different categories of angels, each with their appropriate missions and activities which, over time, have been both added to and elaborated upon. A selection of angels and their areas of expertise are illustrated in Table 1.3 below and over to following page.

Archangel	Role
Metatron	Chief angel in the Cabala's tree of life and guardian of psychic and sensitive children.
Michael	Served as a warrior and

	advocate for Israel. Gives courage and protection to those who ask.
Gabriel	The messenger, who assists with all aspects of conception and birth. Cares for those whose job it is to communicate such as journalists, writers, speakers and teachers.
Raphael	The supreme healer and bringer of comfort, also helps those who take to the healing professions.
Uriel	Angel of the earth who brings us peace, wisdom, light and harmony.
Ariel	The overseer of guardian angels and humans but also has an affinity with animals and the environment.
Raziel	The keeper of the wisdom of the universe, offering help to understand dreams, the earth's secrets and esoteric knowledge.

Table 1.3

Other religions too have a special affinity with angels including the Mormons, Buddhists, Muslims and the Malaysian Baha'i.

The earliest depiction of an angel in art is to be found in the catacomb of Priscilla in Rome and dates back to the 3rd century AD. The image is shown without wings as is the case in many early representations, in fact the earliest image of an angel with wings is a 4th century painting on the Prince's sarcophagus discovered near Istanbul in the 1930's.

An explanation of why angels were given wings in art was offered by St John Chrysostom, Archbishop of

Mrs Darley's Pagan Elements

Constantinople during the 4th century. He suggested that their wings were symbolic of the sublimity of their nature. From that date forward, with only a few exceptions, angels have been both represented and imagined to have wings.

Angelic dress code has varied according to time and religious culture and they have been depicted in many guises from warrior beings such as Archangel Michael, to Byzantium Emperors and from magnificent creatures of light to the long white robed beings of the Middle Ages.

Today there is a growing belief in the existence of angels due perhaps to the fact that they are non-denominational and as such have the ability to span the religious and spiritual divide.

Many people lay claim to having seen, encountered, or simply felt the presence of one at some point in their life and writers such as Doreen Virtue and Diana Cooper have brought angels very much into the public eye.

The following poem on the next page , 'Masnavi', by the Islamic Sufi, Jalal al-Din Muhammad Rumi, offers a suggestion as to where all beings might fit in the great mystery that is pondered as life:

I died as inanimate matter and arose a plant,
I died as a plant and rose again an animal.
I died as an animal and arose a man.
Why then should I fear to become less by dying?
I shall die once again as a man
To rise an angel perfect from head to foot!
Again when I suffer dissolution as an angel,
I shall become what passes the conception of man!
Let me then become non-existent, for non-existence
Sings to me in organ tones, 'To him shall we return.'

The Magic and Alchemy of Air

Carl Jung, the great psychologist believed that just as the four elements exist on the material plane in the forms of air, fire, water and earth, so these energy types also exist in our inner world or subconscious and can be described as thinking, intuition, feeling and sensation, or in relation to the old humours can be likened to the temperaments of sanguine, choleric, melancholic or phlegmatic.

He believed that in an individual who he would describe as 'unconscious', one energy type would always dominate, but that in order to become balanced we must learn to develop each category even though we would always retain the main aspect of our personality.

Jung went on to divide the four categories into two groups, namely perception and judgement. Perception, he stated, tells us what is happening through intuition and sensation, whilst judgement takes us through the decision making process by thinking and feeling.

In terms of human existence, air symbolizes the thinking aspect, the function of the logical mind. Air allows us to think constructively and to build upon what has gone before. It encourages us to be analytical and base our decisions upon the basis of cause and effect, separating what we perceive to be good from what we perceive to be bad.

Jung believed that those with a dominant air aspect to their personality or the thinking types have the ability to step outside the box in order to evolve intellectually and consider things that others have yet to dream of. If however someone is too dominant in this area and employs little sensation, intuition or feeling when dealing with life's challenges, then they may find themselves full of bright ideas that sadly never reach fruition. On the whole however, the thought processes of the air dominated personality fly just a little higher than those of a more tangible nature.

Our language illustrates beautifully the many aspects of air. When someone appears to be rather scatterbrained we describe them as an 'air head' or when someone is shouting or offering words with little substance we say they are 'full of hot air'. When a situation occurs that knocks us for six we turn to the wind for our metaphors and refer to it as 'a bit of a blow', or when someone surprises us with something we say 'well blow me down'. When we eat a delicious sponge cake or dance with someone who glides around the floor we may describe them as being 'as light as air'.

In traditional cultures air is often seen as a universal power or pure substance and derives from the Latin word, '*spirare*', meaning 'to breath'.

There were originally two words for air; the first was '*aer*', which referred to the dim lower atmosphere, whilst the second was '*aether*', referring to the bright upper atmosphere above the clouds.

One of the early Greek philosophers, Anaximenes referred to air as '*arche*', or the first principal of the world, in so much as he considered everything to derive from it. He saw warm air becoming rarefied and eventually turning to fire and cool air condensing into water and eventually earth.

A similar belief was attributed to Diogenes Apolloniates, who was also thought to have linked air with intelligence and the psyche.

Empedocles of Acragas however selected four roots for his archai, rather than just air and these became the classic elements of Greek philosophy; air, fire, water and earth, a philosophy which Plato later expanded upon.

In ancient Greek philosophy, air is considered to be

both hot and wet, hence its association with the humour of the blood and the sanguine temperament which is thought to be sociable, responsive, outgoing, easygoing, talkative, lively and carefree.

The alchemical symbol for air is an upright triangle crossed with a horizontal line.

In the Hindu tradition air is one of the five great elements known as the 'panchamahabhuta'. The Hindu God of Air is referred to by a variety of names, '*Vayu*', meaning 'air', '*Vata*', meaning 'blown', '*Pavana*', meaning 'wind', or *Prana*, meaning 'breathing'.

Magical Air

Ever since mankind has walked upon the earth he has attempted to harness and work in conjunction with her natural forces especially when making magic.

In earliest times the natural world was the domain of the wise woman and cunning man for they knew how to attract love, good fortune and health by working in conjunction with the seasons, the moon's cycles, and the elements of air, fire, water and earth.

The practice of ceremonial magic in its many forms also incorporates the element of air into its teachings. In Wiccan ritual the element of air is placed in the cardinal direction of the east and is protected by sylphs as guardians of the eastern quarter. This direction is associated with birth, sunrise and the spring. It is symbolically represented by the colour yellow, the athame (black handled knife), the wand, woodwind instruments, creatures of flight or the tarot suit of swords.

Mrs Darley's Pagan Elements

In the casting of a magic circle, the element of air is often symbolically depicted by the burning of incense and the smoke which emanates from it, perfuming the air as it does so. The following ingredients (in Table 1.4) of herbs, spices and resins burned as incense on a charcoal block can help to confer certain magical qualities.

Ingredient	Magical qualities
All spice	Wealth, strength
Clove	Love
Fern	Change, fertility
Frankincense	Peace, courage, joy, success
Juniper	Protection, healing
Lavender	Reconciliation, peace
Myrrh	Healing, harmony
Sage	Wisdom
Sandalwood	Spiritual awareness, healing

Table 1.4

It is said that when incense is burned, the direction of the smoke emanating from it will dictate whether your wishes will come true.

- Vertically rising smoke indicates that your wishes will come true with little effort.
- Smoke drifting to the left indicates that you will receive help in your endeavours
- Smoke drifting to the right means that your own hard work will suffice to bring your wishes to fruition.

Air magic is used to ensure safe journeys, to bring ideas into reality and to expand creativity.

Wind has been used in the practice of magic since earliest times, for its ability to be both invisible and powerful has fascinated mankind. Cornish fishermen throughout the ages have chanted the following rhyme about the direction of the winds and their fortune when out at sea:

> *When the wind is in the east,*
> *'Tis neither good for man nor beast,*
> *When the wind is in the north,*
> *The skilful fisher goes not forth.*
> *When the wind is in the south,*
> *The hungry fish opens its mouth,*
> *When the wind is in the west*
> *It's then the fishing's at its best.*

In times gone by, sailors would buy knotted cords from witches and whenever they wanted the wind to blow in order to speed them on their journey they would undo a knot in the cord.

In East Anglia it was important that the sails of the windmills turned in order that the grain should be milled and to ensure that the wind blew, offerings of milk were placed in naturally hollowed stones alongside the mill or farmhouse in order that the Gods of the Wind would be benevolent.

Today magic is still performed by harnessing the qualities of the wind according to the direction from which it comes as illustrated in Table 1.5 below.

Wind Direction	Magical qualities
East	The east wind is the bringer of new beginnings and heralds the arrival of spring. Magic to do with change, health and clearing out the old is recommended at this

	time
South	The southerly winds are the warm winds of summer and magic which involves growth, expansion, wealth and success are indicated when these winds blow
West	The Westerly's are the autumn winds and mark the time for projects to be brought to completion. They can also be utilised for issues surrounding love, healing and resolving differences.
North	The cold northerly winds bring the winter and offer a time for ridding ourselves of unwanted habits, destructive relationships and concentrating on our spiritual side or developing our psychic abilities.

Table 1.5

Mrs Darley Tale: The Honey Fair

'Is everyone ready?' Eddie shouted down the minibus as we all settled ourselves.

'Yes, dear, I think we're all on board,' called Mrs Darley.

'Then off we go!' Eddie laughed as we set off down the lane on what was one of those pale misty October mornings that promised a golden day to come.

Lucy and her cousin, who had taken the day off school for the occasion, began to get everyone in the mood by giving a rousing rendition of Pooh Bear's 'Isn't it funny how a bear likes honey, buzz, buzz, buzz I wonder why he does?'

'Have you ever been to the Callington honey fair before?' Rose asked as we left the bus and made our way into the bustling street, which was full of stalls, street performers, musicians and beekeepers.

I shook my head, 'No but it all looks very interesting.'

'Look dears,' Mrs Darley's voice was just audible above the accordion music, 'let's all meet up for a honey cream tea in the church hall at two o'clock, OK?'

We all nodded our agreement and then went our separate ways in order to explore the fair. Its origins, I discovered on my travels, could, according to some sources, date back to the 13th century when Henry III was trying to raise funds to build Westminster Abbey and in so doing granted a licence to the town for a market and an annual fair. Other sources however say that the actual 'honey fair' originated much later during the latter half of the 19th century and was only discontinued with the outbreak of World War Two. Its revival came about in 1978 and was due to the efforts of a local man called John Trevithick who re-established the fair and ensured its survival by handing over the organisation and running of it to the local Lions. Regardless of its true origins however, the fair was well worth a visit and as two o'clock approached, our company all met up for the much anticipated honeyed cream tea.

As we all squashed ourselves around a table that was far too small for the ten of us, the conversation turned to the subject of honey and Don surprised us all by imparting his knowledge of bees.

'Fascinating creatures honeybees,' he said, 'I kept half a dozen hives for several years when I lived in Sussex.'

'Did you, really!' exclaimed Phyllis, 'Did they make much honey?'

'Plenty for my needs and some left over to sell, but when my wife and I split up I didn't have the room to keep them in my new place.'

'Perhaps we could look at having a few hives at the

cottages?' Mrs Darley suggested.

'Mmmm, that might be worth thinking about,' said Don, 'I don't mind looking after them as long as a few of us contributed to the setting up costs.'

As we all nodded our agreement, a rather large bee appeared at our table and introduced himself as Jim. Whether Jim was actually as round as he appeared or whether his rotund shape was due to expert padding I will never know, however he brought with him a delicious selection of honey pots for us to try, in return for which he was made most welcome.

Enjoying our 'oh's' and 'ah's' of appreciation as we tasted each pot, he proceeded to squeeze himself into an almost impossible space between Phyllis and Rose and began to impart some fascinating information regarding bee myth and legend.

'Reverence and worship of the bee,' Jim began, 'dates back some 8,000 years and gold plaques from Rhodes, embossed with winged bee creatures can be seen in the British museum. In fact throughout the Greek world the bee was believed to be the sacred insect that bridged the space between this world and the next and even Mycenaen tombs were shaped like beehives.'

'What about Goddesses?' asked Mrs Darley, 'Were there any bee Goddesses?'

'Oh yes,' said Jim, helping himself to a generous scoop of lavender honey. 'In Homer's "Hymn to Apollo" we are told that Apollo's gift of prophecy was bestowed upon him by the "Thriae", a trinity of Aegean Bee Goddesses, whilst the Mycenaean Goddess Potnia, was referred to as "The Pure Mother Bee" and her priestesses all received the name of Melissa, meaning "bee".

The ancient Greeks considered honey coated lips to bestow eloquence and it was said that both Achilles and

Pythagoras were fed on honey as children. Of course, we mustn't forget that one of the oldest intoxicating drinks known to man is made from honey, and is something we all appreciate down here in Cornwall.'

'Ah,' sighed Eddie, 'Mead, one of my favourite tipples.'

'A man after my own heart,' said Jim, 'but it's not just us West Country folk who have the monopoly on mead, the Minoans too were expert bee keepers and mead brewers. In fact mead was a Cretan intoxicant much older than wine and just to show my appreciation for this most ancient of drinks, I shall leave you good people and buzz across to the mead tent over there. Good to meet you all and enjoy the honey fair.'

We thanked him for his knowledge and proceeded to finish our honey cream teas.

'Of course,' said Don, 'you know that scientifically speaking it's impossible for bees to fly? An airplane the size of a bee, moving as slowly as a bee, could not fly.'

'Mmmm,' said Mrs Darley with a wry smile, 'it's a good job the Goddess guards her secrets and doesn't rely totally on science!'

Astrological Air Signs

The twelve signs of the Zodiac are each governed by one of four categories, namely those of air, fire, water and earth, and of the three signs which fall within each group, one is cardinal, i.e. initiatory; one is fixed, i.e. controlling; and one is mutable, i.e. restless.

The three signs that fall under the influence of the element of air are the free thinking signs of Gemini, Libra and Aquarius and although each has their own specific traits they do have certain similarities. All three express freedom through expression of thought and movement and have the potential to be philosophical, creative, eccentric and occasionally volatile. That said, the three are quite different as illustrated in the brief character outlines below.

Gemini

Gemini is the mutable air sign and as such people born under this sign tend to be changeable, expressing freedom of thought at its most basic level, moving erratically from one thought to the next without always seeing their ideas through.

That said, they are alert, careful, intuitive, talented, sensitive, active and occasionally of a nervous disposition, although they are more than capable of producing big ideas.

Often people play on the sympathies of a Gemini as they are easily swayed by a sob story. They do however, have a deep understanding of their fellow man and possess keen judgment and foresight.

Financially, a Gemini's fortunes can fluctuate dramatically throughout their life, having more than enough at some points and feeling considerably unsettled at others. Solid investments in land or buildings are recommended over those of a less tangible nature such as stocks and shares.

Travel can often play a part in the life of a Gemini, although they love to come home and appreciate a neat tidy house.

Gemini ties of affection are deep rooted and they will go to any lengths to help those they love, but care should be taken not to cross them, for their affection will almost certainly be removed. They also make faithful and generous friends, for friendship is very important to a

Gemini and they will do anything in their power to help a friend in need.

Throughout life, Gemini men are often likely to link up with unsuitable friends or partners, whilst ladies will probably have several good friends as opposed to one best friend.

Career-wise: writing, acting, music, accounting, editing, lecturing, and beauty therapies are all appealing careers to the true Gemini.

Spiritually, orthodox religion often falls short of their expectations, however Gemini people often possess highly evolved intuitive skills which can develop into mediumistic qualities should they decide to pursue that path.

The greatest handicap for a Gemini is worry and fear about being unable to accomplish any heartfelt desires, however if these doubts can be controlled then a long and useful life is indicated with time to accomplish all their desired goals.

Libra

Libra is the cardinal air sign and as such Librans express their freedom in creating the type of environment they feel most comfortable with. Those born under this sign are balanced, perceptive, intuitive, loving and honourable, yet can appear somewhat self willed and occasionally selfish.

Overall however, Librans are affectionate in nature, often being too generous for their own good.

Finances for the Libran need to be kept under a tight rein otherwise money can disappear as fast as it comes in. A Libran is capable of earning a great deal of money, but unless saving is part of the equation, then financial success can slip through their fingers.

Although Librans outwardly display a love of their home and good domestic skills, they sometimes desire a change of scenery and often wish that they could up sticks, move elsewhere and start all over again.

With regards to affairs of the heart, Librans need to experience a continual splash of romance and if this is not forthcoming then a certain amount of disillusionment often follows. In matters of friendship Librans can be greatly influenced by unsuitable people and therefore should choose their friends with care.

Career-wise, Librans are highly talented in many areas and as such it may be difficult for them to choose a career. The recommended choices however include; music, art, languages, theatre, mathematics, dancing, teaching, library work, decorating, writing, chemistry, aviation, architecture, tailoring carpentry or mechanical work.

Although many Librans have firm religious beliefs they are, more often than not, usually tolerant of the choices of others and are often intuitive and psychically inclined.

The greatest hindrances in life to a Libran are that they are too easily influenced by the remarks of others, rather than trusting and following their own judgment. They should also try not to jump to conclusions and attempt to temper the sharp remarks which are often made when annoyed.

Aquarius
Aquarius is the fixed air sign, expressing their idea of freedom through free thinking and as such they are electric, magnetic, inspirational, sensitive, alert, studious, affectionate and intuitive. They have strong powers of concentration and usually attract attention regardless of

the area of society they choose to move in. Care must be taken however not to become too impressionistic.

Aquarians have deep feelings, a love of beauty, art, music and nature and a fascination of the mystical or occult sciences. They have an observing mind with great abilities for meditation, investigation and constructive thought.

In financial matters, Aquarians have the power to accumulate wealth, but are often too sympathetic to the cause of others, leading them to give away their hard earned cash. It often seems that the Aquarians lot is to shore up someone else's finances. In later life however many Aquarians will enjoy financial independence.

The Aquarian usually has a love of travel and will often find themselves making several important trips to far flung places which will bring many opportunities and benefits. An Aquarian's home however is very important to them and without a harmonious home life they are unable to function to the best of their ability.

In love, the Aquarian is looking for someone who will appreciate their true nature but they sometimes have to wait until mid-life in order to find their true soul mate. With the right person by their side Aquarians can reach their true potential but without that special person ambition means little. Many Aquarians marry more than once and can often have rather strange marital experiences. They are attracted to people of intelligence and only become intimate or friends with very few people during their lifetime, but to these they are fiercely, loyal.

Career-wise, those born under Aquarius excel at teaching, journalism, astrology, the occult sciences, medicine, theatre managing, acting, floristry, decorating and illustrating. They work best in an intellectual and refined atmosphere and often possess natural talents which ask them to perform or speak publicly.

Spiritually, Aquarians are sincere and broadminded, being far more philosophical than orthodox in their beliefs. They often possess mediumistic gifts and could do much with telepathy.

In early life, Aquarians may feel mounting frustration as they have to learn to wait for goals to be achieved through experience and hard work, whilst in later life they will worry that they have too little time left to develop their spiritual understanding.

Whatever the outcome, Aquarians often lead unusual yet thrilling lives!

Imaginings

Winds of imagining
Flutter through staid minds,
Blowing aside
Dark veils of indifference.

Soft whispered secrets
From fleet footed Hermes,
Dance on his breath
To the realm of the Gods.

One sacred moment
Of Angelic compassion,
Move saddened hearts
Towards divinity.

Connecting with the Element of Air

My childhood was littered with dreams of hovering in the air, usually around ceiling height, accompanied by the overwhelming feeling of never wanting to come back down to earth, an indication no doubt, that I would always have my head in the clouds!

As a child I loved to use my imagination, carving out secret dens inhabited by the elementals and writing stories and poems of myth and magic. Sadly my subsequent journey into adulthood led me into an occupation far, far away from this fantasy childhood, where I became totally left brain dominated, making facts, figures and precise note taking part and parcel of everyday life.

It was not until my meeting with Mrs Darley that I began to understand just how far my mind had narrowed from those days of free thought and creative pursuits to one of rigidity and concise thinking. I once remember her describing me as being 'anally retentive', which was probably closer to the truth than I perhaps cared to admit.

Under her influence I began to see that my conditioned thinking had mistakenly led me to believe that everything I did had to have a precise format. In my working life, perhaps this was acceptable, but Mrs Darley allowed me to see that outside of that environment I could learn to be more spontaneous and, so it was, that I gradually began to set the right hand side, of my mind free.

With regards to the physical aspect of flying, I first took to the skies when I was twenty and considered it to be one of the best experiences of my life. As such I decided to apply to be an air hostess however, my inability to swim in event of emergency, coupled with my inability to reach the overhead lockers due to my limited height of five feet two inches, meant that this career choice was over before it began.

The events of nine eleven brought fear into the minds of many jet setters and aviation entered a new era of suspicion and dread. I suddenly found myself experiencing palpitations at the thought of flying, just at a time when my partner and I were being asked to teach in the Far and Middle East. I knew however that I could either allow my mind to destroy these golden opportunities, or I could use it to make me stronger by changing my thought patterns. In the infamous words of Susan Jeffers book, I chose to 'Feel the Fear and Do it Anyway', a decision I have never regretted.

The mind is an invaluable tool to mankind, but what we must remember is that is simply what it is - a tool for our use. The mistake that many of us make is that we allow the mind to control us rather than the other way around, a practice which will quite often seek to destroy us.

Whilst we are on this earth we have to be grounded in order to survive our human journey, but every so often we should allow ourselves to reach for the stars and fly with the angels for without these flights of fancy how would we ever experience the Divine?

Mrs Darley Tale: Summer Air

The annual jazz night in aid of local charities was, according to all accounts, a night not to be missed and was held at Sheila and Tony's beautiful old cottage garden down in Henwood village.

The whole of our hamlet was going, including several people I didn't know very well and so we, plus a handful of Mrs Darley's friends, all walked down the lane together on what was a very still and balmy July evening.

Once inside the gate, the drinks tent seemed to be the main place of attraction but before long we made our way out into the garden, where a wooden block floor had been temporarily laid over the large rectangle of lawn. To one side, under an old apple tree the band began to play and the sound of sleazy summer jazz seeped out across the garden, tempting would be dancers onto the floor.

After watching the action for some time, I found Eddie tugging at my arm, 'Come on,' he said, 'this is a lively one, let's have a go.'

Rather reluctantly, but aided by Phyllis' cajoling and a few glasses of red wine, I succumbed and although Eddie was not the lightest of men on his feet, I had to admit that I actually enjoyed my sojourn around the floor.

'I didn't know you could dance.' Mrs Darley sidled up to me at the interval as I stood in the refreshment queue.

'Oh I haven't done any for years,' I laughed, 'I'm a bit rusty I'm afraid.'

She wagged her finger at me, 'Mmmm, I think you're a bit of a dark horse, your movements were hardly those of someone who's a bit rusty.'

'It must be Dutch courage then,' I replied anxious to change the subject, 'the band's good isn't it? I've always quite liked modern jazz and that saxophone player is just superb.'

'So you have an appreciation of music too?' asked Mrs Darley.

'Well I know what I like, but then doesn't everyone?'

Mrs Darley shook her head, 'No, I don't think everyone does, I think a lot of people just say they like something simply because others like it. What strange creatures we are, on the one hand we all want to be treated as individuals and yet on the other, we don't want to do anything that makes us stand out from the crowd for fear of being different.'

I nodded, thinking that what she had just said was probably true, as much for me as anyone else, but not wanting to get into a deep and meaningful conversation in the food queue I made another attempt at changing the subject.

'I keep getting the most wonderful smell,' I said. 'Do you know what it is?'

'Probably the jasmine,' she replied, 'there's a beautiful tree just beneath the window over there and the perfume tends to hang heavy in the night air.'

'I wonder why it always smells stronger at night?' I mused.

'Well, Indian legend has it, my dear, that once, many moons ago, a beautiful princess fell in love with Surya-Deva, the Sun God, but sadly her love was unrequited. Heartbroken by Surya's disinterest, the princess killed herself and, where her ashes were scattered, grew a beautiful jasmine bush. Since it was the God of the Sun who was responsible for the Princesses death, the jasmine tree will only ever release its scent at night when the Sun God has departed.'

'What a sad, yet beautiful story,' I said.

'Out of sadness, a moment of beauty is eventually born,' Mrs Darley replied gazing into the far distance. 'Of course, without the element of air, nothing we have spoken about in the last few minutes could be experienced.'

'What do you mean?' I asked.

'Well, dancing demands that you slice through the air with movement. Music and words require their vibration to be carried through the air to our ear drums and evocative aromas are brought to our notice on the air, like tonight's jasmine. In fact our laughter, our words, our very breath are transmitted, carried and made possible by this precious element. We should choose our words and deeds carefully, for they are forever caught within the energy of air.'

'Yet something else in this world I have come to appreciate.' I smiled at her.

'And experiencing appreciation is a step closer to knowing the divine,' she said as she turned her attention towards the buffet.

Conclusion

Air is the element that relies upon no other, intangible, independent, invisible and vital; it is more precious than all the riches of the world. It is a divine gift and one which we should aim to maintain in its cleanest and purest form.

Creation

Creation began with a thought,
A flicker within the mind of the All.
A spark, a light in the darkness,
A catalyst for change.

Energy streamed forth, bearing fruits.
Form, born from a whisper,
Intellect, from an idea, life, from a thought,
Nurtured for eternity in the mind of the All.

Chapter 2

Fire

Fire
In flickering flames
I flirt,
Flamboyant, fleeting, gone.

In lava lakes
I lie
Languid, lambent, waiting.

In boiling blood
I bide
Boundless, bellicose, fervent.

Introduction

Fire, in its many forms has become synonymous with the survival of man here on earth. He has, in times gone by, sat by it to warm his bones, cooked upon it to nourish his loved ones, grown crops beneath it to feed his tribe and gazed into it to stimulate his imagination.

Hypnotised by its beauty and in awe of its power man has been both blessed and destroyed by this mighty element of nature.

Fire is a precious gift, without which we could not survive in our present form, a fact acknowledged by our earliest ancestors who, in their reverence, personified it with fiercesome Gods of fire and thunder, volcanoes and lightning and the ceaseless presence of the sun.

The element of fire however extends far beyond its physical form and enters into the realm of our subconscious, existing on a symbolic level as determination and intuition.

Fire is our will; it is the power that drives us forward, that instinctively lets us know when something is right. It is the raw passion that compels us to procreate and the warm heart that holds compassion for our fellow man.

Mrs Darley Tale: The Secret

I arrived home from work to see a fire engine pulling away from my parking space at the edge of the moor and, feeling more than a little concerned, I left my usual collection of briefcases and laptops in the car and hurried round to the cottages. Here I found a collection of people standing on the pocket of grass outside Mrs Darley's cottage obviously discussing recent happenings.

'Oh hello, dear,' the familiar voice of Mrs Darley rang out as she made her way through the little gathering looking unusually dishevelled and decidedly sooty, 'Now don't worry, everything is alright, but I'm afraid I've had a small chimney fire. Apparently it was all caused by some age old bird nest that suddenly decided to dislodge itself. Anyway, to cut a long story short, I'm afraid it's damaged part of your loft and chimney, but not to worry, the insurance people are coming round tomorrow to assess the damage and any repairs will all be taken care of.'

'Oh dear,' I said, 'I don't mind as long as no one's hurt.'

Mrs Darley shook her head, 'No, no we're all fine, luckily Eddie noticed it as he arrived, so we rang the fire brigade straight away who did a wonderful job of putting it out.'

'Look, I don't mean to intrude or anything,' said Eddie, stepping forward, 'but I was wondering if you'd like me to check your loft for you, just in case there's anything damaged up there that needs to be brought down. I've got some ladders on the van.'

'That would be very kind.' I said gratefully, 'I don't think there's much up there but I would like to know that everything's alright.'

Within ten minutes, Eddie and I were standing with heads bent in the loft space and began to pick our way across the beams towards the chimney. Here we could see the damage for ourselves as blackened stones became evident in the eerie torchlight and the acrid smell of burning hung in the air, catching our throats as we spoke.

'You were lucky,' said Eddie, 'the beams do look slightly singed but I don't think any structural damage has been done. Mind you, the mortar's a little bit suspect between these stones and if I'm not mistaken I think a few of them are loose. Still at least the assessor's coming tomorrow and he'll tell you what needs to be done but I think you'll be safe enough and it doesn't look as though it's done any harm to your suitcases over there.'

'Thanks Eddie,' I said, 'I appreciate you taking a look for me, you've put my mind at rest.'

'No problem,' he said, 'let's go down and see if Mrs D has the top off the whisky bottle yet.'

I laughed and turned to follow him when, in the beam of the torch, I noticed something glint way over by the back wall. I made my way, rather unsteadily, across the beams and, as I bent down to investigate; I saw a small wooden box fastened tight with some sort of metal clasp. Feeling rather excited I picked it up and immediately tucked it under my arm and decided to take it with me round to Mrs Darley's.

Upon entering the cottage, Eddie and I were immediately welcomed with a glass of whisky with which to 'calm our frayed nerves' and were delighted to detect the wonderful aroma of fish and chips wafting from the kitchen.

'Bod and Rose have bought us all fish and chips from the mobile van,' explained Mrs Darley, 'they thought we wouldn't want to be bothered with cooking after all the excitement.'

I for one was particularly grateful, and as we all began to tuck in I realised just how hungry I was.

'What have you got there, dear?' asked Mrs Darley, pointing to the little box I'd placed beside my chair.

'Oh,' I said, 'I'd almost forgotten, I found it in the loft, tucked up against the far wall. I haven't opened it yet.'

'Come on then,' said Bod clearing away the plates, 'don't keep us in suspense any longer.'

Under scrutiny I gingerly opened the box. I'm not sure exactly what I expected to see but the appearance of a small piece of wood and a few tiny bits of paper left me feeling rather deflated.

'Ah well,' laughed Bod, 'Looks as though you'll still have to go to work on Monday morning, not much treasure there!'

'Can I see it, dear?' asked Mrs Darley.

I placed the box in her outstretched hand and she carefully lifted out the piece of wood, peering at it closely under a magnifying glass. 'Ah,' she said almost knowingly.

'What?' we all chorused, our curiosity piqued.

'Look,' she said handing the wood and the magnifying glass over to me.

As I looked closely I saw that it was crudely carved, 'It says "Jack",' I said tracing the name with my finger.

'And these,' said Mrs Darley gently probing the bits in the box, 'look like petals. I think they might be from a daisy.'

'Ahhh,' said Rose looking into the box and counting the petals, 'He loves me, he loves me not, he loves me, he loves me not, he loves me, he loves me not, he loves me....'

'Do you think it was unrequited love?' pondered Phyllis.

'Or perhaps she was married and had to keep her love for Jack secret?' offered Rose.

'I wonder how old it is?' I asked.

'No doubt we will all muse over the contents of this box for some time to come,' said Mrs Darley, 'although none of us will ever know the real story but, it matters not, for although the little box does not contain gold and silver, tonight we have all been given a gift far more precious. This box and indeed the fire that led to its discovery have allowed us an insight into a life past and serve to remind us that no matter how many generations separate us and how different our lives may appear, we can all reach out across time and space and connect with others through our emotional experiences.'

The Natural World

The Sun

The sun is one of more than 100 billion stars in our galaxy and due to the fact that it could contain one million planets the size of earth, it is the largest object in the solar system.

The sun is an enormous ball of hot gas, some 4.5

billion years old, which currently comprises of seventy percent hydrogen, twenty eight percent helium and two percent other metals, although this slowly changes over time.

Every second the sun converts 700 million tons of hydrogen at its core into 695 million tons of helium and five million tons of energy in the form of gamma rays. Since its birth, the sun has used up approximately fifty percent of its hydrogen and will continue to radiate energy for a further estimated five billion years. Eventually, however, it will run out of fuel, bringing about the demise of the earth as a habitable planet for mankind.

This life giving star continuously bathes the earth's atmosphere in radiant energy called the 'solar constant' and it is this energy that drives the atmosphere and global weather. Alarmingly, if the sun's heat dropped by thirteen percent it is estimated that the earth would be covered in a layer of one mile thick ice one, whilst if its heat increased by thirty percent then life on earth would be sizzled.

The earth absorbs this radiant energy produced by the sun, becomes warmed by it and then re-radiates it in the form of heat, back out into the atmosphere, a finely balanced act known as the 'solar budget'.

As the energy travels from the core towards the surface of the sun, it is continually absorbed and re-emitted at lower and lower temperatures so that by the time it reaches the surface, or 'photosphere', where the temperature is a much cooler 6,000 degrees centigrade, it is primarily visible light.

Above the sun's photosphere are two further layers, namely the chromosphere and the corona, which extend millions of miles into the atmosphere but can only be seen with the naked eye during a solar eclipse.

The corona emits a continuous stream of charged particles in the form of electrons and protons, which produce a phenomenon known as the solar wind. This wind moves around the solar system at speeds of 450 kilometres per second and is modified by bursts of activity around the sun's surface called solar flares.

When these solar flares and the solar wind reach earth, they are, in the main, deflected by the magnetosphere or earth's magnetic field, however some weave their way into the earth's atmosphere and are responsible for certain dramatic events such as power line surges, radio interference, geomagnetic storms and the malfunction of compass needles. These solar winds are also thought to affect the tails size of comets and the trajectory of space craft.

When this interference occurs above the magnetic poles it becomes responsible for the spectacular shimmering curtain of lights known as the 'aurora borealis' or 'northern lights' in the northern hemisphere.

This beautiful phenomenon takes its name from Aurora, the Roman Goddess of the dawn who was said to renew herself every morning and fly across the sky announcing the arrival of the sun and Boreas, the Greek north wind.

The Aurora Borealis has inspired many literary greats including Shakespeare when he wrote Montague's speech in the opening act of Romeo and Juliet:

But all so soon as the all-cheering sun
Should in the farthest east begin to draw
The shady curtains from Aurora's bed,
Away from light steals home my heavy son.

A solar eclipse is always revered as a rare event although in actual fact it occurs once or twice during the year. Due however to the fact that it is only visible at different points on the earth's surface we still look upon it with a combination of awe and superstition.

A solar eclipse is merely an optical illusion, for when viewed from earth, the sun and the moon appear to be the same size, although in truth the sun is approximately 400 times bigger than the moon. However as the moon is approximately 400 times closer to the earth than the sun, they both appear to be the same size.

The moon orbits the earth on approximately the same plain as the earth orbits the sun and, on occasions, comes directly between the earth and the sun, preventing the sun's light from falling upon the earth therefore causing a solar eclipse. If the angle is precise, a total eclipse will occur whilst if the angle is slightly out only a partial eclipse will be seen.

In the UK the last solar eclipse visible was over Cornwall back in 1999 when, for a short time daylight gave way to an eerie darkness, the birds prepared for bed and the usually invisible corona came into view.

Without the sun, earth would be a very different place and although it is approximately 149,600,000 kilometres away from the earth and takes 8.3 minutes for its light to reach us, the absence of the sun would be devastating for life on earth, as it is responsible for the following:

1. Energy from the sun supports life on earth via photosynthesis, a process whereby plants capture the energy of sunlight and convert it to oxygen whilst simultaneously reducing carbon compounds.

2. The sun drives the climate and the weather by drawing up water from rivers and seas by the process of convection which, upon meeting cooler air, forms into clouds that ultimately provide rain.
3. The sun's energy can be utilised for direct heating or electrical conversion by the use of solar cells.
4. Energy stored in petroleum and other fossil fuels was originally converted from sunlight by photosynthesis in the distant past
5. Ultraviolet light from the sun has antiseptic properties and can be used to sanitise tools and water.
6. When we go out into the sunlight, its reaction with our skin manufactures vitamin D, ensuring the health of our bones.
7. It is partially responsible for biological adaptors, including variation in skin colour around the globe according to the strength of the sun.

By the same token however, the sun can wreak havoc and bring about devastation through forest fires, drought, skin cancers and blindness.

Sun superstitions
As with most natural phenomenon upon which mankind depends for survival the sun has become the subject of many superstitions.

- Morning sun in August never last the day (Cornish).
- A sunshine shower will not last an hour (Cornish).

- Those born at sunrise will be intelligent and sharp witted whilst those born at sunset will be slow and idle.
- It is bad luck to point at the sun.
- The bride and groom who have sunshine on their wedding day will have a happy life.

Sun Deities

Every ancient culture worshipped a Sun God, from Ra in Egypt to Mithras, the Sun God of the Persians.

The Romans acknowledged the great God Sol, the Latin word for 'sun' and after whom 'Sunday' is named, whilst the great Roman festival of *'Sol Invictus'* initiated by the Emperor Aurelian and celebrated on 25 December, marked the occasion of the return of the 'invincible sun'.

The Greeks on the other hand, although acknowledging Apollo as the God of solar light also worshipped the ancient God Helios, as the personification of the sun itself. Helios was the brother of Selene, the Moon Goddess and of Eos, Goddess of the Dawn. He also gave his name to one of the major gasses present in the sun, namely helium.

Helios was worshipped widely all over Greece, but was especially honoured on the island of Rhodes where his colossal statue spanned the harbour, allowing ships to pass between his legs. It was said that Helios was drowned in the ocean by his uncles, the Titans, and then raised into the sky, where he became the luminous sun.

Volcanoes

Throughout time volcanoes have shaped our history and bewitched mankind with their spectacular, unpredictable and destructive nature. Even today vulcanologists risk life and limb chasing the next eruption as though spellbound by the explosiveness of Mother Nature's power.

Away from the romanticism however, the earth is, in scientific terms, a 4.5 billion year old ball of molten rock with an iron core, a molten mantle and a cool crust. The constant movement of the earth's tectonic plates and the propulsion of convection currents in the mantle, cause faults or fissures to weaken and fracture the earth's crust. Therefore when the build up of dissolved gasses in the molten rock or 'magma' become too much for that particular fault to contain, the phenomenon we refer to as a volcanic eruption occurs, blasting a variety of material into the atmosphere as illustrated in Table 1.6 below.

Material	Description
Bombs	Large rocks that set fire to anything they come into contact with.
Eruption Clouds	These clouds pollute the atmosphere with ash and toxic gases such as sulphur dioxide. It is often thought that eruption clouds will affect the climate around the globe if the eruption is of sufficient magnitude for large quantities of material to be blown into the lower stratosphere some 20 – 25 miles high, a thought first put forward by Benjamin Franklin.
Lava	Fiery molten rock that burns everything in its path
Lahar	Mud flows, swift, silent and lethal, caused by rain or melt water from glaciers and which was responsible for the destruction of Herculaneum.
Pyroclastic flow	Exceptionally hot avalanche of rock and ash that engulfs everything in its path and travels at speeds of up to 100 mph.

Table 1.6

Volcanic Hotspots

According to the classification system used by scientists to determine whether a volcano is regarded as 'active' or not, the total number of volcanoes in the world today varies from 550 to 1,500, dependant upon opinion. To some a volcano is regarded as 'active' if it has erupted within the last 2,000 years, 'dormant' if it has not seen any activity for between 2,000 and 10,000 years and 'extinct' if it is more than 10,000 years since an eruption occurred. For others 'active' means that an eruption has occurred within the last 10,000 years.

Regardless of the exact definitions or numbers however, over half are found within an area known as 'The Ring of Fire', the most unstable region of the earth's crust, situated around the rim of the Pacific Ocean.

Of these, '*Mauna Loa*' in Hawaii, is the biggest in the world and has a volume of some 80,000 cubic kilometres. The largest loss of life however came from the eruption of Mount Tamora in Indonesia in 1815, where 92,000 people died and the following year became known in the northern hemisphere as 'the year without a summer'.

Just fifty eight years later, again in Indonesia, the island of Krakatoa was destroyed on 27 August by an eruption that was heard over 2,200 miles away and which triggered a one hundred foot high tidal wave that drowned 36,000 people. The cloud of ash that circled the globe ensured that this little Indonesian island would forever have a place in history, for the world was blessed by spectacular sunsets for a year following the eruption.

Perhaps the most notorious of all volcanic eruptions however was that of Vesuvius in Italy in 79 AD causing the dramatic destruction of Pompeii and neighbouring Herculaneum. This was an event in history that was preserved for all time in lava, enabling us all to appreciate the sheer terror experienced by its residents.

Below is an extract from a letter written by Pliny the Younger to the Roman Emperor Tacitus about the death of his acclaimed Uncle, Pliny the Elder during the volcanic eruption of Vesuvius. The translation of 'The Letters of Pliny', were made by William Melmoth in 1915 and later revised in a document by W M L Hutchinson in 1927.

'He (Pliny the Elder) was at that time with the fleet under his command at Misenium. On 24 August, about one in the afternoon, my mother desired him to observe a cloud of very unusual size and appearance....It was not at that distance discernable from what mountain this cloud issued, but it was found afterwards to be Vesuvius. I cannot give you a more exact description of its figure than by resembling it to that of a pine tree, for it shot up a great height in the form of a trunk which extended itself at the top into several branches...

My uncle, true savant that he was, deemed the phenomenon important and worth a nearer view. He ordered a light vessel be got ready, and gave me the liberty to attend him. I replied I would rather study...

Hastening to the place from whence others were flying, he steered his direct course to the point of danger... And now cinders, which grew thicker and hotter the nearer he approached, fell into the ships, then pumice stones too... then the sea ebbed suddenly from under them, while the shore was blocked with landslips from the mountains. After considering a moment whether he should retreat, he said, "Fortune befriends the brave, carry me to Pomponianus"...

In the meanwhile Mount Vesuvius was blazing in several places with spreading and towering flames. Upon arriving he retired to rest, but the court which led to his apartment now lay so deep under a mixture of pumice stones and ashes that if he had continued longer, egress would have been impossible. On being aroused they consulted together as to whether they should hold out in the house or wander about in the open. For the house now tottered under repeated and violent concussions and seemed to rock to and fro as if torn from its foundations. In the open air they dreaded the falling pumice stones, light and porous though they were, yet this, by comparison seemed the lesser danger of the two; a conclusion my uncle arrived at by balancing reasons and the others by balancing fears. They tied pillows upon their heads with napkins; and this was their whole defence against the showers that fell round them.

It was now day everywhere else, but there a deeper darkness prevailed than in the most obscure night. They thought proper to go down to the shore to observe from close at hand if they could put out to sea, but they found the waves still ran extremely high and contrary. There my uncle having thrown himself down upon a disused sail, repeatedly called for, and drank, a draught of cold water; soon after flames and a strong smell of sulphur dispersed the rest of the company in flight, him they only aroused. He raised himself up with the assistance of two of his slaves, but instantly fell; some unusually gross vapour, as I conjecture, having obstructed his breathing and blocked his windpipe. When day dawned again his body was found entire and uninjured, and still fully clothed as in life; its posture was that of a sleeping, rather than a dead man....

New Volcanoes

For some strange reason we often consider the manifestation of new volcanoes to be something that happened millions of years ago during the formation of the earth and that those which remain active today are merely a legacy of that period in time.

This however is certainly not the case and in places where the earth moves sufficiently to cause a fissure, new volcanoes are always waiting to be born as was the case in a field in Michoacán, Mexico in 1943.

A local farmer called Dionisio Pulido owned the said field which had, for as long as he could remember always contained a hole around five metres in diameter into which he threw his rubbish, although it never appeared to get completely full.

On 5 February that year, the inhabitants of the nearby village of Paricutin some two kilometres away felt the ground vibrate and heard a strange rumbling sound which gradually grew louder as the day progressed. The noises continued throughout the days that followed and on 19 February, 300 tremors were recorded.

The following day, Dionisio Pulido was preparing his field for sowing when he saw a fissure some fifty centimetres deep that seemed to cut through the hole he used for rubbish. He then noticed that the trees were beginning to tremble and watched as the earth began to rise up through the crack, from which smoke was also beginning to escape along with the unmistakable smell of sulphur. In total panic he and his workers returned to the village.

Next day however, curiosity overcame him and he returned to his field to see a cone of ash some ten metres high which, by midday had grown to a height of fifty metres. After a week, the new volcano now named Paricutin stood 150 metres above the field and the eruptions could be heard 350 kilometres away. Within a year it had reached its final size of 336 metres and the field was no more.

In July 1944 a lava flow came out of the cone and travelled ten kilometres to the town of San Juan and by

September of that year the village of Paricutin was no more.

Luckily for Dionisio Pulido, although he had no farm and no home, he did manage to sell his volcano to an artist called Doctor Atl, who was passionately fond of volcanoes and who made 11,000 drawings and 1,000 paintings of Paricutin as it erupted for a further nine years and twelve days.

A later event occurred on 14 November 1963 just off the coast of Iceland where a fisherman noticed clouds of smoke rising from the sea. Before long steam, smoke and debris were rising 12,000ft into the air, resulting the very next day in the appearance of a new island. This phenomenon of a volcano erupting below the sea is referred to as a 'submarine volcano'.

Eruptions continued in the months that followed until the resulting island covered an area of one square mile and rose more than 500ft above sea level. Local people called the island, Surtsey, after the Norse God of fire, Surtr.

Many other islands have also been formed in this way including the Hawaiian Islands, the Galapagos, the Azores and the Canaries, however, Surtsey was unique in that its actual birth was not only witnessed by humans but also captured on film.

Scientists are still attempting to bring about a fool proof way of predicting a volcanic eruption and although there are scientific measuring devices attached to many known active volcanoes around the world, Mother Nature will always have the last word when it comes to taking mankind by surprise and giving birth to new ones.

The one sign however that many people living close to a volcano will still take most notice of is the behaviour of local animals, for they seem to understand the subtle changes take place in the atmosphere around them and will take flight away from the danger zone.

The Beneficial Aspects of Volcanoes

Although volcanoes often portray nature in one of Her most devastating forms, one in ten people throughout the world still choose to live within a volcanic danger zone, indicating that perhaps the benefits far outweigh the risks.

Due to the rich mineral content of volcanic material, the surrounding areas become extremely fertile and as such encourage farmers and wine growers to venture again and again into the volcanic area in order to take advantage of the beautiful soil which yields healthy crops and rich harvests.

Eruptions of thick viscous lava build steep sided volcanic mountains and often offer protection for delicate plants and animals, which may otherwise have difficulty in surviving.

In these carbon footprint conscious days, volcanoes can provide steam from underground, which is heated by the earth's magma, in order to drive turbines in geothermal power stations therefore providing both industrial and domestic electricity as is the case in Iceland and New Zealand.

Very often mining towns develop around a volcanic area as an eruption can bring to light many valuable metals and minerals such as gold, silver, diamonds, copper and zinc.

Finally, a volcano can increase tourism in the area, therefore creating jobs and helping to boost the local economy.

Volcanic Deities
   * **Hephaestus**

Mrs Darley's Pagan Elements

For the ancient Greeks, Hephaestus was the powerful God of Smiths and Fire and had many earthly volcanic abodes with Mount Etna on the island of Sicily being one of the most popular. Etna was often seen as his workplace and the rumbling sounds emanating from the mountain were thought to be the sound of his hammer as he made weapons for the Gods.

For all this dramatic and often terrifying abode however, Hephaestus was not associated with the destroying element of fire, but rather the beneficial aspect, which allowed men to work metal and foster civilization. He was depicted as the Divine blacksmith, the artisan God, who was always portrayed carrying a hammer and tongs.

Hephaestus was said to be the illegitimate son of Hera and Zeus and, unfortunately was not the most handsome of Gods. Hera was extremely embarrassed by her son's unfortunate appearance, for he was both lame and had twisted feet. His gait was most ungainly and he had to endure the laughter of the Gods as he walked amongst them. She therefore decided to cast him into the sea from Mount Olympus to end his life.

This act however was witnessed by Thetis, daughter of the ocean, who took pity on Hephaestus and provided a home for him beneath the waves. Here he remained for nine years whilst continuing to design and fashion beautiful works of art. His works included the winged chariot of Helios, the arrows of Apollo and Artemis, the golden throne of Zeus and the armour of Achilles.

One day he sent his mother, Hera, an unexpected gift of a golden throne but immediately she sat upon it, she was gripped by invisible hands and could not escape, despite the best efforts of the Gods. Realising that Hephaestus had tricked her, Hera offered him a wish in return for her release, and Hephaestus, without hesitation, asked for the hand of the most beautiful Goddess, Aphrodite.

This was not however a marriage made in heaven and with other loves on both sides, Hephaestus was said to eventually become the father to twins, by the Oceanid, Etna.

Masaya

In Nicaragua belief in the Goddess of Volcanoes, Masaya, led to many terrifying sacrifices. Following a volcanic eruption or an earthquake the Indians would chose their loveliest young virgin and cast her into the crater of the Volcano to drown in the lava lake.

Even as late as 1880 the natives attributed the eruption of the volcano to the fury of the Goddess Masaya, who they said was angry because the government had put a launch into service on a nearby lake. In order to appease the Goddess, a young child, bound hand to foot was thrown into the lake as a sacrifice.

In Christianity

From the domain of the old Gods, it appears that volcanoes also made their way into the Christian texts albeit often personified as God as illustrated in Genesis 19:23-28:

By the time Lot reached Zoar, the sun had risen over the land. Then the Lord rained down burning sulphur on Sodom and Gomorrah – from the Lord out of the heavens. Thus he overthrew those cities and the entire plain, including all those living in the cities – and also the vegetation in the land.

Early the next morning Abraham got up and returned to the place where he had stood before the Lord. He

*looked down towards Sodom and Gomorrah, towards all
the land of the plain, and saw dense smoke rising from
the land, like smoke rising from a furnace.*

Here Yahweh, God of the Hebrews, bears more than a
passing resemblance to a volcano. Likewise in the Book
of Revelations 8: 7- 9, the rumblings of the earth are
referred to as the sound emanating from angelic trumpet:

*The first angel sounded his trumpet and there came
hail and fire mixed with blood, and it was hurled down
upon the earth. A third of the earth was burned up, and
all the green grass was burned up.*

*The second angel sounded his trumpet, and something
like a huge mountain all ablaze, was thrown into the sea.
A third of the sea turned into blood, a third of living
creatures in the sea died, and a third of the ships were
destroyed.*

Volcanoes have had a far more reaching effect on
Christianity than is perhaps initially realised, as
evidenced in Iceland in 1,000 AD. Here the 'Althing', the
world's first democratic parliament, gathered at
Thingvellir to discuss the controversial issue of whether
Iceland should adopt Christianity as their national
religion, just as their European neighbours had done, or
whether they should continue to revere the Nordic Gods.

The debate became quite animated as the various
tribal leaders tried to put forward their own point of view.
During the discussions however a messenger arrived to
announce that lava was pouring from a fissure in the
earth and threatening the village of Thorodd. The Pagan
fraternity were ecstatic and used the event to point out
that the Nordic Gods were angry at the thought of Iceland
becoming a Christian nation.

However, one of the tribal leaders, a supporter of
Christianity called Snorri, turned the news to his

advantage by pointing out that the vast expanse of congealed lava that covered the valley of Thingvellir had been deposited many years previously, long before there was any mention of Christianity on the island and it was with a subsequent powerful argument that Snorri won the vote and Iceland became, mainly, a Christian country.

In the early Middle Ages, Christians often saw the eruption of a volcano as being the gateway to hell. These rumours were especially prevalent throughout the communities of Cistercian monks during the 12th century following the violent eruption at Hekla in Iceland.

The volcanoes of Etna and Vesuvius both have their patron saints, which are said to dwell at the foot of each mountain. St Agatha protects the Sicilian city of Catania, whilst St Januarius protects the Italian city of Naples.

In 1971 during an eruption of Etna the people of the nearby village of San Alfio carried the relics of St Agatha to where the blocks of molten lava lay and begged heaven to spare them. The volcano stopped and erupting and their wish was seen as being granted by God.

In Naples, every great eruption leads to a procession of the relics of St Januarius. In the late 19th century peasants with studied whips flagellated themselves until they bled, whilst others tore at their hair, covered their heads with ashes and sang psalms as they made their way towards the cathedral. Once at their destination the Bishop showered down blessings and absolutions, whilst exposing the bones of the saint in order to make Vesuvius stop erupting.

Even in more modern times the church hierarchy have sought to use volcanic eruptions to their advantage in order to control the masses, as was the case in Washington State on 18 May 1980. On this day, Mount St Helens blew away a third of the mountain in an enormous explosion and Adventist preachers immediately deemed this to be a punishment from God to all those who swore and drank alcohol.

Regardless of whether volcanoes are seen as a Divine blessing or curse, their unpredictable behaviour will always capture the imagination and demand the respect of mankind.

Thunderstorms

One of the most terrifying aspects of a thunderstorm is the sheer volume of noise generated as the storm reaches its climax, regardless of the fact that we cannot be harmed by the sound, only by the accompanying lightning. However, the sheer unpredictability of a thunder storm, coupled the feeling that, as always, Mother Nature has the upper hand, finds many a heart gripped by fear as the thunder begins to roll.

Scientifically a thunderstorm is, quite simply a slow explosion of warm moist air, although when looked at in more detail it becomes a far more complex phenomenon.

Since the Second World War, much research has been carried out on the fascinating subject of thunderstorms and in 1948 American scientists discovered that storms occur in units which they called 'cells' and that the presence of one or more of these cells would determine the severity and composition of the storm.

The majority of thunderstorms are normally referred to as 'single cell' storms where there is just one updraft of warm air, a phenomenon we would normally experience in the UK after a few days of hot weather in the summer months.

There are however two other types of storms which occur in other parts of the world. The first of these is a 'multi cell' storm which usually occurs over mountain ranges, often becoming more severe and larger than the single cell storm as it consists of several updrafts, whilst a 'super cell' storm will, as its name probably suggests, be the most violent, consisting of many powerful updrafts. In some cases the updraft can be so strong that the top of the anvil cloud can break through the troposphere and reach the lower level of the stratosphere. The storm can be up to fifteen miles wide and usually brings severe weather conditions such as tornadoes, hail stones up to four centimetres in diameter, winds of up to eighty miles per hour and flash floods.

Understanding Thunder and Lightning

The bright flash or sheet of light we refer to as lightning is caused by a build up of static electricity in a cloud, which is generated by super cooked water droplets colliding with ice crystals.

The temperature of lightning is five times that of the sun although its duration of 0.2 seconds is relatively short and up to ninety percent of strike victims survive.

Lightning, just like storm types can be many and varied but the three most popular are listed in Table 1.7 below.

Type of Lightning	Effects
In cloud	Occurs within a cloud: usually referred to as 'sheet lightning
Cloud to ground	Causes greatest threat to life: Also known as 'fork lightning
Ball	Very rare: A ball of light forms measuring between 20 and 200 cm

Table 1.7

Mrs Darley's Pagan Elements

We are all familiar with the concept of sheet and fork lightning, however ball lightning appears very occasionally and therefore seems to be shrouded in mystery. It is a strange phenomenon, where a ball of light appears quite close to the ground and seems to take on a life of its own, often entering buildings by breaking through windows and causing havoc, until hitting something metallic at which point it makes a loud bang and disappears.

The famous occultist, Aleister Crowley wrote about such a phenomenon which he called 'globular electricity' in his autobiography in 1989 entitled *The Confessions of Aleister Crowley: An Autobiography.* In the book he recalls a time when he was sheltering from a thunderstorm in a small cottage on Lake Pasquaney, New Hampshire in 1916:

I noticed what I can only describe as calm amazement, that a dazzling globe of electric fire appeared between 6 and 12 inches in diameter and was stationary about 6 inches below and to the right of my right knee. As I looked at it, it exploded with a sharp report quite impossible to confuse with the continuous turmoil of the lightning, thunder and hail, or that of the lashed water and smashed wood, which was creating pandemonium outside the cottage. I felt a very slight shock in the middle of my right hand, which was closer to the globe than any other part of my body.

Strangely, although lightning is the one thing we should be afraid of during a thunderstorm, the majority of us are more afraid of the sound of thunder, especially when it cracks right overhead. This is probably due to the fact that we are born with two inbuilt fears, the first being a fear of falling and the second being a fear of loud noises.

The fearsome noise is caused by the super heated air around the lightning expanding at the speed of sound. However, because sound travels slower than the speed of light, the flash is always seen before the thunder is heard. In reality however, they both occur at the same time and it impossible to have a rumble of thunder without a flash of lightning, even if we do not happen to see it.

Storm Safety

Fork lightning will always find the quickest route to earth and if there is anything metallic in the vicinity then the attraction will be too hard to resist. Therefore if you are caught in a thunderstorm it may be worth bearing the following in mind:

- A car is the safest place of refuge due to the rubber tyres preventing the lightning strike from earthing out. A moving car is particularly safe.
- Take shelter indoors, especially somewhere there is a lightning conductor attached.
- Unplug TV aerials.
- If outdoors try to avoid wide open spaces such as golf courses or playing fields.
- It is better to get wet than put up an umbrella as metal spokes can attract lightning.
- Avoid handling golf clubs on the course until the storm is over.
- Avoid sheltering under broad leafed trees such as oaks, elms and beech as these are regularly struck whereas pine trees appear to be virtually immune. This is probably due to the fact that the needles on pine trees produce an electrical effect that helps to prevent lightning discharges.

Mrs Darley's Pagan Elements

Hopefully the following rhyme may just keep you safe:

Beware of the oak, it draws the stroke.
Avoid the ash, it courts the flash.
Creep under a thorn,
It can save you from harm.

Americans say that wood taken from a tree which has been struck by lightning should never be used as firewood, for this exposes the household to a similar fate.

Thunderstorm Superstitions

Yet again thunderstorms provide us with a glimpse of Nature's shadow side, resulting in the formation of many superstitions.

A useful old English rhyme goes:

Thunder in the morning,
All the day storming;
Thunder at night,
Is the sailor's delight.

- To sleep through a storm is to confer protection for superstition tells that no one is believed to have been killed by lightning whilst asleep.
- To be woken by a flash of lightning is good luck.
- To keep safe during a storm, wind a snake skin around your head, sleep on a feather bed, keep a fire burning in the grate, cover the mirrors and hide the scissors.
- Open all the doors and windows to ensure no thunderbolt will strike.
- If church bells are rung the storm will go away.

- Landlords should place a bar of iron over a barrel of beer during a storm to prevent the beer from going off (the same applies to milk).
- A Cornish saying tells that the harvest will fail to ripen until there has been a thunder storm.

Thunder Deities

Most Pagan cultures had their own God of thunder and war after whom the day of 'Thursday' was named. The German God of thunder and war was called '*Donar*' and the German word for Thursday was 'Donnerstang', In Rome the equivalent God was Jupiter and Thursday was called '*Jovis dies*', whilst in French this metamorphosed into '*Jeudi*' and finally in the Nordic lands the God of thunder and war was Thor, after which the English for Thursday was derived.

In the Nordic countries and particularly in Norway, Thor eventually prevailed over all the other Gods. Temples were erected in his name and filled with treasure of many kinds, whilst many parents named their children after him in the hope that he would place them under his protection. Thor was described as a rude, crude warrior, always ready to face combat and a great adversary of giants and demons. He was a fearless and imposing God sporting a long red beard and wielding a stone hammer, whilst his voice was said to instil fear into his enemies and could even be heard above the fiercest battle.

Thor's infamous hammer was considered to be a meteorite which had fallen to earth during a thunderstorm although some sources state that it was fashioned by a dwarf who was skilled in ironwork. This infamous tool reputedly never missed its mark and, after its work was done, would always return to Thor's hand. The hammer was called '*Mjolnir*', meaning 'destroyer' and was not

101

only for the soul purpose of destroying the enemy for it also gave consecration to public or private treaties, especially marriage contracts. This gave rise to Thor's alternative persona as the patron of nuptials and the protector of married couples.

Thor

Not a whisper
Not a breath
Like death.

Hidden sun
Hidden light
Like night.

Sudden wind
Spinning leaves
Thor breathes.

Thunder rolls
Distant drums
Thor comes.

Forked skies
Warlike
Thor strikes.

Storm fades
Heaven weeps
Thor sleeps.

Rainbows

Rainbows show us a gentler side of Mother Nature, although once again we probably find ourselves captivated by this beautiful celestial spectacle, just as Wordsworth was in his poem, 'My Heart Leaps up When I Behold a Rainbow':

My heart leaps up when I behold a rainbow in the sky:
So it was when my life began;
So it is now I am a man;
So be it when I shall grow old,
Or let me die!

Rainbows occur when it is both raining and sunny and can only be seen when facing away from the sun.

When the sun shines through a raindrop it splits white light into seven different wave lengths by refracting (bending) each one at a different angle. This separation of white light into the seven colours of the full colour spectrum is known as 'dispersion'.

The longest wavelength in the spectrum is red whilst the shortest is violet and these, combined with the five colours in between give us the colours of the rainbow with which we are familiar.

Early morning and late evening are the best times to see a rainbow, for the lower the sun is in the sky, the higher the arc of the rainbow.

Due to red having the longest wavelength, this is always the outer colour, followed by the same sequence of orange, yellow, green, blue, indigo and violet.

Secondary rainbows are often seen outside the main arc, a phenomenon caused by a double reflection of sunlight within a raindrop, although strangely this causes the colours to become reversed as though looking at them through a mirror. Only a fraction of the light entering a raindrop ends up in the bow anyway.

Rainbow Superstitions

It comes as little surprise that the magical phenomenon of a rainbow brings with it a host of superstitions.

- Leprechauns bury their pots of gold at the end of a rainbow (Irish).
- It is a pathway to the Gods along which children can be called (Nordic).
- It is regarded generally as a sign of good luck. and you should make a wish if you see one.
- Rainbow in the morning and the day will be wet, but seen in the afternoon the next day will be fine. Conversely the Cornish say:
  'Rainbow at morn put your hook in the corn,
  Rainbow at eve put your head in the sheave.'
- Rainbow on a Saturday forecasts a stormy week ahead (Irish).
- A rainbow in the west indicates rain whilst one in the east indicates fine weather.

Rainbow Deities

Iris

In Greek myth a rainbow was thought to be a path made by the messenger of the Gods, Iris, between heaven and earth and was thus able to link the Gods with humanity. Iris was also the personal messenger of Hera, wife of Zeus and was said to have angel's wings above a gown of iridescent droplets.

Indra

In Hindu mythology a rainbow is referred to as *'Indradhanush'* meaning 'the bow of Indra', the Hindu God of thunder, light and rain.

Ishtar

In the 'Epic of Gilgamesh' (tablet 11), the rainbow depicts the jewelled necklace of Ishtar, a promise that she too will never forget the days of the great flood which destroyed her children:

Then Ishtar arrived. She lifted up the necklace of great jewels that her father Anu, had created to please her and said, 'Heavenly Gods, as surely as this jewelled necklace hangs upon my neck, I will never forget these days of the great flood. Let all of the Gods except Enlil come to the offering. Enlil may not come, for without reason he brought forth the flood that destroyed my people.'

In Christianity

Echoing the earlier story of Ishtar, the book of Genesis, 9: 13-15 in the Christian Bible, sees God sending a rainbow as a promise that terrestrial life will never be devastated by flood again:

I have set my rainbow in the clouds, and it will be the sign of the covenant between me and the earth. Whenever I bring clouds over the earth and the rainbow appears in the clouds, I will remember my covenant between me and you and all living creatures of every kind. Never again will the waters become a flood and destroy all life.

Domestic Fire

Fire, like its elemental counterparts, is a paradox, it can burn with unbridled passion or smoulder with desire. It has the ability to sustain life through the gentle flames that flicker in the hearth or become the all consuming blaze that destroys. It dances, ignites, heats and shines. The heart is warmed by it, yet also has the ability to strike fear and as humans we are both drawn to it and repelled by it.

To describe fire to someone who had never seen it would be a gargantuan task and to consider what man must have made of this magical phenomenon in the first instance is almost impossible to comprehend. However, according to Greek legend, there was a moment in time when mankind had the gift of fire taken away and it is to the Greek God Prometheus that we should offer our thanks for its restoration.

Prometheus was the son of the Titan Lapetus and, according to the Greek poet, Hesiod, posed a threat, albeit a lowly one, to Zeus' position.

One day Prometheus decided to play a trick on Zeus and placed two sacrificial offerings before him. The first was some bull meat hidden within an oxen's carcass, to represent the good being hidden within a displeasing exterior and the second was the bulls bones hidden within glistening fat, to represent the bad being hidden within a pleasing exterior.

Zeus chose the latter, the one which looked good, however in doing so he set a precedent for future sacrifices as from then on the humans decided to keep the meat for themselves and offer the bones wrapped in fat to the Gods.

This trick made Zeus very angry and as a punishment he decided to hide fire away from mankind. Prometheus was horrified by this punishment and at once went to see Athena in order to gain entry into Olympus. Once inside, Prometheus lit a torch from the fiery chariot of the sun, from which he broke a small fragment of glowing charcoal. This he threw into the hollow of a giant fennel stalk in the world of the mortal and, extinguishing his torch, he crept away from Olympus.

Zeus was enraged and as a punishment, he chained

Prometheus to a rock, where each day his liver was ripped out and eaten by a bird of prey, only to be regenerated each night in readiness for the following day's torture. Many years later however, Heracles shot the bird and released Prometheus from his dreadful punishment.

The Magic of the Fireside

Before the days of central heating the hearth was the focal point of the home. It was the protector from cold, the heat source for cooking and the old fashioned equivalent of the TV, where everyone would gather to talk, sing, tell stories, and watch for omens of the future in the flames. It was by far the most popular place in the home.

Today, real fires are becoming a rarity and although we like the idea of a real fire, our busy and stress filled lives see fire making as both time consuming and messy. Therefore heat at the flick of a switch has become the norm and a real fire the exception.

Fire, however, still holds an attraction for many. It is sacred, hypnotic and alive. In times past, the majority of magical and religious celebrations world wide used fire in their rituals and even today flames can still be found on many an altar, albeit in the form of a candle.

Fire cleanses and purifies, cauterises and seals, cooks and melts, warms and lights and yet, as with all things, it too has a shadow side for fire is also capable of burning and disfiguring, of destruction and death. Fire is the ultimate element of transformation.

Fire Superstitions

In the days when fire was revered, it was most important that the domestic fire was maintained at all times, and the only time when a fire was allowed to die naturally was on ritual occasions. At night the coals were banked up to enable new flames to spring from them in the morning.

If a fire did go out, then this was considered unfortunate for the household, and the only resolution was to fetch hot coals from a neighbouring house with which to restart the fire. If, however, the coals died whilst being transported from the neighbour's home, then it was seen as a sign that the family were in for a troubled future.

Today, however, we do not place any importance on a fire going out, and will simply re-light it when we have cleaned it out however, there is still a certain ritual associated with lighting a new fire.

Fires must have at least 13 sticks before they burn properly, however the lighting of fire is a sacred process and not meant for human eyes, therefore the lighter should always partially avert their eyes. If this rule is disobeyed then it will hinder the fire's burning and may even bring bad luck to the entire household!

The chimney too, is seen as a magical entrance and exit (Father Christmas comes down them and witches are said to fly up them), therefore it is most important that they are guarded.

To ensure protection around the hearth, the following fire rituals are recommended:

- Never let a stranger poke your fire as this will bring bad luck.
- To cleanse the house of the negative energies following an argument, keep a jar of salt on the hearth and throw a pinch into the fire.
- To help to restore health of a household member, burn oak, as this helps to draw off the

illness, aids recovery and protects others from contracting it.

- To ensure an evening spent at home is passionate, burn apple wood.
- To attract money burn pine.
- Leaving a lighted candle in the window at Christmas time or the Winter Solstice will ensure a year of light, warmth and plenty for the family.
- Golden sparks indicate money for the observer.
- A brightly burning fire indicates rain.
- A crackling fire indicates frost.
- A blue flame indicates cold weather.
- A fire that lights quickly indicates that unexpected visitors are arriving.
- If a cat sits on the hearth it is the sign of a contented home.
- Smoke rising from a chimney denotes a happy life for those who reside within.
- A fire that burns one side of the grate indicates a wedding.
- Flames roaring up the chimney indicate there will either be a strong argument in the family or a fierce storm is on its way.
- If a candle will not light or if the flame flickers when there is no draft then there is a storm on the way.

Fireside Deities
With domestic fire being such a focal point in times past, it is hardly surprising that Deities were honoured and worshipped at the hearth of the home, In Greece the Goddess of the hearth was Hestia, whilst her Roman equivalent was Vesta.

Vesta

Vesta was the most beautiful of all the Roman Goddesses, being bright and pure like the flame she symbolised. Her name derives from a Sanskrit word, *'vas'*, meaning 'shining' and every Roman hearth had a special altar dedicated to this popular Goddess, where offerings of food and drink were made at each meal before the family sat down to eat.

Vesta had a special feast day on 7 June called Vestailia and it was on this day that her sanctuary, which normally was only open to her priestesses, the Vestal Virgins, became accessible to mothers and their children. The women who visited Vesta's sanctuary brought with them offerings of food in exchange for the blessings of the Goddess.

The Vestal Priestesses, of which there were six, held a prestigious position in Roman society and were chosen by lots from Patrician families. They entered the college of the Goddess between the ages of six and ten and remained in service for thirty years. During the first ten years they completed their training, during the second decade they served the Goddess and during the last ten years they taught the young Vestals.

The Vestal Virgins took vows of absolute chastity and those who broke them were immediately put to death. Initially this punishment was executed by whipping them to death, but a belief became popular whereby to kill a virgin was to bring about bad luck and therefore the punishment was slightly modified by the Elder Tarquin.

Tarquin decided that although the Vestals should still be whipped as a punishment, they should then be taken, whilst still alive, to a tomb where they would be given enough food and water to last them for a few days, after which time they would die of thirst and starvation.

Therefore their death could not be attributed to anyone in particular. It is said that during a period of 1,100 years, only twenty Vestals broke their vows.

When the Vestals finished their thirty years of service they were free to leave and marry, but very few took advantage of their freedom, preferring to maintain the privileges of their position.

If a Vestal was lax enough to let the sacred fire go out she was whipped by order of Pontifex Maximus, however, if a condemned man was lucky enough to meet a Vestal of the way to his death, then he was immediately reprieved.

Hestia

In Greek, the word, *'hestia'* literally translates as 'hearth' and as such the Goddess Hestia became the Greek deity of the domestic fire and offered protection to individual homes and cities. Each Greek town had an altar to Hestia in the *'prytaneum'* or 'public hearth', whilst temples dedicated to her were always circular.

Hestia was the oldest of the Olympians, the daughter of Cronus and Rhea and as such was greatly revered by man. Hestia was always offered the first morsels from a sacrificial victim and the first and final libations.

Both Poseidon and Apollo sought her hand in marriage, but she wanted neither of them and chose instead, to take a vow of chastity and place herself under the protection of Zeus.

Mrs Darley Tale: The Storm

I awoke one hot Saturday morning to a low droning noise accompanied by the sound of voices calling to one another. Looking out of the bedroom window I saw a tanker parked in the field below and several people congregated in Mrs Darley's garden, one of whom was nodding pointedly towards my lawn and so I dressed and went down to investigate.

'Ah, there you are, dear,' said Mrs Darley as I emerged into the sunlight, 'I was just about to come and knock you up'.

'Is there a problem?' I asked.

'Blockage in the septic tank', she stated in a matter of fact tone.

'Oh dear,' I said, 'That sounds rather serious and rather expensive.'

'Well hopefully not, Black Bill's here with his nephew to try and sort it out. The problem is that this septic tank was put in years ago and wasn't designed to cope with all our modern contraptions and the vast use of water, so I suppose we can't really complain. The thing is, although I have the second chamber of the tank in my garden, you have the first chamber under yours, but no-one can quite remember where, although it's been suggested that it's somewhere down the bottom by the wall.'

'Ah,' I said, as all thoughts of having a lazy day in the garden disappeared like the wind. 'They'll be wanting to dig then?'

She nodded, 'I'm afraid so, dear, but I'm sure they'll try and replace it all as neatly as possible and if they start now at least they'll have it done before the storm comes.'

I wanted to ask her how on earth she knew a storm was imminent on such a glorious summer's morning but I could see she was anxious to get everyone started, so I merely replied, 'OK, go ahead,' knowing that I had little alternative.

Around two o'clock, as I sat reading, there was a knock at the door and Mrs Darley stood in the porch waving a piece of paper. 'I'll leave a copy of the invoice here dear,' she said dropping it on the cane chair, 'we're splitting it four ways.'

I went upstairs to fetch my chequebook and within five minutes was making my way round to her cottage. Black Bill, his nephew Tom, plus Don and Phyllis who had just arrived, were all sitting on the little patch of grass outside Mrs Darley's door with a cold beer as I approached.

'Thank you for making such a good job of replacing the grass.' I said as they all greeted me.

'Well, it'll do for now,' said Black Bill, 'but it's really only a temporary measure, I was saying to Mrs D that what you really need is a new pit dug out, that one's far too small, I should … oh …,' he said suddenly stopping mid sentence, 'was that thunder I heard?'

Mrs Darley nodded, 'The tell tale signs have been around for twenty-four hours now.'

'What tell tale signs?' I asked eager to hear how she could predict a storm.

'Yesterday afternoon, although it was hot and sunny, I noticed fluffy sheep clouds line up across the sky. They often appear as a forerunner of stormy weather, although most people just regard them as benevolent summer clouds.'

'Altocumulus floccus,' stated Don, 'so called because they resemble a flock of sheep.'

'Good Lord!' said a surprised Mrs Darley, 'I didn't know you were a weather buff, Don.'

'I dabble.' Don replied smiling, 'Actually I think this storm might be quite a good one, look at the height of the anvil headed clouds over Dartmoor.'

We all turned to look at the horizon, which was rapidly being enveloped by a threatening indigo sky.

'I don't like it,' said Black Bill.

'Well,' said Phyllis, 'I wouldn't have had you down as being afraid of thunderstorms, Bill.'

'It's not that I'm afraid of the storm exactly,' he said, 'it's more a case of I don't like it when a thunderstorm comes from over Dartmoor.'

'Oh, not the story of Widecombe-in-the-Moor again, Uncle Bill,' laughed Tom standing up, 'Come on, I'll take you home before the storm sets in and you bore these good people with your funny tales.'

'No!' we all chorused.

'You can't take him home now,' protested Phyllis, 'Not when it's just getting interesting. If you need to go, Tom, that's fine I'm quite happy to drop Bill off later on my way home.'

With this, Tom said his goodbyes and the five of us settled down with another cold beer to listen to Black Bill as the storm rumbled ever closer.

'Well,' began Black Bill, 'It was an exceptionally hot and sultry day on the 21 October 1638 and the local church of St Pancreas at Widecome-in-the-Moor on Dartmoor was packed with three hundred worshippers when, without warning, the great storm hit.

Eyewitnesses at the time told of a strange darkness and thunder the like of which had never been heard before and then …,' he said dramatically, pausing, 'out of the gloom came a great ball of fire, ripping through the window of the church and tearing part of the roof open. The fire was said to have split in two, causing the death of four parishioners and injuring sixty others. One poor victim called Robert Mead struck a pillar so hard it left an indentation, whilst his skull was shattered and his brain was hurled to the ground!'

'Oh dear, that's rather graphic, Bill!' Said Don

'I'm not making this up for effect you know,' said Black Bill rather defensively, 'you can read all the historical documents if you want.'

'Oh, I'm not doubting it for a minute,' Don said quickly.

'Well,' continued Black Bill, 'the ball of fire left behind the most unpleasant smell of sulphur and burning. Now, don't forget we are going back to suspicious times when witchcraft and the devil meant the same thing in the eyes of the Christian fraternity and so, this naturally led to much speculation as to what or, more to the point, who had just visited the church.'

At that moment a flash of lightning, followed almost immediately by a loud crack of thunder, rolled around the surrounding tors and much to my relief Mrs Darley suggested that perhaps we should go indoors.

'We'll be OK here,' said Don, 'if the lightning's going to strike anything it will go for Caradon mast up on the hill.'

'No, I think she's right,' said Black Bill rising to his feet quicker than I'd ever seen him move before. 'Anyway,' he said gratefully, 'here comes the rain.'

Soon we were all packed into Mrs Darley's cottage and, as we settled down, she went around lighting a few candles in order to dispel the inevitable gloom that accompanies a storm.

'So then, Bill,' said Phyllis, 'What speculation took place at Widecombe-in-the-Moor?'

'Well, it was said that a local card player and gambler called Jan Reynolds was in league with the devil and had made a pact with him. This pact stated that if ever the devil caught Jan sleeping in church then he would have to forfeit his soul. Now this particular day, because the weather was heavy and the church was hot, Jan Reynolds did indeed fall asleep during the sermon with a pack of cards in his hands. The devil of course had noticed this and with great delight set off to collect Jan's soul.

Now just about the time that the great storm began, the landlady at the Tavistock Inn at Poundstock, just a few miles down the road from Widecombe, reported having a strange visitor call at her inn. The stranger asked for refreshments and directions to the church and feeling a little afraid of him the landlady obliged. She described the man as being dressed in black, with cloven feet who rode a jet black horse and that when he swallowed his pint of ale it hissed as it went down. Upon finishing, he placed the glass down on the bar, leaving a scorch mark on the counter. As he rode away he threw a few coins in the landlady's hand but as soon as he had disappeared the coins simply turned into dried leaves.

The story goes that this frightening stranger tethered his horse to one of the pinnacles at St Pancreas' church, captured the sleeping Jan Reynolds and rode off with him into the storm, never to be seen again.'

'Well, what a story!' exclaimed Phyllis.

'Oh I haven't finished yet,' said Black Bill. 'As the devil flew over Birch Tor with Jan Reynolds it was said that Jan's pack of cards fell to the ground and that if you stand today at the Warren House Inn between Postbridge and Moreton you can still make out in the ancient field enclosures, impressions of the four suits of hearts, diamonds, spades and clubs!'

'How very interesting,' said Mrs Darley, 'A story no doubt used as propaganda by the Christian fraternity of the time, in order to dissuade people from both gambling and falling asleep during the sermon!'

'Yes indeed,' said Phyllis. 'A story like that if told with authority would certainly make you stop and think twice before doing things which the church disapproved of.'

'It's not propaganda you know,' said Black Bill defensively, 'like I said, it's all documented.'

'Yes but you don't have to believe everything you read,' laughed Don.

'Well,' said Mrs Darley, stepping in diplomatically, 'it looks as though we have all escaped unscathed today as the storm seems to be rolling away. Perhaps,' she smiled, 'the devil has had his spoils elsewhere.'

The Fiery Concept of Hell

The modern English word 'hell' is thought by some to derive from the old English *'hel'* or *'helle'* which was brought into common usage during the 8th century AD with which to refer to the world of the dead. This in turn comes from the Saxon word *'halja'* meaning 'one who covers up or hides'. A second school of thought however considers the word as being derived from the Old Norse word *'Hel'*, which was the name for the Nordic underworld, ruled over by a being of the same name.

For many belief systems, hell is an alien concept and although there is often a place for those who have left this plane to rest and evaluate their earthly experience, the idea of eternal damnation or punishment does not even enter the equation.

In Christian beliefs however, especially in the Middle Ages, the concept of hell was the place where all those who did not accept Christ as their saviour were destined to burn whilst being separated from God for all time.

According to most Christian teachings, hell is presided over by Satan or the Devil and is described as a great lake of fire where the fallen are burned and tortured for eternity. The New Testament makes several

117

references to hell with regards to murderers, adulterers and those concerned with material possessions as opposed to working for the greater good of others. The following extract is taken from the Gospel of Luke 16: 19-24:

There was a rich man who was dressed in purple and fine linen and lived in luxury every day. At his gate was laid a beggar named Lazarus, covered with sores and longing to eat what fell from the rich man's table .The time came when the beggar died and the angels carried him to Abraham's side. The rich man also died and was buried. In hell, where he was in torment, he looked up and saw Abraham far away with Lazarus by his side. So he called to him, 'Father Abraham, have pity on me and send Lazarus to dip the tip of his finger in water and cool my tongue, because I am in agony in this fire.'

Islam too has a very similar version of hell to Christianity, although the Muslims refer to it as *'jahannam'*. The main difference however is that jahannam is divided into many different levels and the punishment experienced depends on the level of evil committed during a person's lifetime. The gate of jahnnam is guarded by Maalik, leader of the angels who presides over this fiery domain, whilst the fuel needed to stoke the fire comes from once worshipped stone idols and evil human beings.

As a general rule hell is depicted as being a hot torturous place, however within the Islamic tradition there is one place known as *'zamhareer'*, which is a place of extreme cold, comprising of blizzards, ice and snow at temperatures that no human can bear and is meant for those who commit crimes against Allah. The Qur'an, 20:25 states that all non-believers who have received and rejected Islamic teachings will go to Hell on one of its many levels:

And Ibrahim (Abraham) said: 'You have taken idols instead of Allah. The love between you is only in the life of this world, but on the day of resurrection, you shall disown each other, and curse each other, and your abode will be the Fire, and you shall have no helpers.'

Many belief structures have an equivalent to the Christian or Islamic hell, albeit the concept may vary slightly according to the core doctrine. For example some religions who believe in reincarnation such as the Chinese Diyu, perceive hell (or heaven) as a temporary measure rather than an eternal state.

The most elaborate description of hell is probably depicted in Dante's 'The Divine Comedy', written during the 15th century at a time when the medieval church was all powerful and the general populous was controlled by terrifying portrayals of the afterlife or hell.

In *The Divine Comedy*, Virgil leads Dante (Dante Alighieri - 1265-1321) through the nine concentric circles of Hell. Each circle becomes increasingly more horrific and supposedly corresponds with the degree of wrong doing a person has committed during their lifetime. At the centre of the nine circles lies an icy lake, in which sits Satan in bondage. As Dante enters through the gates of Hell, he himself became scared when he read the inscription above the gate, the words with which we have all become familiar with, 'Abandon all hope ye who enter here.' Dante thought he was included in this inscription, which implies the horror of total despair. Table 1.8 over on the following page illustrates Dante's description of Hell.

Circle	Sin committed	Punishment
1st	The Unbaptised, the virtuous pagans i.e. those who did not sin but did not accept Christ	Held in Limbo

Mrs Darley's Pagan Elements

	e.g. Virgil, Aristotle, Socrates, Julius Caesar	
2nd	The lustful, e.g. Cleopatra, Achilles	Souls constantly blown to and fro by a violent storm just like lust.
3rd	The gluttons	Souls forced to lie in slush made by freezing rain, black snow and hail, symbolic of the waste of a life on earth
4th	The avaricious and miserly who hoarded material possessions or the prodigal who squandered them	The miserly push great rocks to the centre of the circle whilst the wasters take the rocks back. Each group is made to do the opposite of what they did in life.
5th	The wrathful, the sullen and the slothful	In the swampy water of the River Styx the angry fight each other on the surface whilst the sullen and slothful lie gurgling beneath the water
6th	The Heretics	Souls trapped in flaming tombs
7th	Divided into 3 rings: The outer: Those who were violent towards people and property during their earthly lives The Middle: 1. Those who have committed suicide. 2. Those who profligate or are extravagant or wasteful. The Inner: The blasphemers (violent against God), the usurers (violent against order) and the sodomites (violent against nature)	Divided into 3 rings: The outer: Souls immersed in a boiling river of blood flaming arrows fired at those who attempt to escape. The Middle: 1. Souls transformed into gnarled thorny bushes and torn at by the Harpies. They will not be resurrected after the final judgment day, but remain as bushes draped with their own corpses. 2. Souls chased by ferocious dogs through thorny undergrowth. The Inner: Souls reside in a desert of flaming sand with fiery flakes raining from the sky. The blasphemers lie, the usurers sit and the sodomites

		wander about.
8th	The fraudsters and those who commit treachery	Divided into 10 ditches of stone or 'Bolgie
	Panderers (pimps) and seducers.	March in separate lines whipped by demons.
	Flatterers	Steeped in excrement
	Simony (the buying or selling of pardons or other ecclesiastical favours)	Placed head first in holes of rock with flames burning on the souls of their feet.
	Those regarded as Sorcerers and false prophets	Heads twisted backwards as they are unable to see the future
	Corrupt politicians (barrators)	Immersed in a lake of boiling pitch
	Those accused of Hypocrisy	
	Thieves, robbers and burglars	They walk aimlessly wearing lead cloaks
	Fraudulent advisors	Bitten by reptiles who steal their human bodies
	Spreaders of discord or scandal	Encased in flames
	Falsifiers, liars and alchemists	Hacked to pieces by a sword wielding demon.
		They are afflicted with different diseases
9th	Traitors divided into 4 distinct circles.	Immersed in frozen lake called 'Cocytus' on 4 levels.
	Ring 1: Caina named after the Biblical Cain for crimes	Ring 1: These souls are immersed within the Cocytus

against their own kin	in ice up to their necks
Ring 2: Antenora, named after Antenor of Troy who betrayed his city to the Greeks for political traitors	Ring 2: Souls immersed to the same level as those in Caina, but they cannot move their necks
Ring 3: Ptolomaea, after Ptolemy who invited his sons to a banquet and then killed them, traitors to their guests are punished here	Ring 3: The souls are immersed in Cocytus but up to half their faces are covered with ice and as they cry their tears freeze their eyes shut
Ring 4: Judecca, after Judas Iscariot, the betrayer of Christ, for traitors of our benefactors	Ring 4: All souls here are completely encapsulated in ice and distorted in almost impossible positions

Table 1.8

In the ninth circle of hell, right in the centre of the frozen lake of Cocytus, sits a trapped Satan, for he has committed the ultimate sin of treachery against God. He is portrayed as having three faces of red, black and yellow, with the mouth of each chewing on a renowned traitor, namely; Brutus and Cassius who were involved in the assassination of Julius Caesar and Judas Iscariot the betrayer of Christ. Satan is of gigantic proportions and weeps tears from his six eyes, which mix with the blood from the traitors. He sits waist deep in ice and constantly flaps his six wings in an attempt to escape.

Finally there was a glimmer of hope for those who committed one of the Seven Deadly Sins but prayed for forgiveness as they were sent to purgatory as opposed to hell. Here they were placed on one of seven levels according to the worst sin committed and were then allowed to work in order to redeem themselves of their sins.

For the more philosophical, hell is often described as a

state of mind, experienced now in this lifetime, where ill formed thoughts consume our waking hours in a blistering inferno of fear and despair.

Fire: a Matter of Life or Death

Symbolically speaking, the majority of us are created from fire, for the human life is born from a couple's burning passion, resulting in the climatic firing of sperm and the subsequent fertilisation of the egg which holds within the potential of a new life.

In some ancient cultures the element of fire is present in the creation myths. Slavonic mythology tells of the Sky God Svarog, who gave birth to two children, the Sun God, Dazhbog and the Fire God, Svarogich. In the shadows of the clouds, Svarog kindled the lightning so that it glowed with fire and was therefore revered as the creator of celestial fire. He then struck the ground with the lightning, giving the gift of fire to man and this was seen as his son Svarogich. After the storm had passed Svarog caused the sun to appear and lit its torch so that it shone in the heavens and this was acknowledged as his other son, Dazhbog.

In many Slavonic countries rural folk still maintain a healthy respect for fire, which they see as being sacred. The older members of the village forbid the young to swear or shout at the moment when the fire is lit in the house for fear of bringing bad luck.

In the Christian Bible, Genesis 1:16 God creates the sun on the fourth day:

'God made two great lights – the greater light to govern the day and the lesser light to govern the night.'

Fire, heat and light sustain and nurture life though their many mediums but by the same token they also have the power to destroy in spectacular fashion. The heat and light from the sun brings the crops to harvest but too much sun can make them shrivel and die. The warmth of a fire can be a welcome addition to a camping expedition but if it rages out of control devastation can result. Exposing ourselves to the sun enables the body to formulate vitamin D but too much exposure and we can be at risk from skin cancers and although we all love to see the sun, looking directly at it can cause blindness. A candle can light the darkness but leaving it unattended can burn a home to the ground and so since mankind first decided to play with fire he has forever felt its consequences.

Externally fire has killed through both natural means and accidental use, however, one of its most horrific aspects is when it has been used deliberately in order to sacrifice, torture and execute especially as a means of religious persecution throughout the centuries.

In 1534, Henry VIII broke away from the Roman Catholic Church, following the Pope's refusal to grant him a divorce from Catherine of Aragon in order that he might marry Anne Boleyn, an act which eventually resulted in him appointing himself as head of the new protestant Church of England. This dramatic change in the religious values of England was swiftly followed by the dissolution of the monasteries and anything that remotely resembled Catholicism.

Following Henry's death in 1547, his son by Jane Seymour, Edward VI, succeeded to the English throne and continued in his father's protestant footsteps. Edward however was a sickly young man and, following his short reign, Mary Tudor his half sister ascended to the throne.

Mary was the daughter of Henry VIII and Catherine of Aragon and, being a staunch Catholic like her French mother, demanded the restoration of Catholicism as the religion of England and Ireland. Whenever blanket beliefs are imposed upon a population, there will inevitably be resistance and with a 'zero tolerance' policy for none Catholics, Mary managed to acquire the title of 'bloody Mary' throughout her relatively short reign. This was due to both the number of protestants executed and the barbaric method of execution favoured by her; that of being burned alive.

A description of a burning appears in 'Fox's Book of Martyrs', Chapter XV1:

John Noyes, a shoemaker, of Laxfield, Suffolk, was taken to Eye, and at midnight, September 21, 1557, he was brought from Eye to Laxfield to be burned. On the following morning he was led to the stake, prepared for the horrid sacrifice. Mr Noyes, on coming to the fatal spot, knelt down, prayed and rehearsed the Fiftieth Psalm. When the chain enveloped him, he said, 'Fear not them that kill the body, but fear him that can kill both body and soul, and cast it into everlasting fire!' As one Cadman placed a fagot he blessed the hour in which he was born to die for the truth; and while trusting only upon the all-sufficient merits of the Redeemer, fire was set to the pile, and the blazing fagots in a short time stifled his last words, 'Lord have mercy on me! Christ have mercy on me!' The ashes of the body were buried in a pit and with them one of his feet, whole to the ankle, with the stocking on.

Perhaps one of the most infamous executions by fire was that of Joan of Arc who was burned at the stake by the Catholic Church for the crime of being a Christian Heretic with the word 'heretic' coming from the Greek meaning 'free choice'. This was due to the fact that she had said that she had heard and acted upon the voice and commands of God after which she successfully led the

French army to victory.

There have, however, over the centuries been many other explanations offered as to why Joan was executed. George Bernard Shaw stated that it was not for her capital crimes that she died but for her 'unwomanly and insufferable presumption' in so much that she dared to wear men's clothing that so annoyed her prosecutors.

Margaret Murray meanwhile claimed that Joan was actually a member of the 'old religion', and that due to her being referred to as 'La Pucelle' (the virgin) or 'the Maid of Orleans', she was in fact the Grandmaster's right hand maiden, and therefore second in command within her coven. This, coupled with the fact that she was a healer and came from Lorraine, an area which was renowned for its sorcery, magic and paganism, all added fuel to these speculations. It was also rumoured that she was seen alive after her death and was worshipped by her followers as though she was more than a mere mortal. Murray therefore goes on to say that Joan's death represented the ritual sacrifice of the Divine King as described in Frazer's 'The Golden Bough'.

As for the truth of these presumptions and speculations we can never be certain, however we do know that Joan refused to say the 'Paternoster', something that a staunch Catholic would be very unlikely to refuse to do and she also continuously insisted that she had been privy to certain revelations by God, something which was regarded as heretical within the church.

Whatever so angered her persecutors, Joan was finally burned at the stake on 30 May 1431 whilst quite bizarrely, she was heralded the very next day as a martyr by the same people who called for her death and almost 500 years later in 1920 she was canonised and became St Joan.

Witches are often mistakenly thought to have been burned at the stake, however although this was the preferred method of execution in Europe and Scotland, in England witches were normally put to death by hanging. This was due to the fact that English witches were punished for '*malefica*' or 'evil deeds' rather than heresy and witchcraft was classified as a civil offence rather than an ecclesiastical one, hence torture in its extreme form, including burning, was not acceptable.

In France on 13 October 1307, the leader of the religious group known as The Knights Templar, Jaques de Molay, was slowly roasted over a hot smokeless fire for the crime of heresy.

The fire was firstly applied to his feet, and then to his genitals to ensure that the suffering lasted as long as possible. As Molay's flesh blackened and cooked he was said to utter a curse on both the King of France and the Pope and although this was never officially recorded, Geoffroi de Paris, chronicled the event in verse as follows:

Let evil swiftly befall those who have strongly condemned us – God will avenge our deaths.

Regardless of whether or not the curse was responsible, both the King and the Pope were dead within a year.

Punishment by fire for deeds done and the threat of punishment by fire in order to control the masses is also a recurring theme in the Christian Bible as illustrated in Peter 23:10-12:

But the day of the Lord will come like a thief. The heavens will disappear with a roar; the elements will be destroyed by fire, and the earth and everything in it will be laid bare.

Since everything will be destroyed in this way, what

kind of people ought you to be? You ought to live holy and Godly lives as you look forward to the day of God and speed its coming. That day will bring about the destruction of the heavens by fire, and the elements will melt in the heat.

Sacrifice of both animals and humans by fire in honour of the Gods has been carried out by mankind since the making of fire was discovered and it is thought that the aroma of burnt offerings was considered very pleasing to the deities. In this respect the Christian God is no exception and the Bible is peppered with burnt offerings of grain and animals as illustrated in Genesis 22:1-2:

If you bring a grain offering of first fruits to the Lord, offer crushed heads of new grain roasted in the fire. Put oil and incense on it; it is a grain offering. The priest shall burn the memorial portion of the crushed grain and oil, together with all the incense, as an offering made to the Lord by fire.

And in the later book of Leviticus 2: 14-16:

Some time later God tested Abraham. He said to him, 'Abraham! Take your son, your only son Isaac, whom you love, and go to the region of Moriah. Sacrifice him there as a burnt offering on one of the mountains I will tell you about.'

The use of cremation in Europe and the near east as a method of disposing of the dead is thought to have become popular during the stone age around 3,000 BC and gradually spread to the British Isles during the Bronze Age.

The Greeks embraced cremation, encouraging this method of disposal above all others due to the fact that it protected the living from disease, especially where there were hundreds of war torn bodies awaiting interment.

The Romans too copied their Greek counterparts and by the time of the Roman Empire, cremation was the normal means of disposal for the deceased, whose remains were stored in elaborate urns.

With the arrival of Christianity however, cremation fell from favour due to the religion's belief in the resurrection of the dead. As the ultimate punishment however, the Romans often resorted to cremating the Christians thus preventing any chance of future resurrection.

By 400 AD, Constantine's conversion to Christianity and the subsequent Christianisation of the Empire ensured that burial was the order of the day, with cremation only re-emerging at times of war or plague, a practice that was to continue for the next 1,500 years.

Modern day interest in cremation began in the late 19th century when there was general concern about the effects of the industrial evolution on health, sanitisation and overcrowding, including the overcrowding of cemeteries.

In 1873, Sir Henry Thompson, surgeon to Queen Victoria, visited Italy where he saw the demonstration of equipment used for carrying out cremations. The equipment had been designed by Professor Brunetti and upon returning home Sir Henry invited some like minded acquaintances to form the 'Cremation Society of England', in order to promote the use of cremation as an alternative to burial.

The Society bought some land next to Woking cemetery with the intention of building a crematorium on site but strong opposition meant that they had to halt proceedings and instead spent the following few years trying to persuade people of the benefits of cremation and campaign for a change in the law. In 1884 however, an event occurred that totally changed the situation regarding cremation and also people's perception.

It was in that year that a Dr William Price of Llantrisant in Wales, who claimed to be the Arch Druid of a lost Celtic tribe, cremated his deceased five month old son, Jesus Christ, on a local hillside. Although a prosecution was brought against the Doctor for carrying out a private cremation, he was found 'not guilty', a ruling which made cremation legal in the British Isles.

The late 19th and early 20th century saw many crematoriums opening up throughout Britain and gradually the number of people choosing cremation over burial crept into the thousands, especially when the first member of the royal family, the Duchess of Connaught was cremated in 1917. This was followed by other high profile figures such as Ramsay Macdonald and Neville Chamberlain although the real breakthrough came in 1944 when Dr William Temple, the Archbishop of Canterbury also chose to be cremated.

In 1963, the Catholic Church, who had always remained against cremation, declared that it was an acceptable form of disposal and three years later Catholic priests were allowed to conduct services in crematoriums in addition to churches.

In 1885, of 597,357 deaths, only three people were cremated, whilst today over seventy percent of people choose cremation as their preferred method of disposal in one of the country's 245 crematoriums.

During the British rule of India in the early 1800's, it became accepted practice in certain Brahman and royal castes to burn alive, the widow of the deceased, upon her husband's funeral pyre, a tradition which took twenty four years of education and preaching from the missionary William Carey and his associates to outlaw this horrific ritual known as *'Suttee'*.

The word 'suttee' is a derivation of the Hindu Goddess Sati, who was said to have burned herself to death after the humiliation of her husband Shiva, by her father.

Carey made reports to the British government about this unacceptable practice as within a thirty mile radius of Calcutta, up to 400 Suttee deaths were recorded in one year alone.

In 1825 the British Indian governor, Lord William Bentinck finally outlawed the practice and a proclamation was made stating:

The practice of suttee or burning or burying alive the widows of Hindus is hereby declared illegal and punishable by the criminal courts.

Although India is now free of suttee practices, public cremations are still permitted and carried out, especially alongside the Ganges, where the ashes are then thrown into the river.

Thus fire as a means of life, death, punishment and sacrifice has understandably invoked both pleasure and fear in the heart of mankind throughout the ages.

In Celebration of Glow Worms
Strictly speaking British glow worms or *'lampyris noctiluca'* are not worms but female beetles who emanate a beautiful fluorescent green light in the dusk of a late summer evening in order to attract a flying male thereby symbolising the light of fire in the darkness.

Once fertilized, the eggs are laid and it is at this point that the female dies, leaving the eggs to hatch into larvae which will remain in the same state for the following one or two summers, feeding on small snails which they paralyse before sucking them empty. This gap between

131

mating and becoming an adult goes some way to explaining why some years there appears to be a glow worm boom and during other years sightings are very sparse.

To go glow worm hunting is a magical experience, although it must be stressed that they are a rare species and as such each one is precious. It is therefore prudent to look but not disturb. Glow worms favour chalky or limestone areas, usually in the South of the British Isles although sightings have been made in Wales and Scotland. Many people discover them in grassy areas such as gardens, beneath hedgerows, on moorland, beside disused railways and amongst the cliffs or places where there is little disturbance.

Although most species in Britain are *'lampyris noctiluca'* there is a much rarer type known as *'phosphaenus hemipterus'*, found these days only in parts of Sussex and Hampshire.

Passion
Eyes blaze, blood boils,
Heart warms, will calls,
Passion engulfs.

Mythical Creatures of Fire

The Salamander
The legendary salamander is the elemental associated with the element of fire and has, over millennia, been attributed with both the factual traits of the natural salamander and those which are rather more fantastical.

Those of a more exaggerated nature include satyr like creatures, winged dogs and a small bird engulfed in flames. According to Pliny and Aristotle, the abilities of the salamander ranged from being able to extinguish fire to being so poisonous that if they fell into a well then all those who drank from it would die.

Of all the ancient lore attributed to salamanders however, that which is associated with fire has stood the test of time and probably stems from the fact that many species of salamander tend to hibernate under rotting logs. When the logs are brought indoors and placed on the fire, the salamanders seem to mysteriously appear as if by magic from the flames.

In the Talmud: Hagiga 27a, it is said that anyone who is smeared with the blood of the salamander will be safe from burning and early travellers to China were shown garments said to be woven from salamander hair or wool which, when held to a flame, would not burn. Many explanations however have since been offered for this fantastic material from the fact that it was anything from asbestos to silk.

The salamander became the traditional emblem of the black smith, and features in a number of civic coats of arms to symbolise the presence of metal-working industries.

The Dragon
The dragon is a legendary creature whose name derives from the Greek word '*drakon*', meaning 'serpent'. In the West we usually think of dragons as being vicious, scaly creatures with flashing red eyes, fiery breath and bat like wings. They are often portrayed as living in mountain caves and have to be destroyed at all costs by a hero such as St George.

St George, however, is a very sketchy character and is merely based on a legend which stems from early Christian times.

Mrs Darley's Pagan Elements

A child called George was born during the late 3rd century AD to an early Christian noble family in Palestine and, following the death of his father, a Roman army official, George decided to go and present himself to the Emperor Diocletian in order that he too may become a soldier like his father before him. Diocletian was delighted to have George in his army and by the age of twenty he was one of the Emperor's imperial guards.

In 302 AD, Diocletian, who was a staunch Pagan Emperor, decreed that every Christian soldier in the army should be arrested and be made to make a sacrifice to the Pagan Gods. George however refused and, despite Diocletian's best attempts including bribery, remained a staunch Christian. These actions left Diocletian with little choice other than to execute George for his disobedience hence George became a Christian martyr.

The myth involving the dragon however was thought to have been brought back by the crusaders who told the tale of a dragon who made its nest alongside the spring in the city of Silene. To enable the citizens of Silene to obtain water, the dragon had to be distracted each day and encouraged it to leave its nest. In order to accomplish their mission the citizens began by offering animal sacrifices, however when these became scarce they decided to offer a maiden by asking the young girls of the city to draw lots. One day the princess herself drew the short straw, but just as she was about to be offered to the dragon, George appeared, protected himself with the sign of the cross and slayed the dragon, thus saving the princess and managing to covert the city to Christianity into the bargain.

The story has led many to suggest that it is purely symbolic in so much that the slaying of the dragon represented the fall of Paganism in order that Christianity could prevail, or the destruction of the Goddess in favour of patriarchy.

Dragons do however have a more favourable press in Wales as their national flag illustrates. The flag was granted official status in 1959, although the dragon had been associated with Wales for centuries beforehand. It is thought that the Romans originally brought the emblem to Wales in the form of the 'Draco' standards carried by the Roman cavalry and that the green and white background were additions by the House of Tudor, the Welsh dynasty that held the English throne from 1485 to 1603.

Welsh mythology tells us that King Vortigern watched a lengthy battle between a red dragon *'Y Draig Goch'* and a white dragon. Eventually the red dragon seized victory and the wizard, Myrddin (Merlin) explained to Vortigern that the red dragon symbolized the Welsh or native Celtic race, whilst the white dragon symbolised the invading Saxons, a prophecy that the Saxons would eventually be defeated by the native Britons.

In China, dragons are particularly popular and are thought to bestow longevity and good fortune upon mankind. Their five claws are said to represent the Chinese Emperors and their snake like appearance is a familiar sight at many Chinese festivals, representing the fluidity of nature. They are considered to have supernatural powers and are often associated with wisdom.

Although most European dragons are fire breathing creatures, Chinese dragons are strangely associated with water and, in particular, moving bodies of water such as waterfalls, rivers, or seas. The four seas surrounding China were once represented by individual dragon kings and many coastal dwellers built temples dedicated to their local king. In times of flooding or drought the local dignitaries would lead their community in making sacrifices to appease him.

Even today dragons are still a popular feature in modern literature including *Harry Potter*, *The Hobbit* and *Eragon*.

The Phoenix

The phoenix is said to be a beautiful mythical bird of eagle like proportions that sports a magnificent plumage of gold and scarlet, although some accounts also mention the colours of blue, purple and green.

The bird's life cycle lasts between 500 and 1,000 years, at the end of which it builds a nest of twigs, self ignites and burns away to ash. Eventually however, a new phoenix rises from the ashes and is destined to live exactly the same time as its predecessor. Its tears are thought to have healing properties.

Legends of this mythical bird span both time and cultures, with the Persians, Chinese, Japanese and Russians all having their own version of the tale.

It was however from India that the original story is thought to have originated. Here the Phoenix is said to be based on Garuda, the sacred bird of the Hindu God Vishnu and was symbolic of sunlight.

The Phoenix is mentioned in the Egyptian Book of the Dead, where it was given the name of Benu and likened to a stork or heron. It became a sacred symbol of worship at Heliopolis and was associated with the Sun God Ra.

It was the Greeks who actually referred to their mythical bird as a Phoenix and was depicted as an eagle or peacock. The Phoenix was said to live beside a well in Phoenicia where it always bathed at dawn and sang most beautifully, a sound which encouraged the Sun God, Helios to stop his sun chariot each morning as journeyed across the skies.

The phoenix became very popular in early Catholic art and literature for it was seen as being symbolic of the resurrected Christ's immortality.

The Magic and Alchemy of Fire

Carl Jung, the great psychologist believed that just as the four elements exist on the material plane in the forms of air, fire, water and earth, so these energy types also exist in our inner world or subconscious and can be described as thinking, intuition, feeling and sensation, or in relation to the old humours can be likened to the temperaments of sanguine, choleric, melancholic or phlegmatic. He believed that in an individual whom he would describe as 'unconscious', then one energy type would always dominate, but that in order to become balanced we must learn to develop each category even though we would always retain the main aspect of our personality.

Jung went on to divide the four categories into two groups, namely perception and judgement. Perception, he stated, tells us what is happening through intuition and sensation, whilst judgement then takes us through the decision making process by thinking and feeling.

In terms of human existence, fire symbolizes the intuitive aspect, the function of the imagination. Fire lets us dream of how things might be or of how things might develop if we give our imagination full rein. Fire encourages us to go one step further, not simply to think but how to intuit, to look in two directions instead of one.

Jung believed that those with a dominant fire aspect to their personality, the intuitive types have the ability to push the boundaries, to visualise great things, to imagine

137

far off places, to invent, to pioneer and to experience things that others can only dream of. They tend to gather people around them and excite them with their far-seeing ideals, inspiring and infusing them with confidence.

If however someone is too dominant in this area and little sensation or practicality is employed when dealing with life's challenges then they may find themselves full of ideas that sadly never reach fruition. On the whole however, fireflies are like the flame, enigmatic, captivating and always just out of the reach of other mere mortals.

Our language illustrates beautifully the many aspects of fire. When we fall for someone our love is 'ignited' and we become consumed by the 'flames of passion' or 'burn with desire'. We describe someone who is enthusiastic about a project as being 'all fired up' or when someone is performing at their best we say they are 'firing on all cylinders'. When a person is angry we say they are 'boiling with rage' or have become 'inflamed with anger' whilst if someone sails a little to close to the wind they are likely to 'get their fingers burned'. If we become tired and stressed we say we feel 'burnt out' like a spent fire. Those who are a delight to be with are described as 'warm' or a 'little ray of sunshine' or when someone says something kind you may feel a 'warm glow' inside.

In ancient Greek philosophy, fire is one of the four classical elements, considered to be both hot and dry and, according to Aristotle, occupies a place between earth and air amongst the elemental spheres. Fire is associated with the humour of yellow bile, which is hot and dry and also the choleric personality which is considered to be touchy, changeable, restless, aggressive, excitable, impulsive, active and optimistic.

The ancient Greeks distinguished between destructive fire known as '*aidelon*', a derivative of the word 'Hades', referring to the Greek underworld and creative fire which was associated with the revered creative smith, Hephaestus.

The symbol used by Plato to depict fire was the tetrahedron (pyramid shaped) whose sharp edges and points were considered to be symbolic of the sharp stabbing pain of fire as it burns.

In alchemy, however, the chemical element of sulphur became associated with fire and therefore its symbol of an upward pointing triangle became the alchemical symbol of fire, depicting metals being incubated in the womb of the earth.

In the Hindu tradition the God of Fire and acceptor of sacrifices, Agni, is symbolised in three forms of fire which include fire, lightning and the sun. The name Agni meanwhile derives from the Sanskrit word for fire. In Latin the name becomes '*ignis'*, the root of the English word, 'ignite'.

Magical Fire
Ever since mankind has walked upon the earth he has attempted to harness and work in conjunction with her natural forces especially when making magic.

In earliest times the natural world was the domain of the wise woman and cunning man for they knew how to attract love, good fortune and health by working in conjunction with the seasons, the moon's cycles, and the elements of air, fire, water and earth.

Mrs Darley's Pagan Elements

The practice of ceremonial magic in its many forms also incorporates the element of fire into its teachings. In Wiccan ritual the element of fire is placed in the cardinal direction of the south and is protected by the salamanders as guardians of the southern quarter. This direction is associated with young adults, noon and the summer and is symbolically represented by warm colours, particularly orange and red, the athame (ceremonial dagger) or the wand. Other correspondences include the tarot suit of wands, candles and predatory animals.

In the casting of a magic circle the element of fire is often represented by the burning of incense or the lighting of candles. The colour of the candle can also play an important part in the overall effect of using candle in magical workings as illustrated in Table 1.9 below.

Candle colour	Qualities
Red	Physical health, courage
Orange	Creativity, joy
Yellow	Communication
Green	Love, balance
Blue	Healing, fairness
Violet	Spirituality, psychic development
White	New beginnings
Gold	Prosperity
Silver	Fruition of dreams

Table 1.9

Fire magic is used to drive matters forward, including job offers, creative projects and lawmaking. In fact fire magic is recommended for anything that needs passion and commitment; it denotes change and speeds its arrival.

Mrs Darley Tale: Signals
Arriving back home after a weekend away with my parents, I smiled as I heard the familiar voice of Mrs Darley's grandson, Rowan coming from the garden,

whilst Mrs Darley and Phyllis were leaning over the half stable door of the cottage.

'Danger!' they shouted as I approached and, feeling rather alarmed, I wondered if I should run or duck.

'Oh it's alright, dear,' called Mrs Darley, 'we're just translating smoke signals, 'have you had a good weekend?'

I nodded, 'Glad to be home though, bank holiday traffic isn't my idea of fun.'

'Well, rather than having to start cooking a meal, why don't you come round when you've sorted yourself out, we're going to have a barbeque in the garden and there's plenty of food. Anyway,' she added, 'Rowan will be delighted to have a different audience for his new found skills.'

Within half an hour I was in Mrs Darley's garden, having brought Mum's lemon drizzle cake as a sweet offering.

I said my hellos to Peter and Rowan and was immediately ordered into Mrs Darley's porch with a smudged piece of paper tucked into my hand in order that I might read their smoke signals. I glanced down at the paper and read; 'one puff = attention, two puffs = all's well, three puffs = danger.'

'Ready?' They called.

'Ready,' I replied.

I waited and, to my surprise, saw a puff of smoke rise into the air, quickly followed by a second. Satisfied that there was to be no third, I looked at the piece of paper and shouted, 'All's well!'

'Good,' came the reply, 'what about this one?'

The single puff of smoke came and after giving my response of 'attention', I made my way into the garden where the wonderful aroma of barbequed food greeted me.

'That was excellent,' I said as Rowan came running up the garden, 'How did you do it?'

'We lit a fire and put some damp grass on it to make the smoke rise then we flapped a blanket over it to make the puffs.' He explained.

'Ah,' I said, 'I didn't realise that was how it was done. So are smoke signals a type of universal language?'

Peter shook his head, 'No not at all, each Native American Indian tribe had their own smoke signal meanings, otherwise their enemies would know what they were saying. Mind you having said that, when I was a boy scout we learned a few smoke signals which are pretty much known by everyone and these are the ones that Rowan has been making today.'

At this, Mrs Darley called us all to eat and as we sat around the barbeque the conversational theme of smoke signals continued.

'Of course,' said Phyllis, 'Smoke signals aren't just the domain of the Native American Indians, the ancient Chinese also had their own smoke language. Chinese soldiers who were stationed along the Great Wall of China used smoke signals to warn their colleagues who were up to 300 miles away of an impending attack.'

'I don't think you'd see smoke signals from that distance,' laughed Peter, 'normally they can only be seen between twenty and fifty miles away, dependant on the height of the elevation on which the fire is lit.'

'You're quite right, Peter,' agreed Phyllis, 'but what the soldiers actually did was signal from tower to tower along the wall and in that way the message was passed on across hundreds of miles.'

'Ah,' said Peter, 'now that makes perfect sense.'

'I think it's all rather romantic,' I said, 'It's a shame we don't use smoke signals for anything useful any more.'

'Oh but we do,' said Mrs Darley. 'Each time the Catholic Church chooses a new Pope, the Roman cardinals use smoke signals to indicate the success or failure of the ballot. The ballot is carried out in secret and continues until one person receives two thirds of the vote plus one.

Black smoke indicates that the ratio has not been reached and is therefore deemed to be a failed ballot, whilst white smoke indicates the successful appointment of a new Pope.'

'I stand corrected,' I smiled.

'In many of today's religious ceremonies,' continued Mrs Darley, 'incense is still used, no doubt echoing the actions of the ancients who believed that the aromatic smoke would carry man's prayers to the heavens.'

'That's a nice thought,' I said.

'Then that is what we will do,' said Mrs Darley rising to her feet and indicating that we all follow her to the still smouldering fire at the bottom of the garden.

Here she gave us all a handful of damp grass and a couple of sprigs of rosemary and, as the smoke began to rise, our heartfelt wishes spiralled to the realm of the Gods.

Astrological Fire signs
The twelve signs of the Zodiac are each governed by one of four categories, namely those of air, fire, water and earth, and of the three signs which fall within each group, one is cardinal, i.e. initiatory; one is fixed, i.e. controlling; and one is mutable, i.e. restless.

The three signs which fall under the influence of the

element of fire are the wilful signs of Aries, Leo and Sagittarius and although each has their specific traits they do have certain similarities.

All three have a desire for freedom but whereas the air signs seek freedom of thought and expression, the fire signs seek freedom of action and the power to do as they wish. This can result at times in them being aggressive, courageous and commanding, possessing the ability to move things forward in order to achieve their desired result. The three are, however, quite different as illustrated in the brief character outlines that follow.

Aries
Aries is the cardinal fire sign and as such Arians have the desire to initiate and tend to push the boundaries further and aim higher, both mentally and spiritually than their fiery counterparts. They will be quick both of temper and of action, making sharp and prompt decisions. They are often the trail blazers of the zodiac and do not tolerate fools gladly.

That said, Arians do have a soft side and this can often lead them to be taken advantage of because of their loyalty, sentimentality and service to others. In marriage it is important for them choose a mate who is an intellectual equal otherwise boredom could easily set in.

Financially, Arians can be impulsive which could prevent projects from coming to fruition. Arians are also born roamers or travellers and rarely find themselves wanting to stay at home for too long, although they do like to have a welcoming place to come back to once in a while.

Career-wise, music, literature, art, journalism, banking, medicine, decorating, designing, contracting, managing and handling property are all appealing careers to the Arian.

Spiritually, orthodox religion does not normally appeal but they will have their own philosophies on life. They are also interested in scientific research and have a tolerance of others beliefs.

Arians often have a tendency to engage in too many lines of interest or employment and will go out of their way to help others, even at cost to themselves. It is advisable for Arians to concentrate on what is most important to them and in so doing they will accomplish their goals and benefit from a prosperous career.

Leo

Leo is the fixed fire sign and seeks the freedom to manage what others have created and as such is fiery, impulsive and hasty, often acting without too much thought. When roused, the sign of the lion can be erratic, wild and occasionally violent in their actions. It is as if they become blinded by their own temper.

That said, Leo people have an underlying sensitive and emotional side in addition to their outward fiery character. Whereas Arians are ruled by their head, those born under the sign of Leo are ruled by their heart and when emotions and fire fuse, fireworks and passion can be the order of the day.

The Leo personality is proud, ambitious, masterful, good natured, generous, fearless and determined but although the temper may be quick to flare, forgiveness is just as quick to materialise. Friends are plentiful and loyal, although they may tend to take advantage of the Leos generosity of spirit.

Finances for the Leo born can be varied, up one minute and down the next, although normally they are given opportunities to travel during their lifetime in order to increase their wealth.

The Leo home is loved, although the practicalities of house work are not relished by either sex. With regards to relationships, these can be very stormy due to the emotional and fiery mix of the Leo personality. Many Leo people marry early and become hopelessly romantically entangled at an early age, but they can be quite demanding and should choose someone of a tolerant nature as their mate.

Career-wise, it is easy for Leos to become Jack of all trades and master of none. The following are considered to be advisable careers for Leos: law, medicine, banking, photography, teaching, music or acting. Leo people will always be far happier working for themselves or at least being given some sort of autonomy rather than being in a subordinate position.

Leos usually have a strong spiritual or religious belief although do not tend to be particularly tolerant of the beliefs of others.

Leos do have a tendency to be nervous and restless and whilst they do not bear a grudge, they also never forget past hurts. Many Leo born will have issues to overcome in early life, but if they manage to accomplish this then they will have a happy and well rounded life.

Sagittarius
Sagittarius is the mutable fire sign and desires the freedom to expand limiting horizons through religion, philosophy, education and travel. As such Sagittarians are in love with the world and everything in it, often wanting to make a good impression through the display of material goods but not wanting to think about the meaning of life too deeply and would prefer others to point them in the right direction.

That said, Sagittarians are positive, hard working, honest, generous, kind, ambitious and very jovial. They come across to others as being sound thinkers, logical in their reasoning and endowed with a generous helping of common sense. They are resourceful and capable of both making and hanging onto money. During their lifetime they long for far off lands and exotic travel which will often come to fruition.

The Sagittarian loves their home life and will always be an attentive host to visitors. They will also be quite affectionate to those they love, although it may not always be shown in a conventional way, which can often lead to misunderstandings. In choosing a mate, they require a companion as well as a lover.

Career-wise, those born under Sagittarius excel at journalism, astrology, law, medicine, inventing, nursing, commercial travel, and printing.

Sagittarians are sincere in their beliefs although they tend to be more philosophical rather than follow an orthodox religion.

The greatest hindrances to a Sagittarian are bluntness and a quick temper, coupled with an extremely generous nature, both of which can be detrimental to progress in different ways.

The Yule Log
Honouring the phallus,
Fanning,
Licking, loving,
Raising.

Inflaming the phallus,
Devouring
Greedy, Gluttonous

147

Consuming.

Transforming the phallus,
Impotent
Sapped, spent
Ashen.

Connecting with the Element of Fire

How do you feel about fire? Is it something you love to be near, or something that makes you feel afraid?

My dad was a keen fan of the 'Parkray', a 1960's version of a wood burning stove and, as such, we had them both in the kitchen and the dinning room and although they were wonderfully warm, more often than not the glass became black and smoky and the ultimate effect was lost. On high days and holidays however, we went into the lounge and that was where the real fire was, a treat that went beyond all those of the festivities and one which sits warmly within my memory still.

When I began to buy properties of my own, all of them had, for some strange reason, their fireplaces blocked up. I now believe that this was perhaps a message advising me that I had closed down my intuitive abilities, my passion and my will.

When I first went to see the cottage in Cornwall, not only had the fireplace been blocked up but the beautiful stone walls had been covered in plasterboard and the slate floor buried beneath two carpets, plastic sheeting and tar paper. Sitting sadly against the wall was an old electric fire, which on that first cold November day remained off due to the fact that the lady, who then owned the property, was afraid of fire.

My first job, when moving in, was to have the walls, floor and fireplace restored, in order that the cottage could breathe again and, upon seeing Mrs Darley's wonderful wood burning stove, I decided that I too would install the same, a decision I never regretted.

During my subsequent encounters with Mrs Darley, I came to appreciate just how powerful, evocative and necessary fire actually was and that many of our celebrations, rituals and even simple times spent together would often involve the magical effect of an indoor or outdoor fire, a candle or the position of the sun.

Gradually she encouraged me to develop my intuition and my imagination, all of which led me to expand my horizons and cast away the blinkers which had always ruled my life. As a result, I danced, sang and dreamed around the fire, sat beneath the sun and meditated upon the candle flame, allowing each act to bring a little more warmth and positivity into my life.

Today I have a chimnea on my balcony and I am lucky enough to live in the middle of the woods, which provide an endless supply of firewood. I am pleased to say that more often that not I allow my intuition to guide me and have also discovered that somewhere deep within me there was a pot of passion just waiting to be discovered. I feel there is nothing in the world quite like sitting around a real fire with the person you love and casting your imagination into the flames.

Take a few moments to consider your own reaction to fire, how does it make you feel; afraid, exhilarated, alive, intimidated or adventurous? Does fire appear during your dreamtime and if so, how does it behave? Is it warm and comforting or is it raging out of control?

Whatever the imagery, it comes with a wise word from the Goddess regarding the use of your imagination and intuition something we should all take time to note and act upon.

Mrs Darley's Pagan Elements

Mrs Darley Tale: Mariella

It was a beautiful summer's evening as a crowd of us stepped out onto the lane and walked down towards the pretty village of Henwood, which nestled peacefully beneath the shadow of Sharp Tor. The copse dropped steeply away to our right, whilst on the left, the moor rose dramatically towards the old railway track. The familiar smell of warm ferns scented the evening air and I felt full of eager anticipation at the evening that lay ahead.

We had all been invited to Mia's cottage, on the outskirts of the village, for a Midsummer party. I had met her once before at one of Mrs Darley's Samhain celebrations where she foretold the future by means of the tarot and palmistry. Mia was one of those people with whom everyone felt comfortable. She was a large lady, swarthy, welcoming and dressed in what seemed to be an endless mass of multi-coloured material that always seemed to float dutifully behind her.

As we entered her garden by means of a gate in the dry stone wall, she immediately caught me up in an all consuming hug that made me feel curiously cared for, whilst the smell of her perfume engulfed me in a cloud of exotic spices and the promise of distant lands.

The evening was a heady mixture of Eastern Mediterranean music, deliciously spiced food and the most intoxicating bowl of liquor which I found so hard to resist that it reminded me of the compulsive Turkish delight in *The Chronicles of Narnia*.

Around 9.30pm I was just about to try some of the tempting homemade sweetmeats, when I felt a tug at my skirt. I looked down and was surprised to see a child of five or six years of age smiling up at me. I put my plate back on the table and bent down to ask her name. She told me it was Mariella and held out her hand as if

150

inviting me to follow her.

Fascinated by what she wanted me to see, I trailed behind her as she made her way over to the far side of the garden where a gap in the wall opened up into a small wood, in the centre of which stood an old gypsy caravan. I gasped with delight at such a spectacle, for it was just as I had imagined a gypsy caravan to be. It was painted emerald green with bright red flower pots hanging either side of the door whilst beside it burned a huge fire, growing in intensity as dusk began to fall.

'Hello.'

I turned, startled by a man's voice and was both surprised and shocked to see the familiar traveller who had called at Mrs Darley's cottage the night of the Lughnasadh celebrations the previous summer.

'Oh,' I said, 'you took me unawares I'm sorry, I didn't mean to intrude, it's just that Mariella brought me here.' I looked around expecting to see her, but she had seemingly disappeared.

'Mariella?'

'Yes, the dark haired little girl, she....'

'Oh, I know Mariella,' the man said in the attractive Irish lilt I remembered, 'but fancy her bringing you here.'

I smiled, unsure of what to say, 'Look, I'll go and leave you in peace, I didn't mean to disturb you.'

'There's no need to run off,' he said, 'after all, I never did get round to reading your fortune last summer did I?'

I shook my head, a strange feeling of pleasure washing over me at the thought that he had remembered who I was.

'Come and sit by the fire,' he said, dragging a couple of logs closer to the flames, 'and throw these sticks into the fire.'

I was suddenly aware of my heart beat as I took the

sticks from his outstretched hand and was unable to decide whether it was apprehension about what he might say or the fact that I felt strangely attracted to this man's free spirit and unorthodox approach.

Following my throwing of the sticks into the fire, he remained silent for what seemed like an eternity, staring unwaveringly into the flames before he finally spoke.

'I remember saying to you last summer that you were lonely but that no one would ever know and, sadly, I feel that's still the case,' he said gently.

I looked down with embarrassment, thankful for the heat of the flames and the ever growing darkness to hide by blushes.

'You work too hard,' he said, 'and work is your life, but gradually I see a progression, a realisation, an epiphany almost, whereby you will embrace a new understanding of what is important to you. There's a significant other in your life, although not in a romantic way, but that's OK for now. Now is a time of learning, of discovery and it's important that you get to know and understand who you are in order for you to attract the right partner. Does that mean anything to you?'

I looked across at him, 'more than you know.' I said.

At that moment the door of the caravan flew open and I saw a woman of about my own age standing at the top of the steps, the firelight only serving to accentuate her dusky beauty.

'Niga!' my fortune teller smiled, patting the log beside him, 'come and join us.'

'Oh no, I must go,' I said quickly, making an instant appraisal of the situation and jumping to my feet. 'I've intruded long enough and my friends will be wandering where I am ... but thank you.'

He nodded and rolled back the logs, stepping aside to

let me pass.

A few hours later as we were walking up the lane towards the cottages, I found myself momentarily alone with Mrs Darley at the back of the crowd.

'That was a lovely evening,' I said, 'and everyone was so friendly, especially Mia, she made me feel very welcome.'

'Ah,' said Mrs Darley, 'Mia is one of life's rare creatures,'

'Tell me,' I said, 'who's Mariella, is she Mia's grand-daughter?'

Mrs Darley suddenly stopped in the light of the waning moon, 'what made you ask about Mariella?'

'Well because she came up to me and introduced herself as I was getting something to eat,' I said.

Mrs Darley sighed, 'Mariella, my dear was Mia's daughter.'

I suddenly shivered in the cool night air, 'was?'

Mrs Darley nodded, 'There was an accident about thirty years ago, Mia was driving, when a car coming in the other direction spun out of control, hitting them head on. Mariella was killed outright but Niga, her twin, survived.'

I stood quite still and stared into the darkness, trying to make sense of what I had just heard until I felt Mrs Darley's hand on my arm, 'If Mariella came to you tonight you should feel very honoured, for those in spirit only reach out to us when they have a message to deliver ... I trust it was a message with meaning?'

I nodded trying to fight back the tears, 'Yes,' I said, 'yes, indirectly I suppose it was, in fact it was the same message you have tried to give me on several occasions.'

'Ah,' said Mrs Darley, 'sometimes we have to hear the same message in many ways from many people

153

before we are ready to take it on board.'

'Perhaps it's about time I listened?' I asked.

'Whenever you're ready, my dear,' she said.

Conclusion

Fire is a basic requirement of every human life here on earth, the many aspects of which depict Nature at her paradoxical best. Fire heals and burns, destroys and nurtures, cauterizes and sterilizes, transforming everything it touches in spectacular fashion.

Fire stirs something deep within us it fires our will, our determination and calls us to action. It beats the drum of passion in our breast at high noon, when we are in the prime of life, when we have the strength and power to drive forward our life's purpose. The element of fire calls us to blaze along our path and burn brightly, not to flicker and die, smothered by the passing whims of others.

Fire Dance
Suppressed passions rise
Amid grey ash.
Tangible longing ignites the flame.
Greedy eyes dance
Across naked flesh.
Burning desire
Consumes reason.

Chapter 3

Water

Water
In the mountain spring
Lies freedom from thirst.
In the flowing river
Lies freedom from hunger.
In the raging seas
Lies freedom from extinction.
In the acts of man
Lies freedom from pollution.
In the heart of the Goddess
Lies Hope for a better world.

Introduction
Since the beginning of time water has held a fascination
for mankind and, notwithstanding that it is the essence of
life, we have eaten from it, lived beside it, sailed over it
and have attempted to harness it in its many forms, for
power, for energy and for pleasure.

It is hardly surprising then that we have also
throughout the ages come to revere and worship it,
personifying it with Sea Gods, freshwater elementals and
dark Goddesses of prophecy. Mainstream rivers, holy
wells and underground springs have all become sites of
ancient pilgrimage and a plethora of archaeological finds
have confirmed the reverence with which these sites were
held.

Mrs Darley's Pagan Elements

Water is essential to every aspect of our lives, for we ourselves comprise of between seventy and ninety percent water, whilst sixty percent of the earth's surface is covered in it and we cannot survive more than a few days without drinking this precious liquid.

Water carries boats, turns water mills and is home to a myriad of marine life, many of which use it as a medium through which to communicate across the world's oceans.

Even before we take our first breath, we spend nine months protected by the amniotic waters of our mother's womb and feed purely on fluids provided via the placenta.

Water has the power to hold universal cellular memory, for the water we drink today is the same water used by the dinosaurs. This valuable fact is one recognized by homeopaths as their remedies are continually diluted until only the memory or energy of the original material is contained within the purified or spring water that we consume.

Water is cyclic, falling from the clouds as rain or snow, consumed and used by the inhabitants of the earth, passed back to the rivers and oceans and finally drawn back up into the atmosphere once again.

It bubbles up as cool or hot springs from the depths of the earth in order to flow as brooks and streams, rivers and lakes. Finally it empties into our magnificent seas and oceans and has, over millennia, prompted many ancient cultures to worship and honour their revered deities beside the sacred waters.

Water supports our bodies as we swim whilst in sharp contrast it can completely overpower us and pave the way to our physical death. We bathe, cook, cleanse and heal with this magical liquid, whilst it has played a major role in many rites of passage throughout millennia. Water is our life blood.

Mrs Darley Tale: Meeting the Goddess

Finding myself on dog sitting duty for the weekend, I decided to take Fudge, the golden Labrador, down to Golitha Falls for his afternoon walk. The falls were a favourite beauty spot of mine some four miles south of the moor where the river Fowey tumbles and turns on its way down to the sea.

As I passed Mrs Darley's cottage I saw her sitting quietly on the doorstep and asked her if she would like to join me.

'Thank you, dear, that would be lovely, I'll just get a waterproof if you don't mind as I think the absence of Dartmoor on the skyline indicates a forthcoming shower of rain.'

Within twenty minutes we were crossing over the small lane that separated the car park from the woodland and began our walk along the path which followed the river as it emerged from beneath the old stone bridge.

After a short while the designated path disappeared, allowing Mother Nature to come into Her own and, with Fudge snuffling on ahead, Mrs Darley and I were left to absorb the beauty of what I considered to be a special place, since coming upon it quite by accident the previous summer.

We picked our way over sprawling tree roots as they sought to bury their toes into the dark yielding earth and watched the river as it meandered tirelessly along the bed, carved out by centuries of time.

Before long the river turned dramatically to the right and the roar of the falls was immediately apparent. The terrain became increasingly uneven and we soon found

157

ourselves clambering over large rocky boulders in order to appreciate the full splendour of the falls as they thundered over the rocks far below.

It was only the onset of persistent drizzle that made us move away from the falls and continue our rocky climb onto the high path. Soon the sound of the falls faded away and the peace of the woodland returned.

'Well, although I'm wet and muddy, I'm glad Fudge gave me the incentive to come out,' I said.

'Yes indeed,' said Mrs Darley, 'because I know full well that under normal circumstances you'd have been stuck at that computer and the idea of a walk would never have entered your head on a drizzly Sunday afternoon.'

I nodded reluctantly, 'You're right.'

'I know I am,' she smiled, 'and then of course you'd never have met the Goddess!'

I laughed, 'Wouldn't I?'

Mrs Darley shook her head. 'This afternoon you have come into contact with Her Mother aspect and She has demonstrated to us just a few of Her many moods.'

'Why the Mother aspect especially?' I asked.

'The Maiden lives out there,' she said waving her hand ahead of her. 'On the high moor at the source of the river, where She manifests as the spring, clear, pure, refreshing, full of the joys of life, unsullied by the hand of man and with the unlimited potential to sustain and produce life as she journeys from spring to stream. You can follow her back from here across the old road to Bolventor. Drive up there one day, stop anywhere along her banks and ask her to show you how to recapture your maiden aspect.'

'Are you insinuating I'm old before my time?' I asked in a half teasing manner.

'I'm saying that no matter how old we may be, or how

serious life's responsibilities become, we should never neglect the Maiden, for She reminds us how life was before work, before relationships, before financial responsibility and before having to grow up. She is the one who helps us recapture fun, frivolity and childlike wonder.'

Knowing full well that Mrs Darley considered my life too work orientated and somewhat lacking in fun, I decided to try and change the subject before she inevitably broached the other topic I wished to avoid which was that of my love life.

'So where does the Mother aspect begin?' I asked.

'At the bridge really, I suppose,' she said pondering, 'here the river widens and takes on a more mature role. She becomes a little slower, a little more thoughtful but is still capable of laughter as She tumbles over the small rock formations along Her path. She twists and turns, influencing the landscape as She does so until She explodes into a cacophony of noise and foam, symbolic of her creative energy bursting forth upon the world, perhaps as a mother, perhaps as a carer, perhaps as an artist or a writer. And that of course is where we left Her, back there in Her creative mode.'

'So what about the Crone, where does She fit in?' I asked.

'Ah,' Mrs Darley replied, 'eventually the ferocity of creativity is spent and the Crone takes us into calmer, bottle green waters, those which offer us stillness and peace before merging with the incoming tide, where all becomes one before the cycle begins again.'

With these words I noticed that we too had come full circle and were once again back, at the little bridge.

'I suppose there's a lesson in that journey for me?' I asked.

159

'There's a lesson in that journey for everyone.' She said.

The Natural World

Clouds

Everything in nature forms a cycle, from the seasonal wheel to the phases of the moon. In keeping with this cyclic pattern is the formation and release of rain, leading to a constant supply of water, one of the most important ingredients for life on earth. The oceans contain around ninety seven percent of the earth's water and it therefore follows that almost all of our drinking water originates from this source.

The heat from the sun evaporates water from the oceans, whilst rising air currents carry it skywards as water vapour. The higher the air current rises, the cooler the air becomes, until it reaches what is known as the 'dew point'. The dew point is the temperature at which air becomes saturated with water.

At this critical point the water vapour in the atmosphere begins to condense around minute pieces of dust, soil or salt from the oceans and begins to form visible drops of water or ice crystals which remain suspended in the air. As more and more of these droplets congregate together, clouds of various types begin to form.

The height at which this process occurs is determined by the stability of the air and the amount of moisture present. The clouds formed at high altitude, known as *'cirriform'*, only contain ice crystals, whilst those formed at a lower altitude and which contain only water droplets are referred to as *'cumuliform'*. Positioning themselves mid-way between these two types of cloud are those known as *'nimbostratus'* and *'altostratus'*, which, perhaps rather predictably contain a mixture of both ice crystals and water droplets.

Cloud Formations

Clouds appear in many strange and often beautiful shapes, with no two ever seemingly alike and have, for millennia, been heavenly messengers to mankind, foretelling the weather and communicating in their own specific language about what is happening in various layers of the atmosphere.

Aristotle in his manuscript entitled *Meteorologica*, commented on the clouds as foretelling the weather to come, however it wasn't until 1802 that an attempt at a scientific cloud classification system was suggested by the French naturalist Chevalier de Lemarck. In 1778 he wrote in six months the first complete account of the flora of France, *Flore française*.

Sadly his work *Meteorologica* was looked upon with some suspicion, for not only were the names rather simplified and included; hazy, massed, dappled, broom-like and grouped, but he also made references to the moon and its influence on the weather, a theory which at that time proved to be quite unacceptable to the scientific establishment.

In 1803, however, Luke Howard, an English pharmacist and weather observer wrote an essay entitled, 'On the Modification of Clouds', which formed the basis of the cloud classification system used today and also introduced the Latin names with which we are now familiar.

Howard originally used three main classifications of cloud, although a fourth category was later added as illustrated in table 2.0 on the next page.

Mrs Darley's Pagan Elements

Cloud Classification	Description
Cirrus (curl, tuft, wisp)	High wispy fibrous, parallel strands of cloud
Cumulus (heap or mass)	Masses of cloud with dome shaped tops that spill out from flat bases
Stratus (layer or spread out)	Low horizontal continuous sheets of cloud that billow out
Nimbus (rain)	Thick, dull, grey masses of rain cloud

Table 2.0

In 1891, a meeting of the International Meteorological Conference in Munich took place in order to recommend that Howard's system be adopted by all the weather services.

Five years later the *International Cloud Atlas* was published and remained as the meteorological bible until it was updated until 1987. At this point far more detailed information was included namely:

- Ten cloud genera.
- Fourteen cloud species.
- Nine cloud varieties.
- Three forms of accessory clouds
- Six supplementary features.

Today the *International Cloud Atlas* still remains the standard reference for meteorological services in the identification of cloud conditions.

Precipitation

In order for precipitation to occur, the water droplets or ice crystals have to grow large enough and heavy enough

162

for them to fall, whilst the various types of cloud determine the area over which the water falls and how powerful it will be, namely: drizzle, showers or continuous downpours.

The precise type of precipitation however depends upon several factors. These include:

- Whether the water vapour comprises of water droplets, ice crystals or a combination of both.
- Their size.
- The temperature of the air through which they fall.

Precipitation however does not have to fall from the sky, for it is also the term used to describe water that forms on objects on the ground such as dew or hoar frost.

Dew is formed when grass or leaves cool below the dew point but stay above freezing and the usually invisible water vapour becomes visible as tiny drops of dew. This is caused by the underlying soil being insulated by the slightly warmer air lying between the leaves and the ground.

Hoar frost also owes its existence to the formation of dewdrops and forms when the dew cools to zero degrees centigrade but does not freeze immediately, leading to the beautiful frosted patterns on windows and trees. If the temperature falls still further to around minus three degrees centigrade then the dew drops will freeze and this leads to what is known as 'white dew' or 'silver frost'.

Mist and Fog
Mist and fog are formed in exactly the same way as drizzle, rain, snow or hail and are also caused by cloud formations, but rather than being thousands of feet up in

163

the air, they occur at ground level.

The official definition of a fog is when visibility is reduced to below 1,000 metres, whilst a mist is defined by visibility of more than 1,000 metres.

When fog becomes super cooled, its water droplets remain as a liquid until they hit a solid object at which point they instantly freeze, creating feathery ice or 'rime'.

Glaze meanwhile is formed from drizzle, rain or fog, where the liquid has enough time to spread itself into a thin layer on a road or other object before freezing. This leads to the dangerous phenomenon often referred to as 'black ice', which gives the impression of a wet road to a motorist until they skid and lose control of their vehicle.

Oceans and Rivers

Ours is a world dominated by water, from soft rains and still lakes to iced glaciers and flowing rivers. None however can compare, either in size or temperament, to the wild, untamed oceans that surround every outcrop of land.

These vast bodies of water once provided the beneficial environment in which life began to develop and even today still support the greatest variety of living organisms on earth, from microscopic algae to the largest living creature; the blue whale.

Water is the most extensive and powerful of earth's natural domains with 1.35 billion square kilometres constantly moving back and forth between the landmasses, either as gentle placid seas or whipped up into oceanic frenzies. This constant motion and change in mood manifests from a variety of complex conditions, involving the rotation of the earth, the phase of the moon, the pressure of the air and the temperature and salinity of the waters.

Ocean Currents

The oceans are never still, for deep below the surface currents pull and push the water between the equator and the poles. Each current however differs in its depth, width and speed offering a combination of surface and deep currents.

Surface Currents

Surface currents are driven by prevailing winds, namely the North East and South East Trade Winds which govern the area around the equator, the Westerly's, which inhabit the mid-latitudes and the Polar Easterlies around the Poles.

The friction built up by these winds, pulls the mass of water beneath them in the same direction, albeit at a slower speed and even when the wind drops, the movement of the water continues, due to the build up of its own momentum.

The most well known of the surface currents is the Gulf Stream, first documented in 1513 by the Spanish navigator, Juan Ponce de Leon, who described it in his log whilst crossing the Straits of Florida as:

'*... a current more powerful than the wind'.*

The Gulf Stream is the most powerful surface current in the world and raises sea temperatures by ten degrees centigrade, which in turn affects the whole climate of Western Europe. Without it the UK would be a far colder and bleaker place to live, for London lies on the same latitude as central Canada and Northern Mongolia. Therefore, if the Gulf Stream became disrupted in any way, our climate would begin to chill dramatically; leading to colder climates throughout the UK and Northwest Europe

Deep Water Currents

Deep water currents are due to a combination of temperature variation and the salinity (salt content) of the water.

As water becomes saltier and cools, it sinks to the bottom of the ocean floor, displacing the water that is already there and forms a very slow moving body of water with average speeds of only one metre per day. These currents are also moulded by the shape of the sea bed and therefore often take strange twists and turns.

In places, these deep water currents run to the surface, forming a continuous looping system which links all the oceans together and is collectively referred to as the 'ocean conveyer belt'.

This ocean conveyer belt has been operating since the end of the last ice age and now scientists are worried that its existence may be threatened by global warming, for as the polar ice caps melt, the salinity of the oceans will decrease, which will, in turn, prevent huge amounts of cold water from sinking to the ocean floor. This will affect the formation of deep water currents and ultimately cause the breakdown of the ocean conveyer belt with devastating results to both the fisheries and the weather.

The Mysterious Depths

Sea water is the most abundant substance on earth and one of the most complex, containing more than ninety different chemical elements, including magnesium, potassium and calcium, although sodium chloride (salt) is the main component at eighty five percent.

The saltiest sea is found between Africa and Arabia at the North end of the Red Sea. The reason for the dramatic increase in salt around this area is due to the fact that the heat of the sun evaporates the water at record rates which, in turn, intensifies the salt content. At the other extreme, the least salty seas occur in the Baltic where extremely high rainfall dilutes the salinity.

Vessels sailing in seas of a high salt content are able to carry heavier cargoes because of buoyancy. This is reflected in the ship's Plimsoll line, a gauge painted onto the hull indicating the maximum safe load in different types of sea.

The oceans and seas originally formed from fresh water vapour which fell as rain over 4.3 billion years ago whilst the salt content was introduced gradually from volcanic eruptions, the erosion of the land and the constant movement of the tectonic plates. This whole process is naturally very slow, resulting in the water from the world's oceans only being circulated every five to ten million years.

It is this fine balance of continued salinity which has led scientists to speculate that these were the perfect conditions for life on earth to begin and thrive. The earliest evidence of life comes from 3.85 billion year old rocks, which contain carbon fingerprints of living organisms and although these were no more than simple bacteria they were the basis for the beginnings of life on this planet.

Around two billion years ago new life forms known as '*eukaryotic organisms*' appeared in the waters, which although still single celled, were more complex than bacteria as they had a nucleus and these became the ancestors of today's algae. The increase in their population increased the amount of oxygen in the water which inevitably led to the evolution of more complex life forms.

It is however quite bizarre, even in this modern age, to consider that scientists know more about the landscape of

167

the moon than they do about the ocean floor.

Understandably it has been a long and arduous process to explore the depths of the ocean with the first attempts being made by early ships which simply lowered lines until they reached the ocean floor. In the 19th century this became routine practice on research vessels in the Caribbean and the Atlantic and little by little a rough outline of what lay beneath the seas and oceans became known.

In 1855 a *'bathymetric'* chart of the Atlantic was published, which was the first chart to show evidence of mountains. During the First World War primitive sonar, which was used to hunt down submarines, provided the means with which to produce a more detailed chart and confirmed that there was a rugged chain of mountains in the mid Atlantic.

We now know this as the 'Mid Atlantic Range' and, like many of the oceanic mountains it was formed by underwater volcanic activity, which not only provided a new crust but also began to house pockets of extraordinary sea life.

These underground volcanoes or 'black smokers' as they are often known, were first discovered by scientists in 1977. This subterranean activity heats the surrounding water to extraordinarily high temperatures of 350 degrees centigrade, therefore becoming the ideal breeding ground to support life unknown anywhere else on earth.

An example of one of the unique life forms which has evolved in this fascinating environment is the giant tubeworm, which thrives in a most peculiar way compared to other living creatures. These worms obtain their food and vital nutrients from the bacteria that live inside their body, whilst the bacteria survive by converting the sulphur found in this mineral rich water into food.

In many parts of the oceans the mountains give way to deep trenches caused by the oceanic plates sinking below the thicker crust of the continents. The deepest trench is the 'Mariana Trench' in the Pacific Ocean, which measures a depth of 10,920 meters and would cover Mount Everest with two kilometres to spare.

To date only one percent of the ocean floor has been explored, therefore we can only imagine what fascinating creatures may live within its depths. In a world without sunlight and without warmth some sea creatures defy life as we know it and challenge us to reconsider our rigid thoughts about the requirements for life on earth.

Wave Power

All waves are caused by the wind and the larger the area of water (known as the 'fetch') over which the wind blows, the greater the size of the waves. Naturally the two largest oceans, namely the Pacific and the Atlantic can produce some magnificent waves; however the largest waves in the world are to be found in the Southern Ocean, where the wind is able to literally blow right around the earth without interruption.

In the absence of wind the seas are almost flat but when a breeze begins, tiny movements only a few millimetres deep can be detected upon the surface of the water known as 'capillary waves'. As the wind increases, more energy enters the water, which both raises the height of the waves and propels them forward, increasing the distance between the peaks. In a relatively short period of time the surface of the water is covered in waves several centimetres high and this is often referred to as a 'choppy sea'.

When the wind blows at storm force for over an hour,

a choppy sea can very quickly become a turbulent sea, with waves reaching heights of a meter. At this point the waves become unevenly spaced and rather unpredictable due to a phenomenon known as 'wave interference'.

Wave interference is caused by the wind blowing in many directions and in varying strengths over a wide area, which sets up differing wave patterns. When two waves collide, a larger than normal wave is created but when a wave collides with a trough, a smaller wave than normal is formed, therefore giving rise to a completely unpredictable and chaotic sea.

Meanwhile, several hundred kilometres away from the action, these powerful wave trains gradually begin to dissipate in order of their size resulting in a long lasting series of regularly spaced waves known as a 'swell', a phenomenon which, in the open sea, will cause a boat to rock from side to side.

As waves move towards land they grow larger and come closer together due to the change in the depth of the water. In the open sea waves are unaffected by depth, for their circular motion only plummets down a few meters according to the size of the wave. As a wave approaches the land however, the water becomes shallower and when its circular motion comes into contact with the sea bed the wave begins to slow down and the distance between each wave decreases. The energy carried by the wave however remains the same therefore increasing its height.

As a wave hits the shore the friction at its base becomes so powerful that the top of the wave begins to overtake the bottom and eventually gravity drags the overhanging crest of the wave down, therefore breaking it. At this point the water runs up the beach until it is finally stopped by gravity at which point some of the water seeps into the sand whilst the remainder flows back towards the sea and into the base of the next wave, a phenomenon known as 'backwash'.

Occasionally however, wave power can be totally devastating and the word 'tsunami' has the ability to strike fear into many inhabitants of countries prone to this frightening phenomenon. The word tsunami comes from the Japanese and means 'harbour wave', which is perhaps a rather innocent expression for one of the most terrifying occurrences involving the sea.

Tsunamis are often referred to as 'tidal waves', which is a somewhat confusing term, due to the fact that they have nothing whatsoever to do with the waves themselves, only what lies beneath them. In most cases tsunamis are caused by seismic activity beneath the ocean floor, although other causes can include volcanic eruptions, gigantic landslides or the impact of comets or asteroids. Whatever the cause, the result is a huge displacement of water, which in turn gives rise to a tsunami.

Contrary to popular belief, a tsunami is not one huge wave but a series of waves which ripple out from the source. As they move across the open ocean however their behaviour varies slightly from that of a normal wave.

Firstly the wave length of a tsunami is much greater than a normal wave, ranging from between fifty five to two hundred kilometres. Secondly all of the water beneath a tsunami wave is affected, resulting in the waves picking up speeds of between 500 and 800 kilometres per hour. Thirdly their presence in deep water is hardly noticeable because their height compared to their wave length is negligible. Finally the time span between wave crests is much longer and can be anything from ten minutes to an hour.

171

Mrs Darley's Pagan Elements

When the tsunami eventually reaches the shore, the full power of this mighty sea monster is felt, for as the water depth reduces, the waves slow down but the tremendous energy they carry continues to build their height. This often results in a phenomenon known as 'undertow', which drags the water from the shoreline out to sea, giving the appearance of a low tide before the full impact is delivered.

Although a tsunami can be up to thirty meters in height, more often than not it arrives as a powerful rushing sea without the classic wave breaking but nevertheless, destroys everything that lies within its path. The first impact sadly is often not the only one or the most powerful and others may follow within minutes or even hours.

On 26 December 2004 the most powerful earthquake recorded for over forty years occurred off the North West coast of Sumatra, measuring over nine points on the Richter scale and causing the planet to wobble on its axis. It had the energy of 23,000 atomic bombs.

The tectonic plate of India slipped fifteen meters beneath the Eurasian plate, causing a rupture in the earth's surface below the sea of some 1,200 kilometres. This catastrophic event displaced an estimated thirty square kilometres of seawater, leading to a tsunami that claimed at least 150,000 lives and making many millions homeless, with the worst country affected being Sri Lanka.

The sea can look tranquil and inviting on a beautiful summer's day but as with everything in nature, it can become wild and tempestuous, unleashing its full force upon those unfortunate enough to stand in its way.

Watery Superstitions

Mariners have always both feared and revered the sea, resulting in a belief in many omens and superstitions, which, even today, bring valuable messages to the sailor from an unseen world.

When a sailor or fisherman was about to set out upon a voyage, the meeting of certain individuals did not augur well. This included the sighting of a lawyer or 'land shark' as they were unaffectionately known. It was also considered bad luck to meet a tailor or dressmaker and was even considered bad luck to utter their names before the ship sailed.

The most feared person to encounter before a voyage however was the priest, who was not only synonymous with Jonah but also associated with the burying of the dead. To take a priest to sea was definitely not recommended as they were credited with the power to raise storms and even to mention the word, 'minister' or 'church' on a Scottish fishing boat was enough to warrant being thrown overboard.

This fear of priests also extended to women and in Scotland it was not recommended to set forth on a voyage if you were unfortunate enough to see a bare footed woman with flat feet! French fishermen maintained that the sight of a woman made the sea angry, although in Pliny's, 'Natural History', women are credited with the ability to abate the winds if they present themselves naked. In Brittany nuns and spinsters were regarded as bad luck whilst in other cultures it did not bode well to see a lame man, a red head, a Fin or a Laplander.

If a sailor or fisherman was spoken to whilst on their way to the ship then it was thought that they would not catch any fish that day and in one part of Scotland it was considered necessary to beat up an innocent bystander in order to reverse the ill fortune.

Animals too did not escape the hand of superstition and many were banned from being brought on board such as pigs, cats and hares with the latter name not even allowed to be uttered by Cornish fishermen. In some cases this list extended to horses, dogs and spiders and both English and Scottish mariners were banned from mentioning the name of a four footed animal whilst at sea. In contrast however, rats were considered a good omen and if they deserted the boat then bad luck was forecast.

To lose a water bucket, mop or flag at sea was not a good omen and neither was playing a game of cards. All things black were banned as they were associated with death and to have a corpse on board was looked upon with dread, as illustrated in Shakespeare's *Pericles*:

Sir, your queen must overboard: the sea works high, the wind is loud, and will not lie till the ship be cleared of the dead.

Specific days were also seen as lucky and unlucky. According to biblical events there were supposed to be twenty eight lucky sailing days which the Arch Angel Gabriel revealed to St Joseph, whilst there were fifty four unlucky days upon which no sea journeys should be undertaken.

Among the unlucky days were; the first Monday in April, the birthday of Cain, the day on which Abel was slain and the second Monday in August, being the anniversary of the destruction of Sodom and Gomorrah. The 31 December was also to be avoided due to the hanging of Judas and it was said that if sailors went to sea on that day they would catch no fish but only the bones of a corpse and a shroud.

Certain days of the week were also to be avoided, especially Fridays for it was a popular superstition that the witches reigned supreme upon this day and could weald great powers over the waters. This dread of Friday was said by some to stem from the supposed day of the crucifixion however other sources considered it a Pagan superstition.

Friday derives its name from Frigga, the wife of the God Odin who, in Norse mythology represented the eternal feminine and was highly revered, especially on Fridays. It is interesting to note that this superstition appeared just as Christianity began to take hold during the 5th and 6th centuries, thus demonising the Pagan Goddess' special day.

The renowned poet, Lord Byron shared all the superstitions of his fellow Scotsmen and although he recognized Friday as an unlucky day on which to sail, he nevertheless put his beliefs aside and embarked on a voyage to Greece, where he died at Missolonghi.

The British admiralty once tried to prove the absurdity of this superstition and ordered the keel of a ship to be laid on a Friday; they then named the ship Friday and launched her on a Friday. They gave the command to a man called Friday and set sail on a Friday, however although the ship was new and sea worthy when it left port, neither ship nor crew was ever hear of again!

The ceremony of naming a ship dates back to Pagan times when vessels were placed under the protection of certain Gods and libations were practiced when the ship was launched. Even today many sailors will not go to sea in a boat that has not been named or blessed.

With regards to lucky talismans or omens it was considered fortunate to have an old coin hidden under the mast and for sailors to carry salt in their pockets. A far more peculiar token of good luck was if a fly fell into a sailors drink whilst on board and children were also considered to be lucky.

A strange phenomenon experienced by sailors was that known as 'St Elmo's light', the unearthly phosphorescent light, which appeared at night usually within the rigging of ships and which, gave birth to many superstitions. The Roman writer Pliny mentioned it in his 'Natural History', although it was during the Middle Ages that the phenomenon was attributed to St Elmo, the patron saint of sailors. In reality however there was no St Elmo and the name was said to have derived from a corruption of either St Erasmus, the patron saint of Neapolitan sailors or of Helena, sister of the twins, Castor and Pollux and daughter of Jupiter and Leda.

The majority of seafarers saw the light as a sign of the saint's benevolent presence, a fact which brought great relief to the crew of Columbus' second voyage when sudden winds put them in danger.

Suddenly one sailor saw the strange flame dancing in the rigging and called the crew, all of whom were delighted to see the presence of the light as they considered their protector was near.

Some sailors however attribute the number of lights dancing in the rigging as meaning different things. Often sailors would refer to the appearance of two or more lights as Castor and Pollux, which symbolized the end of the storm and a return to calm waters, whilst if they only saw one light they would refer to it as Helena, which would act as a warning that the worst of the storm was yet to come.

In Cornwall the light is called 'Jack Harry' after the first sailor who was fooled by it.

Considering man's fragility against the mighty power

of the untamed oceans it is little wonder that so many superstitions have blossomed throughout the ages from around the world.

Divinities of the Waters
Regardless of whether a body of water springs from the ground, falls from the sky or thunders onto a sandy shore, mankind has, since his time here on earth began, revered the sacred waters. A fact which, over millennia, has led to many Gods and Goddesses becoming associated it.

Sea Gods
The oldest of all the water Gods was Pontus, produced by Gaea herself at the very edge of time. He is without physiognomy or character and, as time evolved, his name simply became synonymous with the sea.

From the union of Gaea and Uranus, the great God Oceanus was born who, according to Homer, contributed to the formation of the world and whose power was inferior to none but Zeus. Oceanus married his sister Tethys and between them produced three thousand Oceanoids and three thousand rivers known as the Hesiod.

As time passed the Olympians stamped their authority over both the earth and the waters with the domain of the sea and rivers given to Poseidon, whilst Oceanus was guided towards retirement.

River Gods
The Hesiod or three thousand rivers, were so revered by mortals that they would cast living bulls and horses into the watery depths along with burning rams and, in some cases, rather bizarrely their own hair. The Hesiod were depicted as virile men with long beards, whilst their

strength was symbolized by a pair of horns which adorned their brow.

The most sacred of the rivers was the Achelous which gained its name from Achelous who became Hercules opponent in the fight for the hand of Deianeria.

Upon losing the fight, Achelous changed himself into a serpent, then into a wild bull. Hercules however, still angered by Archelous' challenge, ripped off one of his horns, which the nymphs subsequently made into the horn of plenty. Archelous, ashamed by his total humiliation, finally threw himself into the river which then took his name.

Water: our Lifeblood

Water is the essence of life; it carries the hope of future generations, memories of lives past and is present in every living thing. It is the lifeblood of Mother Earth with the rivers and streams being symbolic of Her capillaries and veins.

Seventy percent of our planet is covered by water, all life was born from it and all life depends upon it. However, because it is a universal substance, the majority of us take it for granted, we hardly ever think about it and we certainly don't appreciate it. In many instances we exploit it, manipulate it and pollute it to suit our own ends and then spend our lives looking elsewhere for the magic elixir of life, when it's right here under our own noses.

It is important to remember that as long as we treat water with love and respect, it will love and respect us in return, nurturing our bodies and providing us with the key to longevity.

Tantric scripts tell us that water is *'prana'*, the vital breath that brings life, without which we could not live.

The human body comprises of millions of cells, each of which is filled and surrounded by a watery fluid. In a healthy hydrated body the water outside the cells is less concentrated than that inside, therefore allowing toxins to be drawn out of the cell through the process of osmosis. However when the body becomes dehydrated through a lack of fluid intake, this process can become reversed and the water outside of the cell becomes more concentrated than inside. This in turn interferes with the delicate process of osmosis, which ultimately leads to a build up of toxins that are known to be the cause of a whole host of serious diseases.

Maintaining the balance of this fluid in each cell therefore is the key to health and is achieved by drinking on a regular basis. Just a two percent loss in cellular water can affect our energy levels by up to twenty percent therefore the recommended daily intake of water is six glasses per day to avoid dehydration.

In certain areas of the world, anthropologists have discovered that people frequently live to be over one hundred years old and this they attribute to the quality of their water supply.

The mountains north of Pakistan are home to the Hunza people, who are fortunate enough to drink from melted glaciers, which is probably the purest form of water on earth as it contains a high proportion of carbons and silicates. Interestingly the Hunza's seem to be immune from the majority of the degenerative diseases that we know so well here in the west such as arthritis, senile dementia and heart problems.

Unlike our mineral water where the mineral salts have become dissolved in the water, the Hunza's water actually contains clusters of minerals called colloids, ensuring that the water is electrically and magnetically balanced for optimum health.

Many other ancient cultures have revered and treasured their relationship with this vital fluid and although they may not have been fortunate enough to have the purity of water to which the Hunza's are accustomed, they nevertheless went to great lengths to ensure that their storage methods enhanced their drinking water.

The Chinese chose to store their water in jade vases as they considered Jade to be the gem stone of longevity, whilst the Incas and Aztecs chose obsidian, a stone associated with purification.

Modern science now recognises that gem stones not only contain certain minerals, which when in contact with water, make it more beneficial to drink, but also that the silica content from certain gem stones prevents the water from becoming polluted.

The ancients, however, did not need the confirmation of science, they simply appreciated the miraculous power of water and knew not only how to store it but also where to collect it, recognising that water taken from cool shady places where there was movement, meant that it would be both energised and pure. Likewise water that lay in an exposed pool with little movement, would be lifeless and often contaminated.

Sadly for most of us, this is exactly how our water is stored, in vast, still, open reservoirs, with little movement and little shade. In addition to this, the water companies then have to treat it with a range of chemicals in order to 'clean' it and, although this is unavoidable, what they then fail to do is revitalise it.

Energising and Purifying our Water
The majority of us are not fortunate enough to have

access to such pure water as the Hunza people and it can therefore be worth taking a little effort to energise and purify our water before consuming it as failure to do so can leave us feeling depleted in vital life energy.

Filtered Water
Fit a filter to the sink or use a filter jug or kettle as the carbon contained within it removes excessive chemicals which arise from the purification process.

Magnetised Water
Although magnetic healing is ancient in its origins, over the past twenty years modern scientists have been looking at how magnets are able to change the structure of water. Hans Grander, an Austrian naturalist has developed a technique whereby he is able to restore natural energy to water through a process called 'implosion'. The resulting water is known as 'Grander Water' and is said to dramatically improve the health of all living things.

Making Vortices
Theodor Schwenk, a follower of Rudolph Steiner, spent his whole life working with water and was fascinated by the way in which water responds to the slightest change in its surroundings especially when one layer of water meets with another such as salt water coming into contact with fresh water at which point a series of waves begins to form.

He discovered that air becomes trapped in the hollow between the inner surfaces of the water as the wave curls and is then released as the wave unfurls, producing vertical spirals of energy or vortices, which have their own energetic pulsating rhythm. He went on to note that temperatures at the core of spiralling waters are cooler, which means they are more lively and energetic and that the varying speeds of a vortex means that both positive and negative energies are balanced.

In order to create vortices in your water at home simply swirl the water round with your hand before entering a bath or stir water around in a jug or filter before drinking.

Swirling or stirring the water in a clockwise or deosil direction (the way of the sun) is recommended for inducing positive vibrations.

Using Colour

The Egyptians were particularly well versed in storing their water in coloured glass jars in order that they might harness the energy created in the water for healing purposes, with blue glass being the preferential colour.

Water as Vibrational Medicine

Despite water's ability to change form from a solid to a liquid, from a liquid into a vapour and back again, the molecular structure of water is quite stable which gives it the ability to store information obtained from other molecules.

As water travels, it carries not only physical information but is also capable of picking up more subtle messages and retaining the memory of that information. This theory was brought into the popular domain during the 1990's when French biochemist, Jacques Benveniste attempted to show the scientific world that other molecular substances use water as means of communication and that water acts as a transmitter of both physical and vibrational energy.

Sadly, Benveniste was accused of fraud by the

scientific establishment, regardless of the fact that his experiments illustrated that water does retain and transfer both chemical and vibrational information.

This is however, information that modern homeopaths have known for over 200 years thanks to the pioneering work of Samuel Hahnemann. Hahnemann believed in the principal of 'like curing like' and therefore set out to investigate the theory that anything which can harm the body can also have the potential to cure it. Having isolated several 'remedies' he then placed the specific substance in distilled water, diluted it many times until no trace of the original substance remained and gave it to his patients with some success.

On some occasions however, Hahnemann had to deliver the remedies to patient's homes and every time he did so, the remedies appeared to be more successful. He eventually came to the conclusion that their increased effectiveness must be due to the shaking of the bottle and the subsequent movement of the water, which increased its life force whilst journeying in his carriage. It was at this point that Hahnemann decided to shake or 'succuss' the water, to give it its correct term, before adding the remedy and diluting it.

What Benveniste proved was that homeopathic medicine actually works scientifically, for at dilutions of ten to the power of one hundred and twenty, biological changes do actually take place, despite the fact that none of the original material is present in the remaining water.

He concluded therefore that water molecules retain the memory of the original additional substance and work directly on the energy frequencies of the body.

Types of Fresh Water
There are several types of fresh water although not all are

suitable for drinking due to their journey from cloud to earth.

Distilled Water
Distilled water is what scientists refer to as 'pure water' as it contains no dissolved materials such as minerals and salts. This is what makes it particularly beneficial to homeopaths as it acts like a sponge and will absorb anything that is added to it. It is not recommended as normal drinking water however, for on a physical level it is devoid of life giving minerals and energetically carries no beneficial memories of mountain streams or deep shady pools.

Juvenile Water
Although juvenile water comes from deep underground, it has not had sufficient time to mature as it comes up though the earth and therefore lacks sufficient minerals to be of any long term use as drinking water.

Rainwater
This is often referred to as 'immature water', which again is not recommended as drinking water for it contains very few minerals. It can also pick up toxins as it falls and is therefore best left to make its way into the ground where it is then referred to as 'surface water'.

Surface Water
This is, more often than not, the water that comes from our taps. Originally it falls as rainwater and runs away into pools, dams and reservoirs where it collects a variety of both minerals and toxins as it moves along.

Groundwater

This water comes from deep within the earth, finally materialising on the surface from underground streams. These streams have travelled for many miles beneath the ground, picking up vital minerals and vital salts as they go, although some groundwater these days becomes polluted by the use of chemicals.

Spring Water

This is by far the best water to drink, particularly if it comes from mountain springs for it will be rich in minerals. It is always recommended however that the water is tested regularly to ensure that farm and industry chemicals have not polluted it.

The quality of our water is a reflection of our society, for it mirrors exactly what we put into it, therefore if we treat it well and strive to keep it as pure as possible, the health of the society in which we live will improve.

Mrs Darley Tale: Fairy Rain

I awoke to the sound of something rattling against my bedroom window and, flinging back the quilt, went to investigate. Peering down onto the path through bleary eyes, I was surprised to see Mrs Darley poised with a second handful of rubble.

I quickly opened the latch and poked my head out, thinking that perhaps she felt unwell after our Beltane celebrations of the previous evening. Upon seeing me, she smiled and put her fingers to her lips to indicate my silence and then motioned me to join her.

Glancing swiftly at the clock as I pulled on my jeans, I was rather disgruntled to see that it was only 5.30am and that this rather rude awakening had deprived me of a good one-and-a-half hour's sleep.

Mrs Darley's Pagan Elements

My face was obviously still displaying these thoughts as I appeared through the porch door and was something that did not go unnoticed by Mrs Darley.

'Hello, dear,' she whispered, 'I know you're not happy with me disturbing your beauty sleep, but what I'm going to show you will more than make up for it. Come.'

She took my arm and lead me along the path, through the five-barred gate, across the lane and up onto the moor. Here the landscape was dotted with smooth granite boulders that protruded from the coarse tufted grass-like sleeping giants. Our ascent gave us cold wet feet and led us towards the old railway track where a striking gnarled hawthorn stood out against the skyline in all her May Day beauty.

'Isn't she lovely?' Mrs Darley asked, more of herself than of me, as she reached up to caress the pale pink May blossom which hung in swathes from the dark branches. 'What a gift to be greeted with on the Goddess' special day.'

I nodded in agreement, my earlier grumpiness now almost forgotten as I drank in the beauty of the first day of the Celtic summer.

'Now,' said Mrs Darley, turning her attention away from the hawthorn and sinking down beside one of the smooth granite boulders, 'look what we have here.'

I looked down and to my disappointment could see nothing particularly unusual. Noticing my obvious blank response, she dipped her hand into a small pool of water, held within a depression in the rock and splashed my face.

'Fairy rain,' she laughed as I flinched from the shock of the cold water, 'a gift from the elementals.'

I looked at her with some suspicion, unsure as to

186

whether to take her seriously.

'We always refer to dew as fairy rain, my dear, and, when it collects in a pool like this, it means we can avail ourselves of its most precious gift.'

'Which is?' I asked.

'Which is; *"The fair maid who the first of May, goes to the fields at break of day and walks in the dew of the hawthorn tree will then ever handsome be."* And here we are on May Day morning, sitting beneath the thorn, (the portal to the realm of the fairy), under which, in a hollow of granite, (the stone renowned for its powers of insight and hallucination), lies a pool of fairy rain.

Now that my dear is what I would call magical!'

I laughed, suddenly feeling as though I had become part of another world which only few had known, 'So do we give it try?' I asked.

'Why of course!' replied Mrs Darley, scooping a little of the water into her hands and splashing her face.

I followed suit and began to feel wide awake as the cold water tingled against my skin. 'That feels good,' I said.

'Water, my dear, is the universal healer, the life giver. We often turn to chemically produced lotions, potions and medicines, when all we need is to bathe in and drink more of this magical liquid in order to maintain our inner health and outward beauty.'

At this point she rummaged in her pocket and produced a small hip flask, which she immediately offered to me. I took it and braced myself for the obligatory taste of whisky, which had become part of many seasonal and moon phase celebrations. To my surprise, however, I found myself drinking cool refreshing water that tasted almost sweet.

'Mmmm that's lovely,' I said, almost reluctant to

hand back the flask.

'It's from the spring at the back of the tor,' she said, 'and is quite different from tap water. This water is alive and energized, which of course is exactly how it makes you feel when you drink it. In reality you need nothing more.'

'Not even a tot of whisky?' I asked smiling.

'Ah,' she said, waving her finger at me as the fairy rain shone on her face, 'all good whiskies use flowing water as their base ingredient, for this alone is the elixir of life!'

Water: A Matter of Life and Death

In almost every creation myth the element of water is involved. The Gods create it, are born from it, breathe life into it, reside in it and preside over it.

In Babylonian mythology water was the primordial element and from the fusion of sweet water personified as Apsu, which encircled the earth and salt water personified as Tiamat the sea Goddess, the world was born.

In Egyptian legend Nun or Nu was chaos, the primordial ocean in which lay the germs of all things and all beings. He was sometimes personified as a man plunged up to his waist in water holding up his arms to support the Gods who were created by him.

Yet for all its life giving and enhancing properties water is a paradox, for what it gives it can also take away.

A still pool can look deceivingly welcoming and yet has the power to suck us down, a calm sea will tempt us away from shore and yet has the ability to whip up a devastating storm, the rich and abundant harvest fields can hide many a menacing presence beneath the depths and a shower of rain can prolong itself into a destructive flood an event documented in the records of many religions and cultures.

In Babylonian mythology the Gods one day resolved to destroy the human race, albeit the reason was not revealed. They gathered on the banks of the Euphrates and decided to bring about a great deluge which would drown mankind. The God Ea however felt sorry for the mere mortals and told a reed hut in a loud voice what they should do in order to avoid the forthcoming flood.

Man of Shuruppak, son of Ubar-Tutu,
Destroy thy house, build a vessel,
Leave thy riches, seek thy life,
Store in thy vessel the seeds of all of life.

As the reed hut told his secret, an inhabitant of the village called Uta-Napishtim overheard him, just as Ea had intended and set to work without delay. He built a ship a hundred and twenty cubits high and loaded it with all he possessed in gold and silver. He took his family aboard along with his cattle, animals and birds of the land. That evening the Lord of Shadows caused the rain to fall and so fierce and furious was the storm that even the Gods who had initiated it were afraid.

For six days and six nights the winds were abroad and the deluge descended. At last on the dawn of the seventh day the evil wind grew peaceful, the sea became calm; the voices of men were stilled, and all mankind were changed into mud.

At this point the vessel came to rest on the summit of Mount Nisir, and Uta-Napishtim let loose a dove and a swallow, who both soon returned to the vessel having found no other place to land. A while later a raven was released which did not return, and Uta-Napishtim took

189

this as a sign that waters were receding. As a token of thanks he made a sacrifice, which pleased the Gods, all that is except Enlil, who was most displeased to see that some mortals had survived. Ea however managed to appease him and eventually his anger subsided and to make amends gave Uta-Napishtim and his family a home at the mouth of the river, where they would be safe from future floods.

The similarities between this and the later Christian story of Noah detailed in the biblical book of Genesis are startlingly similar in nature.

For each of us, earthly life begins in water, for within the safety of the mother's womb we quietly develop within the amniotic waters and, following our birth, we are often initiated into a specific religion or belief system through a christening or baptism using the symbolic aspect of water in order to represent purification and cleansing.

Water, however, can also be the substance responsible for our death through drowning from within, via pneumonia or oedema or drowning from without in a body of water.

It is also the element that has been used throughout history for far more sinister purposes such as torture and murder and none more so than during the witch hunts of the fifteenth to the eighteenth centuries.

Here water was the medium into which suspected witches were cast, hands bound, in order to determine their guilt or innocence. If they floated they were found guilty and subsequently put to death, whilst if they sank they were deemed innocent and their name cleared, which was little consolation for those who breathed their last on the muddy bed of a cold dark river.

Water was also used as a punishment for 'scolds' and

'nags', more as an act of humiliation rather than torture. Here the poor unfortunate was wheeled around the village in a ducking stool, whilst the inhabitants were at liberty to jeer and name call. The accused finally ended up at the local duck pond or river where they were unceremoniously ducked several times into the water.

For sailors worldwide, burial at sea has often been a necessity and in early times the body was simply sewn into a shroud made of a sail cloth and cast over the side of the boat, usually accompanied by a religious ceremony. Today, however, the rules appertaining to this means of disposal are slightly more stringent, details of which can be obtained from DEFRA.

For Pacific Islanders and some North European cultures, burial at sea was a natural act and consisted of the body being submerged until the flesh had disappeared from the bones, at which point the bones were often lifted from the sea and buried on land.

In Celebration of the Mollusc

There are many creatures which would have been an obvious choice for this section as each has their own vital role to play in the eco system of our precious planet with the most popular being dolphins, whales, sharks or perhaps coral, especially in view of its fragility.

However, many creatures tend to be overlooked because of either their size or simplicity and yet are some of the most fascinating to study. Among them are the molluscs, the forgotten creatures of the sea.

One of the first molluscs many of us come into contact with as children is the limpet. British beaches are often littered with their empty shells. The limpet, however, has an intelligence which belies its simplistic make-up, as many children discover when they try to pull one away from a rock without success.

When the tide is in, limpets move around in the shallows in order to feed on algae but as the tide ebbs, the limpet makes its way home and suckers down on the rock in readiness for exposure to air by means of extremely sticky mucus. Limpets have, in fact, one of the strongest grips in the animal kingdom and have the ability to cling firmly to rocks even through the fiercest storms.

Limpets are gastropod molluscs and belong to the same family as slugs and snails. Like all gastropods they move around on a single large foot, leaving a trail of mucus behind them, which acts as their map, enabling them to find their way home. As the tide falls the limpet simply follows its trail back to the same place and, over time, the shell begins to wear a groove into the rock which eventually makes for a very snug fit. This tight fit helps the limpet to retain water beneath its shell which is vital to its survival once the tide has fallen.

A second member of this fascinating mollusc family is the Bubble-raft Snail, a four centimetre long creature that looks both delicate and harmless as it floats along the surface of the subtropical oceans. This peculiar snail is encased in a paper thin shell and yet, its appearance is quite deceptive. The Bubble-raft Snail is, in fact, a floating carnivore and devours any suitable victim it happens to bump into including stinging jellyfish and the Portuguese Man o' War, which most other creatures tend to avoid.

The Bubble-Raft Snail is, rather strangely, unable to swim and so secretes a stream of mucus covered bubbles from its foot which quickly harden in order to make a raft like vessel strong enough to carry the creature across the high seas. The snail is however, completely at the mercy of the tides and comes upon its food by accident rather than design.

Once in contact with a food source the snail climbs onto it and feeds by rasping at it with a muscular tongue called a *'radula'*. The radula is covered with numerous tiny teeth which give it a texture rather like sandpaper and the poor victim is slowly devoured over a period of days or weeks.

Perhaps next time we kill molluscs in our garden or eat them in a fancy restaurant, whether they be snails, whelks, or muscles we will give thanks to these fascinating creatures that live their lives almost unnoticed and unappreciated by humankind.

The Yew
Beneath the yew,
Beside the stream,
Lies the land
Of long lost dreams,

Where through the mists
Of yesterday,
The lore of magic
Still holds sway.

Where Naiads sing
And Ondines dance,
The human soul
Becomes entranced.

Beneath the yew,
Beside the stream,
Lies the land
Of long lost dreams.

Mrs Darley's Pagan Elements

Mythical Creatures of the Deep

The power, scale and overall mysterious nature of the waters which inhabit our planet have, over millennia, given rise to many tales which weave their way into our dreams and capture our imagination.

Every culture around the world has their own tales of terrifying sea creatures and enigmatic elementals and in our enlightened times, many explanations have been offered by scientists and biologists as to what these mysterious creatures can actually be. For the fishermen who have encountered them however or for the land dweller that has seen them, no scientific offering will suffice.

Selkies

Selkies, also known as *'silkies'* or *'selchies'*, are normally found in Icelandic, Irish and Scottish mythology and have the ability to transform themselves from seals to humans.

Stories surrounding selkies are normally associated with romance but sadly, few have a happy ending. It is said that the pelt of a selkie gives them power over mankind, but without it they will become trapped on land and a slave to the human who entraps them.

Female selkies are quite beautiful and should a human male be lucky enough to steal the pelt of a selkie, then she can be forced into becoming his wife and will remain so as long as the pelt is kept hidden. Often the selkie provides her human husband with many children and although they are said to make good wives and mothers they do spend much of their time looking seaward, splashing around in the shallows and gradually dying of a broken heart for want of the ocean.

If the selkie is lucky enough to find her hidden pelt,

she will immediately return to the sea and although she does not see her human husband again she does return to see her children in the shallows of the waves.

Just as female selkies are very beautiful so male selkies are extremely handsome, with great powers of seduction over mortal women. They are said to prey particularly upon the wives of fishermen who are left alone whilst their husbands are at sea.

In the film entitled *The Secret of Roan Inish*, a fisherman sees a beautiful woman sunbathing on the rocks and immediately falls in love with her. He realizes however that she is a selkie because of her discarded seal pelt and knows that if he steals her pelt she will be forced to go to with him as she is unable to return to the sea without it. The fisherman ensures that the pelt is well hidden and as times goes by he marries the selkie and, in turn, she provides him with many children.

One day one of her children finds the pelt and asks her what it is. She immediately reclaims the pelt and returns to both the sea and her selkie husband without a word to her human family.

Selkies are not always selfish lovers however, for there is one tale which tells of a very happily married selkie woman, whose human fisherman husband, Cagan, goes to sea late in the year when a storm is forecast. Knowing that her husband is in trouble, his selkie wife dons her seal pelt and returns to the sea to save him, although she knows that she will never again be able to return to him in her human form.

Ondines
According to the works of Paracelsus, the controversial 15th century surgeon and alchemist, Ondines or Undines are water elementals which appear in European folklore

as fairy-like creatures. They are said to be found in forest pools and waterfalls and sing beautifully above the noise of the water.

These enchanting creatures are born with the gift of eternal life, but sadly do not possess a soul and are only able to acquire one by marrying a human and bearing his child. There is however, as always, a price to pay for wants and desires and so it is that if an Ondine acquires a soul, so they must give up their right to eternal life.

In German mythology the term 'Ondine' was used as a proper name for a beautiful water nymph who fell deeply in love with a handsome and brave knight called Sir Lawrence. The couple married and, when making their vows, the handsome Sir Lawrence stated that his every waking breath would be a pledge of his love and faithfulness to Ondine. The couple were very happy and a year after their marriage, Ondine gave birth to a beautiful child. From this moment on however, Ondine began to age and as her looks diminished, so Sir Lawrence's interest waned.

One afternoon as Ondine was passing the stables, she heard her husband's familiar snoring and, upon entering, she found him sleeping in the arms of another woman. Ondine was enraged and pointing her finger at him, reminded him of their wedding vows when he said that his every waking breath would be a promise of his love and faithfulness to her. She then went on to curse him by saying that as long as he stayed awake he would have the breath of life, but if he should ever have the misfortune to sleep, then his breath would fail and he would die.

Interestingly there is a medical term known as 'Undine's Curse' which is used to describe a rare condition whereby the autonomic control of breathing is lost, resulting in the need for every breath to be made consciously. If the problem is untreated then the patient will, like Sir Lawrence, die if they fall asleep and are unable to breathe consciously.

Water Nymphs

Just as every large body of water had its own Deity, so every stream, brook, spring and pool had its own nymph, each of which was classified in Greek mythology according to their place of abode. Potamids were river and stream nymphs, Naiads, looked after brooks, Crenae or Pegae were carers of springs, whilst Limnads were nymphs assigned to stagnant waters.

As a general rule, nymphs held a lower rank than the Gods, but were occasionally admitted to Olympus where mortals honoured them with offerings.

As a group, their functions were varied. They were, on the whole, benevolent creatures but could become dangerous to any mortal whom they found beautiful, as they often carried them away to their watery abode where the unfortunate mortal subsequently died. They could also be fickle with their affections, as Selemnos, a gentle shepherd, discovered when he fell in love with the fountain nymph Argyra. Having initially returned his love, Argyra eventually tired of Selemnos and deserted him. Selemnos was so broken hearted that the great Goddess of love, Aphrodite took pity on him and turned him into a river, thereby granting him oblivion to ease the sickness of his heart. Thereafter, the river Selemnos became a place of pilgrimage for those who were suffering from the sorrows of love.

The nymphs also had the gift of prophecy which they would share with mortals who wished to know their fate. They also had the ability to cure the sick and cared for flowers, fields and flocks, whilst much of their time was

197

spent weaving and spinning.

Despite their Divine character, however, they were not immortal and, according to Plutarch, their average lifespan did not extend much beyond 9,620 years. However, their one privilege was that they remained for their lifetime young and beautiful, for they fed upon ambrosia, the food of the Gods.

Mermaids

Tales of mermaids have existed for thousands of years, with the first reference to a fishtailed God being in the form of a Babylonian Deity called Oannes.

The classic British mermaid with which we are all familiar with is thought to have originated from a mixture of Celtic legend and seafaring lore.

Generally the mermaid's upper body is that of a beautiful woman crowned with a head of golden blonde hair, whilst their lower body is that of a fish. The classic mermaid is to be found sitting on a rock just off shore, combing her long tresses and admiring her beauty in a small hand mirror.

It is however their singing that entices men to follow them, in much the same fashion as the Sirens. Once entranced, mermaids either spirit the mere mortal away to their watery world never to return or simply lure the victim to their death by drowning them amongst the waves.

It is said that Mermaid Rock at Lamorna Cove, on the south coast of Cornwall was one such place where the resident mermaid would sing local fishermen to their deaths. Whilst on some occasions mermaids themselves are tempted away from their watery home by the sound of a beautiful mortal voice.

There have, over the last few hundred years, been

several recorded sightings of these enigmatic and often feared creatures, especially where seafaring lore still holds strong such as the Celtic lands of Scotland, Wales, Cornwall and Ireland.

The Loch Ness Monster

Perhaps the most famous creature of the deep is the enigmatic 'Nessie' thought to inhabit Scotland's Loch Ness.

Although sightings of what we would now term as 'The Loch Ness Monster' became popular in the 20th century, the loch has always had an eerie reputation as far as strange sightings have been concerned and even as early as the 6th century, St Columba was said to have had a confrontation with a 'fearsome beastie', which fled at the sound of the saint's voice.

Non-believers have offered many explanations as to what the monster could be, including wave patterns caused by the wind, tricks of the light, fish, animals swimming, boats and floating pieces of wood.

Even scientists using highly developed equipment, have been unable to discover any evidence of a monster in Loch Ness and of the many people who have claimed to see 'Nessie', none have been able to take a conclusive photograph or capture its existence on film.

The Kraken

Tales of the terrifying sea monster, the Kraken date back to ancient times when both Aristotle and Pliny felt the need to mention it. It is however into Nordic mythology that the Kraken has crept for there are actual historical accounts from Scandinavia of what is considered to be a mighty sea monster.

In 1520 Eric Falkendorff, Bishop of Nidros, wrote to

199

Pope Leon a long letter on the subject of the sea monster. Apparently whilst the bishop had been at sea one Sunday he was feeling quite upset that he was unable to celebrate mass on dry land, when suddenly from the sea, emerged an island upon which he and his crew were able to land and celebrate mass. With mass over, he returned to his ship, however upon looking back at the island he was aghast to see that there was no land in sight and that the island had totally vanished.

Many accounts of meetings with the Kraken are recorded, which provide the seeker with more information. The monster is said to be several miles in length, hence the reason for it often being mistaken for an island, and only appears in calm water, but when it emerges it seems to cover the whole sea. Many fish are said to swim alongside the monster whose presence encourages fishermen to cast over their nets and hooks albeit they are unaware of the monster's presence. Unfortunately for the fishermen, whenever the monster feels the hooks piercing his back he is said to rise up and devour the fishing boat.

However, for fishermen who know the Kraken's secret, they are able to avoid destruction by softly calling the sea monster by name, at which point he will immediately sink gently down into the watery depths without causing any harm.

Morgawr

Cornwall too has its own sea monster, a creature known as Morgawr, the Cornish word for 'sea giant' which is said to live in and around Falmouth Bay.

In 1976 there were many sightings, with two local fishermen describing the monster as having a long neck and a huge grey head like an enormous seal. They described the body as being black with humps and estimated it to be approximately twenty two feet in length. Since that time there have been many more sightings although, as always, the mystery remains unsolved.

The Magic and Alchemy of Water

Carl Jung, the great psychologist believed that just as the four elements exist on the material plane in the forms of air, fire, water and earth, so these energy types also exist in our inner world or subconscious and can be described as thinking, intuition, feeling and sensation. He believed that in an individual who he would describe as 'unconscious', one energy type would always dominate, but that in order to become balanced we must learn to develop each category even though we will always retain the main aspect of our personality.

Jung went on to divide the four categories into two groups, namely perception and judgment. Perception, he stated, tells us what is happening through intuition and sensation, whilst judgment takes us through the decision making process by thinking and feeling.

In terms of human existence, water symbolizes the feeling aspect, that of love and compassion, hatred and despair. Its constant and unpredictable movement is akin to our emotional state, one minute calm and controlled, the next tempestuous and angry.

Jung believed that those with a dominant water aspect to their personality, the feeling types, have an understanding of their fellow man. They take into account the emotions of those whom they come into contact with and often consider how they would feel if they were in that same position. They have the ability to make others realize their worth and inspire them to achieve their goals. If however someone is too dominant in this area and uses little logic when dealing with life's challenges then they may find themselves in difficulties, for talking nicely to someone and being sympathetic to their feelings is not always enough to encourage forward movement.

Our language illustrates beautifully the unpredictability of our emotions through imagery with water. We feel 'waves of emotion', we describe minor upsets as 'a storm in a teacup', we cry 'rivers of tears' when we are upset, we often have 'that sinking feeling', when realization of what we have done hits home, we describe someone as 'wishy-washy' when they are unable to make a decision and refer to feelings of being overwhelmed as 'drowning in a sea of despair'. Perhaps what we should all attempt to do as we journey from the cradle to the grave is simply ebb and flow with the tides of life.

In ancient Greek philosophy, water is one of the four classical elements, considered to be both wet and cold and, according to Aristotle, occupies a place between earth and air amongst the elemental spheres. It is associated with the humour of phlegm which, like water is cold and wet and also the phlegmatic personality which is considered to be passive, thoughtful, careful, controlled, even tempered, calm, reliable and peaceful.

The symbol used by Plato to depict water was the icosahedron (formed from twenty equilateral triangular faces), making water the element with the greatest number of sides, a fact that Plato regarded as appropriate due to the fact that water flows as though it is made of tiny balls.

In alchemy, the chemical element of mercury was associated with water and therefore its alchemical symbol became a downward pointing triangle (see next page).

In the Hindu tradition, the element of water is associated with Chandra, the Moon or Shukra, for all represent the realm of feelings, intuition and imagination.

Magical Water
Ever since mankind has walked upon the earth he has attempted to harness and work in conjunction with her natural forces especially when making magic.

In earliest times the natural world was the domain of the wise woman and cunning man for they knew how to attract love, good fortune and health by working in conjunction with the seasons, the moon's cycles, and the elements of air, fire, water and earth.

The practice of ceremonial magic in its many forms also incorporates the element of water into its teachings.

In Wicca ritual the element of water is placed in the cardinal direction of the west and is protected by the ondines as guardians of the western quarter. This direction is associated with maturity, the evening and autumn and is symbolically represented by cool colours, especially blue, the cup or chalice, sea creatures, watery domains, shells and the tarot suit of cups.

In the casting of a magic circle the element of water is simply depicted by itself contained within a bowl or chalice.

Water magic is used for alleviating emotional trauma, promoting emotional well being and is often a key element when trying to attract love.

Dew has always been acknowledged as a mystical

manifestation and has, over millennia, been referred to as 'cosmic semen' and 'fairy pearls', to name but a few. In rural communities it has been used in a myriad of ways from soothing sore eyes to alleviating skin diseases, gout and strengthening those of a delicate disposition. The dew formed on May Day morning was not only thought to keep fair maidens beautiful but also had the power to enhance fertility, confer protection and offer all those who rolled or washed in it good luck throughout the year.

The liquidity of essential oils can also represent the element of water along with the added dimension of smell.

The essential oils listed in Table 2.1 below offer their own magical qualities and can either be burned on an incense burner or used in the bath.

Please note: If you are using essential oils in the bath do not use more than six drops diluted in a teaspoon of oil, milk or alcohol before entering. Please do not use oils marked with * in the bath or if you are pregnant.

Essential Oil	Properties
Chamomile	Healing, harmony
Geranium	Love
Frankincense	Peace, success, joy
Lavender	Peace, harmony
Lemon	Releasing negativity
Patchouli	Wealth
Peppermint *	Protection
Rose	Love
Tea Tree	Purification
Thyme*	Wisdom

Table 2.1

Mrs Darley Tale: Beyond the Land

To the west of St Ives there lies a wild barren land where mighty tors rise from an ancient landscape and blackened rocks plunge into an unforgiving Atlantic. It was to this remote corner of Cornwall that ten of us were ferried via minibus, one balmy evening in mid summer in order to experience a 'sea shanty' evening courtesy of Bod's long time navy friend.

Tucked away off the main road somewhere between Porthmeor and Zennor, the ramshackle granite cottage had seen better days, but the warmth with which we were greeted and the enchanted garden in which we sat set the tone for a magical evening.

Lobsterpots were scattered around the garden, topped with occasional cushions on which to sit and upturned packing cases were our tables, each housing a sea urchin shell and tea light for lamps.

'How beautiful,' I said to Phyllis as we arranged ourselves around a corner table towards the top of the garden in order to avail ourselves of the breathtaking view of the coastline and the immanent sunset.

Very soon the music began with fiddles, accordions and a rather lively lady who rhythmically thumped a substantial stick on the ground complete with a boot at the foot and a myriad of ribbons and bells down its length. Although many of the songs were unfamiliar to me, the richness of the voices drifting through the warm night air made the whole experience quite enchanting.

After a while the musicians downed their instruments and took a break whilst our hosts brought out a huge cauldron of seafood stew accompanied by great chunks of crusty bread and eternal refills of Cornish ale and cider.

'I'd just like to propose a toast before we eat,' boomed our host, a huge man with a ruddy face and a rough dark beard.

I'm not quite sure what I expected him to say but what followed quite surprised me.

'This celebration is in honour of our lady Penardum,

who once again has blessed the harvest field which surrounds our sacred land. It is with our love and thanks that we drink to you. To Penardum!'

We all stood and raised our glasses, 'To Penardum!' we toasted.

Just as we sitting down again Mrs Darley leaned over and said, 'How lovely!'

'Who's Penardum?' I asked.

'An ancient Celtic sea Goddess, wife of Llyr, God of the sea and the term 'harvest field' is the terminology the old Cornish would use to refer to the sea.'

Explanations over, we all turned to concentrate on the wonderful seafood stew courtesy of the benevolent Sea Goddess, after which I was delighted to learn that there would be a period of storytelling.

'The area of Penwith is a strange and mysterious place, where the realm of the mortal meets that of the fairy and where the voices of those who once lived upon the drowned land can still be heard.'

Our host's words hung in the still night air and I shivered a little as I looked down towards the darkening sea.

'And so, I turn to my learned friend Clemo to tell us the tale of Matthew Trewella, a young carpenter lad who lived a mere stone's throw from where we are now.'

Clemo drew his lobster pot a little nearer to his audience and in a rich Cornish voice began his tale.

'Now young Matthew Trewella was a quiet lad, a carpenter who still lived at home with his parents and who was blessed with a beautiful tenor voice. Every Sunday the inhabitants of the little village of Zennor turned out to hear him sing in the choir.

One Sunday morning when the air was clear and warm and the doors of the church were left open to let in

206

the first breeze of summer, Matthew's voice drifted across the village and down the valley to the sea where, beneath the waves, a mermaid sat looking into her mirror and combing her long blonde hair. So bewitched was she by such a beautiful voice that she decided to discover who was singing and made her way up to the village via the stream that ran from close by the church down to the sea. Once on dry land she disguised her long tale beneath an elegant sea green gown, swept up her long tresses beneath a velvet hat and, with great difficulty, made her way into the church, knowing that she only had a short time upon the land before she needed to return to the sea.

Once inside the church she could see the young man to whom the voice belonged and, as he began to sing, she joined in harmony with him, mesmerizing the whole congregation with the beauty of their duet.

Matthew naturally hoped to speak with the young woman after the service but to his disappointment she had already left. The following Sunday, however, she returned and once again their voices lifted the hearts of all those who heard them. This time, however, Matthew decided that he simply must speak to her and, leaving the church before the service ended, he waited for her in the churchyard.

Seeing him waiting, she slowly made her way towards him. She praised his singing and asked him what he did for a living. Matthew told her he was a humble carpenter and that the partially carved rood screen in the church was a piece of his work in progress. She smiled, touched his arm with her hand and moved away in the direction of the stream. For many months following this meeting she continued to appear at the church each Sunday to sing in harmony with her Cornish tenor.

One foggy day in late November, Matthew was just

about to finish carving the final piece of the rood screen when he sensed someone watching him from the doorway of the church. Turning around with his lantern, he saw that it was the beautiful woman who appeared in church every Sunday.

She smiled as she walked towards him, "I see the screen is almost complete," she said.

Matthew nodded, his heart beating a little faster as he looked into her sea green eyes.

"Then your work here is done," she said, "and you are free to follow your heart."

Matthew moved towards her, dreaming of how she would feel in his arms, but at that moment she pulled away and said, "But first you have one more job to do. I would ask that you carve my likeness on the end of this pew before we leave, for I am the daughter of Llyr, God of the Sea."

Upon hearing Matthew's agreement she turned up the light on the lantern and posed for him. First of all she let down her long golden locks, allowing them to fall about her shoulders before taking out the comb and mirror from her robe. Then slowly she removed her emerald green robe, revealing to Matthew the true nature of her identity as his eyes fell upon her beautiful bare breasts and silver fish tale. And so as dawn broke across the sky he finally completed the carving of his mermaid upon the pew end.

When the sexton came to open the church before the morning service he found the door unlocked, wood chippings covering the floor and the carving of a mermaid upon the pew. Immediately he went to the home of Matthew Trewella where his parents were worried that his bed had not been slept in. For days and weeks the inhabitants of the village of Zennor searched for Matthew Trewella without success, although it was not long before they linked his disappearance with the beautiful woman who had once attended church to sing with so beautifully with him and had also not been seen since.'

A tangible silence of expectancy hung in the still evening air. Surely the story couldn't end there, I wanted more.

'And so,' Clemo's voice once again pierced the silence, 'one day some two years later, a schooner called the Endeavour anchored in Pendower cove, having been sent on a mission by the admiralty to investigate the puzzling growth of Japanese kelp, which was not to be found anywhere else in Europe.

But, within minutes of the anchor being dropped, the surface of the sea began to bubble and break as a golden haired mermaid rose from the waves and called out to the captain of the ship asking him to raise his anchor as it had landed on the door to her home, preventing her from opening it and returning to her husband.

Well, like all true seafarers, the captain considered it unwise to argue with a mermaid and gave immediate orders to raise the anchor. As the crew sailed away, they saw the mermaid rise from the waves holding a merboy in her arms that, so the captain said, bore more than a passing resemblance to Matthew Trewella.'

An appreciative round of applause immediately erupted but Clemo put up his hand, indicating that he had more to tell.

'Don't think however that Matthew Trewella was never heard of again, for still today, so some men say, his beautiful voice can be heard amongst the waves. He sings soft and high if the weather is to be fair and deep and low if Llyr is about to brew a storm and it is from his songs that the fishermen of Zennor know when it is safe to go to sea.'

Mrs Darley's Pagan Elements

This time the applause progressed into a standing ovation swiftly followed by the resurrection of the band and a further round of lively shanties. Thinking that the evening would soon be coming to a close I was delighted to learn that yet another story telling session was planned by our very own Black Bill, who loved nothing more than to hold an audience with tales of the sea passed down from his somewhat colourful ancestors.

'I want you to imagine standing on the western cliffs of Land's End, a place where the wild ocean meets with the seething sea and where once the lost land of Lyonesse stood proudly above the waves almost joining the mainland to the now Isles of Scilly. This was a land of plenty, a warm fertile land, abundant in livestock and crops where beautiful towns once stood.'

Black Bill's eyes twinkled in the candlelight as he savoured this dramatic pause.

'But, on 11 November 1099, a huge tide unlike any anyone had known drowned the beautiful land of Lyonesse and all those who lived there.'

'How can you be so sure?' asked a lady sitting at a table opposite ours. 'How can you possibly know that this was the date and more to the point how can you be sure that Lyonesse even existed? It may simply be the figment of someone's overactive imagination.'

'It could well be my 'andsome,' replied Black Bill, 'but certain details of its existence were recorded by the Emperor Maximus during the Roman occupation, whilst the great flood of 1099 and the total destruction of life that it caused was documented in both the Anglo Saxon Chronicles and the Chronicles of Florence of Worcester.'

'How dreadful,' murmured Phyllis shivering next to me.

'Destruction that is, of everyone except …,'

210

whispered Black Bill raising his finger into the air, 'one, who's name was Trevilian, long time ancestor of a well known Cornish family hereabouts. He was said to have knowledge of both the tides and the moon and, knowing that some terrible storm was brewing, he moved his family and livestock to what we now refer to as the mainland to ensure their safety. For all his knowledge, however, Trevilian himself had a rather narrow escape, for as he returned to Lyonesse to collect the last of his belongings, the sea came thundering in and, so the tale goes, he had to ride with all the speed of the wind on his pure white stead in order to escape. Legend has it, for we are in legendary territory now, that that is why the present day Trevelyan family still has the white horse in their coat of arms.'

'What a wonderful story!' exclaimed Rose, 'imagine Cornwall having its very own Atlantis.'

'Yes but has anyone actually done any research for this supposed lost land?' asked the lady who had previously doubted Black Bill's story.

'They don't have to,' replied Black Bill, 'for there are many who can vouch for the existence of Lyonesse, including my great, great grandfather, a once infamous free trader of these shores who spoke to those who had seen the evidence.'

I couldn't help but repress a smile as I recalled Bod's fiftieth birthday party when Black Bill entertained us with tales of his smuggling ancestor, whose notoriety made him very proud.

'And what evidence might this be?' The lady persisted.

'Oh there's plenty, my 'andsome, plenty. The old Cornish name for St Michael's Mount is "Careg cowse in clowse" meaning "hoary rock in the wood", which

211

indicates that the Mount once stood in woodland. They say that between Mounts Bay and Penzance when violent storms disturb the sea bed, petrified tree trunks have been seen, still in their natural position, whilst many a fisherman both old and new have dredged up windows and pottery from the watery depths and ...,' Black Bill lowered his voice, 'when the tides are at their lowest and fishermen sail close to Lethowsow, or the Seven Stones as the English would call them, they often glimpse ruined buildings beneath the waves. Some even say, or so I've heard tell, that they've heard church bells ringing on stormy nights.'

'Mmmmm, fanciful tales conjured up by those with an overactive imagination if you ask me, all of which is based purely on flimsy anecdotal evidence and I'm yet to be convinced,' the lady said, folding her arms in a gesture which said both the subject and her mind were now closed.

Mrs Darley however, who had remained uncharacteristically quiet throughout the evening, suddenly leaned forward and said in a soft voice, 'For those who believe, my dear, no proof is necessary and for those who choose not to, no proof is enough.'

Astrological Water Signs

The twelve signs of the Zodiac are each governed by one of four categories, namely those of air, fire, water and earth, and of the three signs which fall within each group, one is cardinal, i.e. initiatory; one is fixed, i.e. controlling; and one is mutable, i.e. restless.

The three signs that fall under the influence of the element of water are the emotional signs of Cancer, Scorpio and Pisces and although each has their specific traits, they do have certain similarities. All three have a

212

great need for security and have the ability to either become emotional themselves or play upon the emotions of others in order to achieve what they most desire. The three signs however are quite different as illustrated in the brief character outlines that follow.

Cancer

Cancer is the cardinal water sign and as such Cancerian's tend to initiate security around themselves. This can be achieved by keeping family and friends close to them and by often making that family unit or group of friends feel guilty if they move away from the nest, by playing out the 'poor me' act or turning on the waterworks.

That said, Cancerian's are sensitive souls, friendly and romantic although sometimes irritable and tend to give a little too much of themselves to others with little regard for their own welfare.

Acquaintances are easily made and they are always interested in the welfare of others although friendships are a little harder to come by. This is a sign that likes to accumulate money and Cancerian's make the best 'savers' in the zodiac, as this adds to their feelings of security.

Cancerian's are usually well balanced, good judges of human nature and although they are fond of travel, they do love their home where they show a penchant for luxury and material things.

In life, success will come via hard work and persistence, often leading to a career in the medical profession, law, teaching, music, public speaking or the financial sector.

On a spiritual basis, many Cancerian's will be loyal to their original doctrine of belief rather than explore new paths.

The Cancerian's greatest limitation is that they tend to help others to the detriment of themselves, including making generous donations to charitable causes, all of which, although very altruistic, can threaten the personal security which they hold so dear.

Scorpio

Scorpio is the fixed water sign and as such Scorpions tend to obsessively need to know the person, or group with whom they connect at the very deepest level in order to feel emotionally secure. Often, this need can make them appear manipulative or controlling.

That said, Scorpios are generous, determined, quick witted, loyal, magnetic and progressive, although sometimes they can be both suspicious and critical and do not suffer fools gladly. Friends are often far more fond of the Scorpio than the Scorpio is of them and they will be most drawn to those who are musically talented or have a good sense of humour. The accumulation of money does not come easily and it is often a case of easy come easy go.

Scorpios enjoy their home life and will attempt to make their home as comfortable as possible although relationships are another matter. This sign is very emotional although perhaps on the surface this does not often show. As such there will often be many ups and downs romantically (and perhaps several marriages or serious partnerships) until they connect with the right person who can understand the deeper side of the Scorpio nature.

At work, nothing is too hard for the Scorpio to attempt and their love of travel often combines with work to take them away from the home environment. Careers in the medical profession, law, teaching, preaching, chemistry, dentistry, astrology, geology, engineering, farming, journalism and music, will all suit.

On a spiritual basis, many Scorpions will have fixed ideas regarding their beliefs and are often outspoken in this respect.

Scorpions are often their own worst enemy because of their tendency to postpone issues and dominate others, but if these obstacles can be overcome then happiness and prosperity will be achieved.

Pisces

Pisces is the mutable water sign and as such, Pisceans tend to feel secure as long as they do not feel hemmed in and are free to follow their dreams.

Pisceans are often credited with a dual personality for their many positive traits often have to overcome a more pessimistic nature before they shine through.

That said, Pisceans are good conversationalists, sympathetic, original, thoughtful, kind and loyal.

Friendships are easily made although friends may be a little wary of their pessimistic trait. Finances fluctuate between being able to earn a fortune one minute and nothing the next.

Pisceans love their home although it's not always quite as they would want it to be, either through lack of money or through those who share it. Travel too is important and Pisceans often travel far and wide during their life time both at home and abroad.

Pisceans are loyal and romantic to their chosen partner although they sometimes have to deal with those who are not quite of the same ilk as themselves and thereby suffer heartache.

Any type of natural outdoor work will appeal to the Piscean such as fishing, forestry concerns or agricultural pursuits.

Other areas of interest may include; nursing, teaching, merchandising, managing, acting, writing, floristry, chiropody, photography and the occult sciences will all suit.

On a spiritual basis, many Pisceans are very orthodox in their beliefs and should refrain from criticising the beliefs of others.

As long as the Piscean concentrates on developing the positive side of his or her nature then success will eventually come, for the greatest hindrance in achievement comes from a lack of aggressiveness, courage and optimism.

She
She is the Goddess of the still waters,
Lie upon Her
And She will lull your mind to slumber

She is the Goddess of the flowing waters,
Ride upon Her
And She will speed your journey

She is the Goddess of the seething seas,
Sail upon Her
And She will call your soul to adventure.

Connecting with the Element of Water

How do you feel about water? Is it something that you dive willingly into whenever you have the opportunity or is it something you avoid at all costs?

I used to think that my fear of water was something that was inherited from my parents. My father learned to swim as a youth in the dark and murky waters of a Black Country canal, warmed by waste water from the engineering works.

He once said he went for a swim in the sea at Blackpool in 1949 and had never been warm since. More to the point however, I don't think he has ever swum since.

My mum too was never quite able to master the delicate art of remaining afloat and I can never remember her even venturing into a body of water during my formative years. I suppose therefore that for me, becoming an Olympic swimmer was somewhat of an outside shot.

My Godmother, bless her soul, decided that it was her duty to teach me to swim during a visit to Cornwall in 1968. She marched me purposefully into the sea, lay me horizontally across the waves and immediately let go, leaving me to sink into the watery depths without trace, a fact she put down to getting her foot entangled in a large bed of seaweed.

Not filled with confidence, school swimming lessons were my next port of call. Here we were instructed to stand at the side of the pool whilst safety issues were discussed. The girl standing next to me whispered something in my ear, I leaned over to hear what she was saying, slipped, fell in and began to drown. My saviour came by way of Mrs Smith, sporting a rather large unglamorous hook with which to fish me out.

217

Mrs Darley's Pagan Elements

Admittedly these experiences did little to help my confidence in the water, but when I think about the symbolic aspect of water and its connection to the emotions, I wonder if my fear goes back much further than this to the time of my birth. Apparently my entry into this world was somewhat dramatic, with little hope of my mother's survival and an awaiting incubator for me. Not being able to bond with either parent for at least a week, I often consider my emotional detachment to stem from this initial experience. Although I had a very happy childhood, I was an only child and spent much of my time lost in the world of books and my vivid imagination rather than interacting with others of my own age.

In addition to this I am an Aquarian, known for their coolness when it comes to emotional involvement and so, when I met Mrs Darley, the feeling side of my nature was almost dormant. Through her teaching however, it slowly awakened and, little by little, the damn, which I had carefully constructed around my emotions, began to crumble.

Today I can swim, I can stand in ecstasy beneath a hot shower for far longer than I actually need to and walk in the rain without reaching for an umbrella. But most importantly for me, I have opened up my closed shop of emotions and allowed myself the sheer luxury of crying through to the pure pleasure of being in love.

Take a few moments to consider your own reaction to water, how does it make you feel; afraid, exhilarated, alive, intimidated or adventurous? Does water appear during your dreamtime and if so, how does it behave? Is it calm or turbulent, do you swim easily in it or struggle to stay afloat?

Whatever the imagery, it comes with a wise word

from the Goddess regarding your emotional state and an invitation to take note and act upon it.

Mrs Darley Tale: Time and Tide

Eddie the poacher's birthday do was held at Mrs Darley's cottage on one of those nights when the moon makes frost sparkle on the ground like stardust as She hangs pale and remote in the winter sky.

When I arrived, I was immediately given a glass of steaming alcoholic beverage in the one hand and whirled into the room by the other. A fiddler sat on the old oak chest in the corner of the room and played a selection of eternally popular Irish jigs and reels to which we all attempted to do justice by stomping our way around the room in a most ungainly fashion.

'Ooooo!' Exclaimed Rose flinging herself down in the nearest chair after a particularly lively jig, 'I had the most peculiar feeling then, just like I'd lived that moment before, it must have been déjà vu.'

'What exactly is déjà vu do you think?' asked Peter.

'I think it's when we've been here before, in this same place, but in a previous life,' said Rose, 'and just for a minute you recall part of that past experience.'

'Rubbish!' said Don, 'I mean, I believe in past lives but I don't see how you can possibly have been dancing here with all of us in a previous life.'

'Oh I don't know then,' said Rose waving her hand dismissively in the air, 'I don't know what it is. Perhaps I've just slipped in and out of time.'

'Now there's an interesting concept,' said Mrs Darley.

'What do you mean?' asked Eddie.

'Well time doesn't really exist,' stated Mrs Darley, it's merely an abstract concept, around which we mere mortals organize our lives. The only thing that actually

219

exists is now, this eternal moment in which we can make a difference and change the world.'

'Oh dear, that's a bit deep for a birthday party!' laughed Don.

'Actually, I was finding it rather interesting,' said Phyllis. 'So do you think then,' she said directing her question towards Mrs Darley, 'that we can slip in and out of what we would perceive to be different time zones?'

Mrs Darley smiled, 'Do you?' She asked.

The question was left hanging in the air as Bod began to pull on his boots and make his way towards the door.

'Won't be a minute,' he said as Rose cast him a quizzical look.

In his absence the fiddler, who obviously felt that he had been quiet for far too long, began to play the familiar tune of 'Molly Malone', to which we all sang heartily and were just giving him an appreciative round of applause when Bod returned.

'Where've you been?' Rose asked.

'To fetch something which I've never shown to anyone, in fact I almost feel as though I shouldn't have it, but it came into my possession, shall we say, several years ago and I've never quite known what to make of it, but considering the subject matter that we were discussing just a few minutes ago, I thought you may all be interested to hear it.'

We all murmured our approval as Bod put on his glasses, took a few sheets of crumpled paper from his pocket and began to read.

'I have committed the events of the last few days to paper, for my own peace of mind, if, that is, I ever manage to find piece of mind again.

Only two hours ago I stared into the blue abyss from the edge of these cliffs contemplating the fall that would lead to my death and relieve me from the torment I currently feel, but the hand of destiny in the form of a passing surfer made me realize the futility of such an act and so here I sit, wedged in a crevice away from the wind, my mind attempting to make order out of chaos.

It's been a pretty rotten year, one of those where I've felt picked on by the universe; redundancy, wife left, lost the house and, out of the kindness of their hearts and probably to have a rest from my constant moaning, my brothers, clubbed together to pay for this week away in North Cornwall for my 30th birthday.

Three nights ago I entered the dining room of a small, family hotel called "The Gulls" only to be greeted by the wonderful sight and smell of Cornish pasties. I was led to my table by the bustling Mrs Trevannion, who thought it would be a good idea to sit me next to someone around my own age, called Nick.

Nick and I seemed to hit it off straight away and began an easy acquaintance which took us to the Jolly Sailor pub later that evening.

Here I discovered that Nick was taking a year out, wandering around the south west after completing a fine art degree in the summer and was determined to discover more about his great, great, great grandfather who had been some sort of sailor in and around the North Cornish coast. He of course asked what brought me to Cornwall and I bored him until closing time.

After breakfast the next morning, we took ourselves off for a day fishing trip, returning home on the incoming tide around 5pm. On the way back up to The Gulls, we decided to stop off for a pint at a pub halfway up the hill and Nick disappeared into the bar to get the drinks while I sat at one of the picnic benches outside.

Appreciating the rest after the agonizing pull up the

hill, the creaking of the pub sign made me look up and I saw a picture of a ship inscribed with the words, "The Lugger". I was just wondering how long it had hung there when Nick came hurtling out of the pub.

I could see he was shaking and beads of perspiration were sliding down his face. He slammed the change down on the table, apologized for the lack of drinks, muttered something about not feeling too good and began to run up the hill towards The Gulls.

I stopped just long enough to pick up the change and ran to find him, catching up with him outside the hotel. I asked what had happened, but he just muttered that perhaps he'd imagined it all and that I probably wouldn't believe him anyway. I was quite insistent that he told me and, eventually he managed to tell me a garbled story about him going in and ordering drinks, but when the barman turned round to give him his change, he was different. When I asked what he meant by "different", he said the barman's clothes, his demeanour and even the pub itself had changed. He said he felt as though he was in a dream where there were familiar things like the fireplace and the door and yet at the same time something was odd, as though he'd been transported back in time.

I didn't know what to say and Nick looked bewildered obviously trying to make sense of what he'd seen. I offered him his change that I'd picked up from the pub table, but he told me to keep it and give his apologies to Mrs Trevannion as he wouldn't be down for dinner.

I went up to my room, trying to form a rational explanation as to what Nick could have seen. Sunstroke, an artists overactive imagination, and even dim light playing tricks on the eyes after being in bright sunshine, all came to mind, but nothing could account for the look of pure terror in Nick's face as he ran out of that pub and it was that fact alone I found difficult to dismiss.

I pulled the loose change out of my pocket before lying down on the bed and was surprised to see a small dark coin roll against the pillow. I picked it up and saw what looked like a cutlass engraved onto it with some kind of worn inscription underneath and decided to place the coin in my wallet with a view to finding out a little more about it.

At dinner that evening Mrs Trevannion was all tea and sympathy as I gave her Nick's apologies, going on to say that Cornish sea and sun was a lethal combination and asking for confirmation of this diagnosis from an elderly gentleman sitting close by whom she referred to as Mr Clark. The man momentarily looked up from his soup to agree with her, adding that many men had perished over the centuries from just those natural phenomena.

Mrs Trevannion went on to proudly tell me that Mr Clark was a permanent resident at the hotel, a retired historian and that his knowledge on the history of Cornwall was second to none, a fact which I decided to make the most of once dinner was over.

Whilst Mrs Trevannion was serving coffee I walked over to join him at his corner table and asked if he could tell me anything about the small coin with the mark of the cutlass. He stared at the coin I had placed in his hand, remained silent for a moment or two and then, removing his glasses he said quietly, "It's the mark of a traitor."

I could feel the hairs begin to prickle on the back of my neck and asked him what he meant. He went on to tell me that the coin was some 150 to 300 years old and was used by smugglers to give to those who betrayed them to customs and excise. He asked where I'd found it, at

223

which point I immediately lied and told him I'd picked it up on the beach at low tide.

I thought I detected a slight frown, but put this down to my imagination as he went on to say that at least finding it didn't have such sinister connotations as actually being given it. I asked him what he meant and he went on to explain that if you were given it by someone it was said to signify that not only was your end nigh but that it was almost certain to be unpleasant.

I thanked him for the information and went upstairs in a state of disbelief, still trying to make sense of it all in my own mind. Nick had definitely been given that coin in his change from the pub, but then odd coins were always being found, it could have come from anywhere, however try as I might I couldn't stop the overwhelming feeling of doom that seemed to engulf me.

I stopped outside Nick's room on the way back to my own and was relieved to hear the gentle snoring of restful sleep. Back in my own room I threw myself onto the bed but couldn't settle and decided to walk down to the harbour to clear my head.

As I came down the stairs, Mr Clarke was just coming out of the dining room and asked me if I was going out. I told him I was going to take a walk down to the harbour and that I might call into The Lugger for a drink.

It was at this point that he gave me a strange look and said, "The Lugger?"

He went on to tell me that there wasn't a pub in the village called The Lugger, only The Jolly Sailor down by the harbour and The Ship halfway up the hill. It was at this point he went to turn away, but almost as an afterthought said that he seemed to recall an old document mentioning the fact that The Ship used to be called The Lugger over a century ago. It was at this point that he wished me goodnight and, no longer having the enthusiasm for a walk, I returned to my room to embark on a night of disturbed sleep.

I didn't see Nick until the following evening and spent the day alone surfing. When I returned to the hotel for evening meal Mrs Trevannion was buzzing round Nick like a bee round a honey pot and went on to ask us both if we would be going down into the village to celebrate the festival of the sea. She told us that it was a local tradition to bless the fish by taking a few drinks and that we would be very welcome to join her and her family.

I saw that Nick looked a little better and was pleased to hear him agree to an evening out. By nine 'o clock we were all jammed into The Jolly Sailor alongside the harbour and I could just see Nick across the other side of the bar, deep in conversation with some red head.

At 10.30 the gang, to which we now belonged, began to move out and onto the street before making their way up the hill. "To The Ship," someone called and there was a race up the hill to see who could be first into the pub. In my mellow state, I only had a momentary twinge of anxiety about going into The Ship, which immediately eased as the bright lights of the pub came into view.

There was a traffic jam of people trying to get in through the doors and, as we stood waiting, I suddenly froze as I heard a familiar creaking sound above my head. I looked up and saw the sign of "The Lugger" swinging menacingly in the cool night air.

Panic stricken, I called Nick and began to push my way through the crowd towards the door, praying that he wouldn't have gone inside.

I felt myself being carried into the bar on a wave of people and for a moment could see very little through the heavy swathes of cigarette smoke which hung in the air. I

225

became immediately aware, however, that the jovial atmosphere which prevailed outside had now disappeared and had been replaced by something dark and menacing.

Gradually I became accustomed to the dim light and heard someone breathing in short shallow gasps on the floor in front of me. He was on his knees, hands tied behind his back and face pushed into the floor by the owner of a booted foot. I watched in horror as the boot was removed from the man's face, his head pulled sharply back and a knife held to his throat, for I could clearly see that the man in question was Nick.

I rushed forward shouting his name and immediately felt the breath leave my body as I was completely winded from a punch in the stomach. I fell to the floor and was dragged to my feet by someone who leered into my face and made my stomach churn with the stench of his rotten breath.

It was only at this point that I began to realise that I was no longer in my own time. Lamps were burning on the bar, a sea of hostile swarthy faces peered at me through the gloom and the sickening smell of old sweat mingled with stale beer. I suddenly felt very afraid.

My attention was brought back to the moment in hand as a voice from the crowd spoke with authority.

"Traitors must suffer, just as John Lancey did." At which point there was a roar of approval from the crowd.

I remember hearing Nick speak in a broken voice asking them who they were and what they wanted with him. The explanation came from a huge bearded man, with a filthy shirt and dark bulbous eyes whose voice echoed around the room.

"John Lancey died because of you, he was one of our own kind, a respected smuggler."

I heard Nick's voice, pleading and eager above the jeering of the crowd, "But wait," he said, "my great, great, great grandfather was a smuggler here too, he was one of you .. .James, James Bunce."

The information was received by a deafening roar from the crowd and the bearded man hauled Nick to his feet by his neck, "James Bunce was no smuggler, he was a traitor, he reported John Lancey to customs and excise and John swung for it."

I could see the terror of realisation in Nick's eyes as the horror of what was happening began to dawn on him. "I didn't know ... I didn't know," he whispered.

A hushed silence suddenly descended and I was aware of someone appearing out of the crowd. The figure was dressed in a long black robe and had a cowl covering his head. He stopped in the centre of the room and pulled something down from the low ceiling. It was at this point that I was physically sick as a noose was lowered from the beams and I saw that Nick was standing over the cellar doors.

The rope was hung about Nick's head and above his shrieks of protest the hooded man pronounced sentence upon him telling him that the debt of his ancestor could now be repaid and the death of John Lancey could be avenged.

He went on to announce that following his execution, his body would be cut down and thrown into the cellar below where it would be washed by the tide to prevent a curse upon the house.

I tried to break free from those who held me and I remember screaming "In God's name, no ... this is barbaric...."

I felt strong hands restrain me and tasted the iron in the blood which ran into my mouth as a knife easily

227

opened up my cheek.

"Please ... please...." I begged.

At this point the robed man turned his attention momentarily to me and as he stood before me he pulled back his hood, but all I can remember was the face of Mr Clarke from the hotel before succumbing to the sickening blow to the head which heralded oblivion.

I woke to find the sun streaming in through my window and a pot of tea by my bed. My head felt as though it belonged to someone else and slowly the memories of the previous night began to flood back. I suddenly felt nauseous and staggered to the bathroom where I was violently sick.

Eventually I stood and looked in the bathroom mirror hardly recognising myself with twelve stitches in my cheek and a blackened forehead.

I realised however that I had to do something, I had to find Nick. I sank down onto the bathroom floor, how could I find someone who had been murdered two centuries ago? All I knew was that I had to try.

I struggled painfully into some clothes, and made my way along the landing to Nick's room. I knocked on the door and was aware of my heart pounding as footsteps approached.

To my overwhelming disappointment a woman in her mid-thirties peered out, obviously annoyed at having been woken. I muttered my apologies and slowly dragged myself down the stairs to be greeted by Mrs Trevannion.

In her usual mother hen fashion she made a great fuss as to why I was up and about after such a terrible fall, saying that the doctor had told her to keep me in bed all day. I ignored her concern and demanded to know where Nick was.

She looked at me with a look of pity on her face,

"Who?" she asked.

I could feel frustration and anger beginning to boil up inside me

"Nick ... Nick, the chap who shared my table," I yelled at her, grabbing her shoulders. "Where is he?"

She told me in no uncertain terms to remove my hands and venomously denied all knowledge of ever having heard of him. Undeterred I asked her about Mr Clark, the historian, who again she denied knowing, all the time muttering that this fall had affected me more than they all thought and that she would get Mr Trevannion to help me back to bed.

I brushed past her and began to stumble as fast as I could manage down the hill towards The Ship. Hurling myself at the door, I hammered it relentlessly until the disgruntled landlord finally opened up. I immediately pushed past him and rushed into the pub.

"Hey," he said, "just a minute, you can't barge in here, who do you think you are?"

"Someone was murdered here last night," I blurted out. "I need to see that cellar," I said pointing at the trap doors.

"Oh yes," he replied "and who are you, the police?" I shook my head.

"Then get out."

I was suddenly aware just how weak I felt and how futile my quest had become and so I turned towards the door. "Can I just ask you one question?"

Without waiting for an answer, I continued, "Does the sea ever come into your cellar?"

He shook his head, "Not now, no, the floors were raised to stop it some 100 years ago, but before that I believe it flooded at high tide, and that the barrels had to sit on raised platforms."

Mrs Darley's Pagan Elements

There was no one around when I returned to The Gulls to collect my belongings which are now sitting in my car in the lay-by, while I sit in my tiny crevice amongst the rocks.

I feel helpless and hopeless, I have no real knowledge of Nick, his surname, or where he came from. I have no evidence of his murder, no witnesses and no body. The only thing I have is the coin, the fateful coin which portended Nick's death.

And now I am about to stand up and walk to the edge of the cliff, ignoring the surfer's earlier warning of a dangerous overhang and with all the venom I can muster will condemn the coin into the tormented sea while I bid a silent farewell, to Nick, the man for whom both tide and time waited.

Tom Minton
23-7-81.'

Bod took off his glasses and slowly put the papers back into his pocket, while we all sat in silence trying to make sense of what we had just heard.

'Well,' said Don, finally breaking the silence, 'do you think it's true?'

Bod shook his head and sighed, 'I don't know, but I have no reason to doubt that it was real to Tom.'

'It matters not, my dears,' said Mrs Darley, 'for time is but an illusion though which we pass and who is to say that we cannot revisit that which we perceive to have gone before?'

Conclusion

Water is the elixir of life, one of the great gifts of the Goddess. Its numinous aspects provide a force of nature that cleanses and nourishes nurtures and heals. Water invites us to drink, bathe, sail and wish in order to experience the wisdom of the ages.

Water is a paradox, benevolent and life giving yet cruel and destructive but wherever we go upon this earth we eventually come to stand before it. During the span of a human life time, many choose to stand upon the shore and simply gaze at the waters, quite content to spend their lives without risk or adventure whilst others run headlong into the waves, an act that may carry them effortlessly to distant shores or crush them mercilessly against the rocks.

Eventually, however, we are all called to the waters edge where Charon, the ferryman, carries our soul to experience the greatest adventure of all.

Liquidity
I am the liquid mirror
Within a moonlit pool,
I lie within the wine of kings
And bless the ale of fools.

I speed the flowing river,
I bend the winding stream,
I form the blood of life on earth
And fuel your wildest dreams.

I dwell in mighty oceans,
I swim in open seas,
I am She for whom you search,
I am Divinity.

Chapter 4

Earth

Earth
Rich, dark, nurturing,
Fine, light, drying,
Damp, thick, cloying,
Soil, sand, clay.

Smooth round cold,
Grey, soft, flat,
Firm, dense, hard,
Stone, slate, rock.

Sacred Earth.

Introduction
Earth is our home, the solid, dependable mother figure upon whom we rely for shelter, protection and food. Yet we misuse and abuse Her, taking for granted Her unconditional love which always hold firm, regardless of how we treat Her.

Capable in equal measures, of ferocity and benevolence, she illustrates through her moods the very nature of mankind, the anger of her earth shattering quakes, the parental shelter of a mountain cave, the enduring beauty of her rolling hills and protective forests.

Planet earth provides the surface upon which mammals walk and in which trees plant their roots. It contains the seas in which marine creatures swim and is the place upon which we build our lives.

Over millennia we have exploited our planet, blasted minerals from her belly, mined her secret passageways, concreted her forests, driven over her, drilled into her, buried our rubbish within her, polluted her seas and atmosphere, genetically modified her food sources and often forgotten to give thanks for all that She is and all that She provides.

The element of earth is a physical manifestation of the rarified element of air and thought. Earth gives birth to the material world in its basest form through procreation. It allows the soul to experience human form with all its agonies and joys, from pain and disorder through to the ecstatic pleasures of the senses.

Mrs Darley Tale: Earth Secrets

My weekend explorations of Cornwall varied in direction according to my mood. Often I would drive down to the south coast where sheltered coves and quaint fishing villages would speak to me of close knit communities and man's close relationship with the sea. Occasionally however, the lure of the north coast would prove too much to resist and although it was further to drive, the promise of the rugged coastline and the deep cobalt blue of the Atlantic would call me across the wild windswept moor to the sea.

One particularly hot Saturday in late August, the calling came and just as I was closing the door to the cottage, Mrs Darley waved at me from her garden. 'Are you going out, dear?'

I nodded.

'Would you be so kind as to get me some demerara sugar? I forgot when I went to the supermarket yesterday and I'm making pissed pears for pudding.'

I managed to repress a smile for I had little doubt that the pears would be well and truly inebriated knowing Mrs Darley's generosity when it came to alcoholic measures.

'No problem,' I replied, 'although I'm going over to Tintagel for the day so I won't be back until late afternoon.'

'That's fine,' she said, 'I don't need it until tomorrow. What are you going to look at over in Tintagel?'

'Oh nothing in particular, I'm just going for a wander round really.'

'Have you been to the castle?' she asked.

I shook my head, 'No, but I've got some friends coming down next month so I might save the castle until then. It's never much fun going round things like that on your own.'

'Look, dear, I don't want to push myself on you, but if you'd like some company, I would be more than willing to come with you.'

That was an offer too good to refuse and two hours later we found ourselves sitting on Tintagel Island, our backs up against the warm stone of the ruined castle and surveying all the wonder and rugged beauty of the North Cornish coast.

'Isn't it stunning?' I said.

'It is in deed, my dear, but the beauty of Tintagel is far more than skin deep, for this is sacred earth; a place where legends are made.'

'Are you referring to King Arthur?' I asked.

'In part, yes, although the castle you see today is far too modern to have any connection to King Arthur, as it's 12th century.'

'Oh,' I replied somewhat disappointed by this piece of information.

Mrs Darley's Pagan Elements

'Ah, but don't let that put you off any romantic notions you may have about the possibility of Arthur having lived here. The history of this place dates way back to Roman times, when it was a renowned trading post for Mediterranean merchants. Ten years ago however, in the early Eighties, a series of fires swept across this little island, unearthing the remains of buildings which proved archaeologically that the island was occupied from Roman times up until the end of the 7th century when it appears to have been abandoned. This of course covers the time of King Arthur and, if this is the legendary Camelot, it is the place where King Arthur is said to have been conceived and born.'

'So where does Merlin feature in all of this?' I asked. 'The stories of King Arthur have always confused me somehow.'

'Well, my dear, as with all legends, there are often several versions, but mine is quite simple. In order to claim the throne of England, Uther Pengragon had to conquer all those who stood in his way, one of which was Gorlois, Duke of Cornwall. Now you may think that all Uther had to do was kill Gorlois and all would be well. Gorlois, however, was married to the beautiful Igraine whom Uther Pendragon desired beyond all measure and try as he might, he could not think of a way in which he could seduce her, especially if she knew he was her husband's murderer and so he turned to the magician Merlin.

Now Merlin promised to help him on condition that any child conceived from Uther's union with Igraine would be immediately handed over to the wizard in order that he may educate and protect him until he was old enough and wise enough to rise up against his enemies. Uther's desire for Igraine was so powerful that he agreed

236

to Merlin's demands.

In due course, Uther Pendragon murdered Gorlois, but before the news of his death was disclosed to Igraine, Merlin altered Uther's appearance to that of Gorlois in order that he might gain entry into the castle and ultimately to Igraine's bedchamber. Here he made love to Igraine and Arthur was conceived. Following Arthur's birth he was handed into Merlin's care where he remained until he could stand alone in the face of his enemies.'

'Mmmm,' I mused, 'So was Merlin good or bad? I can't quite make up my mind?'

'Oh, my dear,' laughed Mrs Darley, 'no one is either good or bad, everyone is penumbral, even wizards. Just think how boring and totally predictable we would be if we were "either/or"!'

I blushed a little, feeling somewhat foolish for what must have seemed a rather naïve and childish comment. Noticing my obvious discomfort however, Mrs Darley leaned towards me, put her hand over mine and lowered her voice to an audible whisper

'Here,' she said, 'lies a place where the Goddess dwells, where earth meets with water and yields to its power, where religions fuse yet the old ways prevail. Here is a place where reason meets with magic, yet magic defies all reason. Beneath us, my dear, lies the cave of Merlin, a place of mystery and transformation, where natural laws become suspended and only enchantments prevail. Here is a place of contrasts where sunlight dances upon shadowed walls and chastity is consumed within the fires of passion....'

She stopped speaking and stared out to sea for what seemed an eternity before turning to me with a smile.

'Over time,' she said, 'this place has been an ancient

Roman trading post, a Celtic monastery and the ruins of Camelot with its turreted towers. It has housed the cave of Merlin, a 12th century castle and is now a modern tourist attraction. Each era has left its impression on the landscape and the spirit of its inhabitants in the stones. All of these things have been embraced by the Goddess throughout eternity which explains the feeling of sacredness we experience here and, just like the Goddess, we should embrace old and new, black and white, good and bad, for it is in the celebration and appreciation of differences that we grow, learn and begin to understand the wonder of being human.'

The Natural World

The Earth
The earth is our home, a place that is solid and dependable or is that simply what we want to believe? In reality, earth is a volatile planet, rotating on its axis at around 1,036 miles per hour at the equator, tied in allegiance to the sun, pushed and pulled by its only satellite, the moon and constantly in a state of flux beneath our very feet. It is however this movement and unpredictability that makes earth not only a breathtakingly beautiful place to live but also a constant source of fascination to mankind.

The earth is the third closest planet to the sun at a distance of approximately 93 million miles and formed some four-and-a-half billion years ago when a solar nebula contracted, causing a cloud of hydrogen and dust to form. This cloud grew extremely hot and at its centre a star began to form, whilst around it swirled a great disc, comprising of the same material.

Over millions of years, the star began to grow in both

size and energy, whilst the disc surrounding it began to cool. Certain components of the disc such as silicon, magnesium, aluminium and oxygen began to freeze into small dust sized grains and eventually the grains settled together, forming larger and larger pieces until they were big enough to exert their own gravity. Over time these pieces collided with others where they both melted and vaporised, resulting in the heavy metals joining together to produce a central core whilst lighter materials encased the core, forming the mantle, a process we now refer to as 'differentiation'.

During this time the sun ignited, a phenomenon referred to as the 'T Tauri Phase', an event which was powerful enough to blow away most of the gaseous remains of the disc. This process left in its wake, a handful of large stable bodies set in well spaced orbits, of which earth was one, a process that took approximately ten million years from the initial event.

Eventually the earth began to cool and acquired a solid crust comprising of the constantly moving tectonic plates. These plates have, over billions of years, repeatedly moved towards and away from each other causing the formation of both continents and super-continents. The oceans meanwhile, appeared courtesy of collisions with icy meteorites and comets, whilst volcanic activity and water vapour created an atmosphere devoid of oxygen.

A chain of chemical reactions in this volatile environment eventually lead to the formation of a molecular structure that had the ability to reproduce itself and so life was born on planet earth. From a single celled organism came more complex forms of life, which gradually changed the atmosphere of the earth from one that was carbon dioxide based, to one that was oxygen

239

charged, leading to the eventual creation of the ozone layer. The rest is evolutionary history and gradually life forms became more and more complex and varied, colonising the air, the oceans and the land to produce a fairly constant biosphere.

Over millions of years, life has come and gone, species have evolved and become extinct but somehow, against all the odds, Mother Nature has filled every void with new species of life, which will continue to evolve and adapt to their ever changing environment for as long as planet earth orbits the sun.

The Structure of the Earth

The earth is a layered planet as defined by its chemical make-up, but basically comprises of a core, a mantle and a crust, knowledge of which stems from volcanic and seismic activity.

The Core

Seismic activity illustrates that the core is divided into two parts, a solid inner core made of primarily iron and nickel, which is approximately 1,600 miles in diameter and a liquid outer core comprising of iron, nickel and trace amounts of lighter elements which is approximately 1,400 miles in thickness. The inner core is too hot to hold a permanent magnetic field, but helps to stabilise the field generated by the liquid outer core.

The Mantle

The Earth's mantle is also divided into an upper and lower part. The lower part is more dense and rigid than its upper counterpart and extends to a depth of approximately 1,800 miles. The upper layer is some 400 miles thick making the mantle in total the thickest layer of the planet comprising of silicate rocks which are rich in iron and magnesium. This upper layer, although solid, is of a sufficiently high temperature to become ductile thereby allowing a certain amount of tectonic plate movement.

The Crust

The crust ranges from between five to twenty five miles in depth and forms the outermost layer of the earth. The thinnest parts are found beneath the oceans and are referred as the 'Oceanic Crusts '. They comprise of iron magnesium silicate rocks, whilst the thicker parts are to be found on land, known as the 'Continental Crusts', which are less dense and comprise of sodium potassium aluminium silicate rocks such as granite.

Many of the rocks that now makeup the earth's crust, formed less than 100 million years ago, however the oldest mineral grains date back some 4.4 billion years, indicating that the earth's crust has been in evidence for at least that long.

Tectonic Plates and Earthquakes

Tectonic plates are pieces of the earth's crust and upper mantle often referred to as the 'lithosphere'. The plates are approximately sixty miles thick and there are, over the surface of the earth, a total of seventy, including the fifteen major ones.

It is the movement of these major plates that have, over millennia along with other geological processes such as glacial and river erosion, created the most amazing transformations and spectacular formations on earth including the magnificent oceans, breathtaking mountain ranges and stunning island paradises.

Conversely tectonic plate movement has also caused

some of the worst natural disasters killing hundreds of thousands of people in devastating earthquakes such as the huge 7.7 Richter scale earthquake that struck the Chinese province of Hebei in 1976 killing as many as 800,000 people.

The major plates are:

- African Plate
- Antarctic Plate
- Arabian Plate
- Australian Plate
- Caribbean Plate
- Cocos Plate
- Eurasian Plate
- Indian Plate
- Juan de Fuca Plate
- Nazca Plate
- North American Plate
- Pacific Plate
- Philippine Sea Plate
- Scotia Plate
- South American Plate

One of the areas most prone to tectonic plate movement is where the Pacific plate meets many surrounding plates and forms what is now known as the most seismically and volcanically active zone in the world; 'the ring of fire'.

One of the most famous faults on the ring of fire is the San Andreas Fault, which runs along the coast from San Francisco to Los Angeles. This fault is present where the Pacific and North American plates meet and grind past each other in a north-south direction. This opposition of movement is caused by convection currents deep within the earth that occur as a natural by-product of radioactive decay.

Not all earthquakes that happen along this fault line take the form of earth splitting devastation as there are in fact, two types of movement.

The first involves 'fault segments' that are subject to a creeping motion and, more often than not, cause little or no damage. The second type are known as 'locked segments' which store a tremendous amount of energy that can build up for decades or centuries eventually unleashing the devastating quakes with which we are all familiar. In 1906, San Francisco experienced an earthquake that measured 8.3 on the Richter scale, rupturing the earth for a distance of 430 kilometres along a previously locked segment of the San Andreas Fault.

The vibrations produced when the ground suddenly ruptures, radiate out through the earth's interior from the rupture point known as the 'earthquake focus', whilst the geographical point directly above the focus is referred to as the earthquake's 'epicentre'. In a major earthquake the energy released can cause damage thousands of kilometres away from the epicentre.

In 1989 the Loma Prieta earthquake registered 7.1 on the Richter scale and occurred along a segment of the San Andreas Fault which had been locked since the 1906 quake. Although it occurred in a relatively remote part of the Santa Cruz Mountains, it still managed to cause sixty two deaths and four billion pounds worth of damage.

One of the most difficult questions for scientists to answer is, 'when will an earthquake actually occur?' And to this end, the midway point between San Francisco and Los Angeles has been littered with seismographs, creep

243

meters, stress meters and all manner of measuring equipment to help them in their quest.

Although today scientists talk about tectonic plates as a matter of course, knowledge of this constant motion beneath our feet is a relatively new concept and one that only came to the fore in the 1960's with the help of ocean surveys.

Treasures of the Earth

Mother Nature has provided mankind with a wealth of treasure within the confines of the earth.

Our construction and manufacturing industries rely on the likes of clay, stone, copper and tin. Beautiful gemstones and crystals have formed the centre pieces of many stunning pieces of jewellery from engagement rings to the crowns of royalty, whilst many people have and still do, place their faith in the healing power of crystals such as quartz and amethyst. Finally the precious metals of gold and silver have underpinned many of the world's economies as well as being fashioned into both jewellery and beautiful works of art.

Regardless of the type of material taken from the earth, each one comprises of one or more minerals combined in various ways.

Minerals were one of the catalysts that directed prehistoric people towards civilization. The discovery of a property of quartz called 'conchoidal fracture' led early man to be able to fashion tools and weapons by splitting or cutting them at their natural weak points rather than waiting until they simply came across a suitably shaped piece of material.

As time progressed, the subsequent discovery of more and more minerals from tin to copper, from silver to gold and a myriad of crystals and rocks accelerated the progress of humanity and paved the way to the world with which we are now familiar.

The earth's rocks are usually categorised into three distinct groups according to their formation.

Igneous

The name 'igneous' comes from the Latin word '*igneus*' meaning burning or fiery and these rocks begin life as molten magma which, as it cools, forms a variety of materials according to the conditions to which it is exposed.

Magma which cools rapidly does not have time to produce crystals and therefore often turns into a natural glass called obsidian.

Magma that cools more slowly begins to form crystals, varying in complexity according to their melting points and chemical compositions.

Magma that reaches the surface of the earth as lava cools very quickly and produces rocks comprising of tiny crystals of which basalt is the most common. Magma which is captured under ground however, solidifies more slowly into coarse grained rocks such as granite.

Sedimentary

This type of rock occurs when layers of water or wind-borne materials are consolidated into stone, such as sandstone.

Metamorphic

This type of rock occurs when existing rocks are subjected to intense heat and pressure. E.g.: shale can become slate, limestone can become marble, sandstone can become quartzite and granite can become gneiss.

Many of our earth bound treasures however, are not

mineral derived and comprise of fossilised living creatures which provide such precious commodities as coal and oil. Certain types of sandstone are formed from the shells and skeletons of marine animals and even some semi precious stones and crystals are plant and animal extracts such as jet, pearls, amber and coral.

Earthy Superstitions

Earthy superstitions are almost too numerous to mention as they can involve anything from gardens to homes and all the objects contained within. The following are examples:

- Spilled salt forecasts trouble, whilst spilling pepper indicates a fight. It is recommended therefore that a grain or two is thrown over your left shoulder to knock off the devil who will be laughing at you.
- It is considered unlucky to run out of salt.
- It was once thought that if food had been salted then it was impossible to be able to 'hex' it or bewitch it, which is probably why many people still throw a pinch of salt into their food even though the medical profession tell us that we should do without.
- It is considered unlucky to lend or borrow salt.
- When laying the table for a meal, the salt should be the first item that is put onto the table and the last to be taken away as it is thought to protect the food that is being served and those sitting around the table.
- Scatter salt into the corners of a home to clear it of negative energies.
- Upsetting the sugar is a sign of money.

- The planting of certain flowers and shrubs in the garden can help with fulfilling personal goals as illustrated in Table 2.2 below.

Goal	Plants
Psychic powers	Bay, celery, honeysuckle, marigold, rose, thyme
Love	Primrose, tomato, pansy, jasmine, rose
Happiness	Hyacinth, lavender, marjoram
Money	Mint, onion, snapdragon, camellia, chamomile, clover, apple trees, oak
Protection	Garlic, thistles, cactus, juniper, hawthorn, rowan, bay
Luck	Sunflower, hydrangea, bamboo

Table 2.2

- Spiders in the house are good luck, whilst seeing one crossing the threshold means news is on its way
- Place five shiny pennies beneath your front door mat to bring money into the house, whilst two crossed needles in the same place will ensure protection
- Many people today do not have real wooden furniture, but for those who do or who are about to purchase some Table 2.3 below may offer timely advice.

Wood	Qualities
Ebony	Protection
Oak	Strength, luck, healing
Pine	Money, healing
Teak	Riches
Mahogany	Protection from lightning
Walnut	Health

Table 2.3

247

- Mining superstitions abound in Cornwall, for the mines are thought to be inhabited by the knockers from the realm of the fairy and therefore the sign of the cross should never be made in or over a mine for fear of offending them.
- Miners were not allowed to whistle underground as it was thought to upset the knockers.
- To meet a woman on the way to the mine in the early hours foretold of a disaster.
- Births and deaths also have their fair share of superstitions including the fact that if more than one lady pours tea from the pot there will be an increase in the family.
- A caesarean birth is the sign of psychic ability, strength and the possibility of uncovering hidden treasure.
- A breach birth child can possess magical gifts
- An easy birth is predicted if all of the doors and windows are left open.
- Death carries its own superstitions as the body returns to the earth and if rain falls on a coffin the deceased is said to have arrived on the other side safely.

Earth Deities

With the ever changing moods and unpredictable behaviour of the planet upon which we live, it is hardly surprising that earth Deities in their many forms have been honoured and worshipped by mankind for millennia in return for their benevolent care.

Gaea

According to Hesiod, it seems that Gaea was the great Deity of the primitive Greeks, the Mother Goddess, and the earth, from where all things came. In the Homeric hymn, this idea is confirmed in the words:

'I shall sing of Gaea, universal mother, firmly founded, the oldest of divinities.'

She was also referred to as 'the deep breasted', whose soil nourished all that existed and was revered and honoured not only by men but also by the Gods themselves.

In later times when the great dynasty of the Olympians was established, Gaea's prestige remained undiminished and it was still She whom the Gods themselves invoked whenever they had cause to make an oath.

Gaea was credited with not only creating the universe and the first race of the Gods but also with giving birth to the human race. The oracle of Delphi was said to have belonged to Gaea long before it passed into the hands of Apollo.

As time progressed, other earth deities such as Rhea and Cybele began to rise in importance and Gaea's role declined, although her cult always continued to some degree in Greece, where she was honoured as the Goddess of marriages, prophecy and oaths, accepting offerings of grain and the first fruits from those who wished to avail of her gifts.

Demeter

Where Gaea was seen as the Goddess of the earth, Demeter was looked upon as the Goddess of the fertile and cultivated soil.

In Attica, she was particularly revered as the Goddess of the fruits and the riches of the fields, with specific dominion over the corn. It was She who presided over the harvest and all the many labours and rituals associated with it.

Her association with the earth also stretched to the underworld where her daughter Persephone was destined to spend four months of the year with the dark Lord Hades.

Dionysus

The name Dionysus stems from the Greek word, *'dithyrambos'*, meaning 'born twice' and stems from the dramatic story of his eventual birth.

The beautiful Semele, daughter of the King of Thebes, had been noticed by the great Zeus, who visited her frequently at her father's palace. Zeus' wife Hera was not amused by yet more of her husband's amorous escapades and, after discovering that Semele was pregnant, assumed the guise of Semele's nurse and entered her room. Here she suggested that Semele ask Zeus to reveal himself in all his Olympian glory.

Semele thinking this was a good idea took Hera's advice and Zeus, flattered by her attention, did as she asked. The light that shone from him however was so brilliant that Semele became consumed by flames but as the fire burned, a piece of ivy which was growing in the palace grounds began to weave its way into the palace forming a protective screen between the flames and the unborn child. Zeus, seeing the child released from his mother but not yet ready to be born, gathered the child up and enclosed him in his own thigh, where he continued to grow until his due time at which point Zeus named the child Dionysus, meaning born twice.

Dionysus spent his childhood on a fabled mountain where he befriended many nymphs and rural divinities such as dryads, satyrs, sileni, centaurs and the Gods Pan, Aristaeus and Pirapus by whom he was educated in the fruit of the vine and the art of winemaking.

One day, whilst walking along the seashore, he was abducted by Tyrrhenian pirates and taken aboard their ship. The pirates mistakenly took Dionysus for the son of a king from whom they intended to demand a hefty ransom, however, when they attempted to tie him up with heavy cords, the knots just loosened of their own accord and fell to the deck. The captain, realising that their captive was probably a divine being, attempted to persuade the crew to release him, but undeterred they continued to try to restrain him. All at once, a river of rich dark wine began to flow about the ship, fragrant and delicious, whilst a vine attached itself to the sail and ivy leaves wound their way around the mast. Dionysus meanwhile took the guise of a fearful lion and in terror the pirates leapt into the sea and only the captain was spared.

Thus Dionysus became the God of wine and from earliest times, wine festivals were dedicated to him at which, devotees of all kinds drank of the vine and paid homage to their God. These faithful followers earned themselves the title of 'Bacchantes', which derives from the Latin *'bacchati'* meaning 'revel' and from where Dionysus' Roman equivalent, Bacchus earned his name.

Satyrs

Satyrs were the elementary spirits of the forests and mountains, a type of wood genii whose sudden appearance would often frighten lone travellers. In early Greek myth they were portrayed as being of a rather lascivious nature, chasing innocent nymphs through the forest.

Their appearance was a combination of a monkey and a goat, with low foreheads, snub noses, pointed ears and a hairy body ending in a goat's tail.

251

In later times their character became gentler in nature, specialising in the pleasures of music and dance, whilst their features also softened and became more youthful. They were always portrayed as faithful companions to Dionysus and played a principal role in his orgiastic festivals.

Sileni

Silenus, although portrayed as a rather gregarious, drunk, fat old man with a bald head and snub nose, was in fact the off spring of the Greek God Hermes and the Earth. Silenus had been a tutor to the young Dionysus and had assisted in the moulding of the impressionable God's character. He followed Dionysus everywhere and was often portrayed in his drunken state as being supported by the Satyrs whilst other times he was shown as swaying precariously upon an ass. For all his drunkenness however, Silenus was a wise old man who knew of both the past and the future and could allegedly reveal the destiny of anyone who was successful in tying him up during the heavy slumber which followed his drinking sessions.

The name Silenus is also a generic term given to a category of rural divinities rather like the satyrs and often confused with them. However, unlike the satyrs, the Selini were from Phrygia rather than Greece and were the genii of the springs and rivers rather than the woods. Their name means 'water which bubbles as it flows'.

The Centaurs

The centaurs also made up part of the cortege of Dionysus and were portrayed in popular myth as having the head and torso of a man whilst the remainder of their body belonged to a horse. In the main their behaviour was questionable, being rude, cruel, lecherous and drunk, however there were certain exceptions to the rule as was the case of Pholus who entertained Hercules and Chiron and who was educated by Apollo and Artemis.

Pan, Aristaeus and Priapus

Pan, the great lusty Arcadian God of nature, was often confused with the satyrs because of his goat like appearance and became incorporated in the entourage of Dionysus. The popularity of Pan spread throughout the classical world and eventually every region in Greece had its own Pan. In Thessaly it was Aristaeus, whilst in Mysia in Asia Minor it was Priapus all of whom became associated with Dionysus.

Mrs Darley Tale: The Knockers

'Sorry I'm late,' said a breathless Phyllis as she struggled into Mrs Darley's cottage with several bags and a bunch of beautiful peonies. 'I got waylaid by Black Bill down the bottom of the lane, who seems to be in a bit of a state over his neighbour having heard the knockers again.'

I wondered momentarily if I had heard correctly and, noticing my somewhat questionable expression, Mrs Darley stepped in with what she considered to be an explanation. 'Mining piskies, dear.'

'Oh,' I said.

Phyllis by this time had dropped her various bags on the table and flopped down into the fireside chair from where she gratefully accepted a glass of whisky from Mrs Darley. 'So,' she said continuing her story, 'now he's expecting the worst.'

'I thought you said that it was his neighbour who had heard them, not Black Bill?' Mrs Darley asked.

Mrs Darley's Pagan Elements

'It was,' said Phyllis, but you know how superstitious Bill is about everything and don't forget, his grandfather died in a tin mining accident. In fact Bill always maintained that his grandfather had heard the knockers every day for a week before that ladder collapsed.'

'Mmmm,' murmured Mrs Darley, 'the trouble is the more you think about something the more inclined you are to attract it to you ... good or bad.'

Unable to contain my curiosity any longer I asked the burning question. 'Why is it a bad omen to hear the knockers?'

'Well, it is and it isn't,' said Mrs Darley, 'it's all to do with what you believe I suppose. The Cornish people are a superstitious lot as are most of the Celtic races and here we have a variety of piskies or little people that each have their own particular characteristics and areas of habitat. The knockers, or Buccas as they are sometimes known, live in the tin and copper mines and are thought by some, to be the spirits of the old Jewish miners who worked the Cornish mines in ancient times. Others however believe them to be the souls of those who are neither good enough to go to heaven or bad enough to go to hell, therefore spending eternity in the dismal darkness of the mines.

So, in answer to your question, some miners believed that to hear the tapping of a knocker's tools meant that these elfin folk must be working on a rich seam of ore, and, in return for the miners respect and a crust from their pasty the knockers would disclose the best place to mine. Other folk however, Black Bill included, believed that to hear the knockers was a bad omen and that it preceded a mining disaster as was the case with his grandfather.'

'Has anyone ever seen them?' I asked.

'Supposedly very few, but according to all accounts,

the descriptions remain very similar. They are said to be thin, ugly creatures about the size of a human dwarf, with large hooked noses and mouths that stretch from ear to ear.'

'And apparently,' added Phyllis, 'they love to pull grotesque faces at humans by crossing their eyes and thumbing their noses, or bending over and grimacing from between their legs.'

'Lovely!' I laughed. 'But on a more serious note, what can we do about Black Bill being so worried?'

'I think I might just have an idea,' said Mrs Darley smiling, 'get your shoes on, it involves a trip to the bottom of the garden.'

The three of us made our way into Mrs Darley's garden and came to a standstill by a small shrub covered in a mass of yellow flowers.

'St John's Wort,' announced Mrs Darley, beginning to pick a few of the flowers. 'Now do be careful not to bruise or crush the flowers when you pick them because they do exude the most peculiar red liquid, which strangely turns your fingers blue and is an absolute nightmare to get off, oh and watch your clothes,' she added as an after thought.

'So how will this help?' I asked.

'Well, since Saxon times St John's Wort has been used as a means of protection against evil spirits and has been attributed with all kinds of magical properties, a fact that the Cornish have long held dear. In fact the old Cornish used to dress the long poles that marked the boundaries of the tin mines with the flowers at midsummer to ensure protection for the mine and its workers.

So I thought that if we made a garland, Phyllis could drop it off to Black Bill on her way home this evening and he can do with it what he will. It's all psychological really; I'm just hoping that if Bill thinks he's got protection then he won't draw negativity towards himself.'

Phyllis nodded her approval, 'Good thinking,' she said.

'And that,' smiled Mrs Darley, 'is what we all need to practice in order to create a joyful life.'

Earth: A Matter of Life and Death

Although a reasonably common theme, not all creation stories include an actual creator. Some creation myths illustrate the world gradually emerging from the latent power of the earth, whilst others show the world being formed from a cosmic egg, or appearing from deep within primordial waters. The vast majority of stories, however, do feature a Divine being from which all aspects of the world with which we are familiar derive.

In Hindu myth the universe existed only in complete darkness, unmarked, unknowing as though it was in a deep sleep. Then all at once the Divine appeared, created by His own self-will and, using his great power, he dispelled the darkness.

His desire was to produce beings of many kinds from his own body and so, with a single thought, he created the waters and placed his seed in them. The seed became a golden egg and within the egg, he himself formed as Brahma, the creator of the world.

Brahma lived within the egg for a year and by a single thought, divided the egg into two halves, one of which became heaven and the other earth, whilst between them laid the eight points of the horizon and the eternal waters.

Brahma then drew from within himself the mind, which he saw as being both real and unreal and from the mind he created the ego in order that the function of self consciousness may be known. He then created the soul and the five sensory organs after which, he took minute particles of each and, mixed them with particles of himself to create all beings.

In the Japanese Shinto tradition, heaven and earth were united as one chaotic mass, rather like an egg with little definition and which contained germs. As time progressed, the purer and clearer part was separated from the heavier element forming heaven, whilst the denser element eventually settled down and became earth.

In Aboriginal myth we are told that there was a time when all was still and that the only being awake was the Father of All Spirits. Eventually the Father awoke the Sun Mother and as she opened her eyes, a warm ray of light spread across the sleeping earth. The Father asked the Mother to go down to earth to awake the sleeping spirits and give them form.

As the Mother walked the earth, plants grew where she trod and eventually she went into the dark caves and awoke the spirits who began to fly out of the caves as insects of many kinds. She watched as the insects fed on pollen from the flowers and was pleased with what she had done.

The Father however urged her on and once again she ventured into the dark caves and as she spread her light, her heat melted the ice from which all the rivers and streams of the world were created and teemed with aquatic life.

Next she awoke the spirits of the birds and animals and they all ventured out into the warm sunshine and the Father was pleased with what he saw. The Mother called all the creatures to her and told them to enjoy the wealth of the earth and to live peacefully amongst each other before rising into the sky and taking up position with the sun.

Initially the animals lived harmoniously together but this soon changed, for one animal would want the traits of another and so, the Sun Mother was forced to revisit the earth to sort out their bickering.

In an attempt to bring peace she gave each creature the power to change their form to whatever they wished. This gift however, did not work out the way she had planned as she witnessed some rats becoming bats, whilst certain lizards and fish began sporting blue tongues.

The Sun Mother decided the time had come to create new creatures for otherwise she felt that the Father would be angry by what he saw.

She therefore gave birth to the morning star and the moon, whose subsequent union brought forth the first human beings. The Sun Mother made these humans superior to the animals because they had within them part of the Divine mind and therefore would never want to change their shape.

The above is, no doubt a rather familiar theme to those who have read the biblical creation story where we are told in the book of Genesis 1:1-2:

'In the beginning God created the heavens and the earth. Now the earth was formless and empty, darkness was over the surface of the deep, and the Spirit of God was hovering over the waters.'

Gradually over the following five days God created light and darkness and day and night. He made the land and seas, seeds and fruit, the sun and moon, creatures of the air and beasts that roamed the earth, including man in the form of Adam.

Finally to mankind he gave dominion over all that lived in and upon the earth, the seas and the skies:

Genesis 1: 26:

'Let us make man in our image, in our likeness, and let them rule over the fish of the sea and the birds of the air, over the livestock, over all the earth and over all the creatures that move along the ground.'

To Adam he gave a warning that he may eat of anything in the Garden of Eden with the exception of the tree of knowledge. Eve, however, Adam's companion, became tempted by the serpent to eat from the forbidden tree of knowledge and then persuaded Adam to do the same.

Immediately the knowledge of consciousness was their's and they became ashamed of their nakedness, hurrying to cover themselves. Realising what they had done, God unleashed his wrath upon them as depicted in Genesis 3: 17-19:

Cursed is the ground because of you. Through painful toil you will eat of it all the days of your life. It will produce thorns and thistles for you and you will eat the plants of the field. By the sweat of your brow you will eat your food until you return to the ground, since from it you were taken; for dust you are and to dust you will return

Therefore within a few verses of the Christian Bible we are given an explanation as to why we are here, why we die and what happens to our physical bodies after death.

Burial of the Dead
The popularity of burial as a suitable method of disposing of a dead body has waxed and waned throughout the ages, often alternating with cremation, due to both space limitation and the constraints of religious beliefs.

We know, however, that burials did actually take

place on these islands long before the Christian creation myths were written, for although human remains from earliest times are few and far between, the Gower peninsula in South Wales has provided archaeologists with substantial evidence. Here a burial, complete with certain grave goods, indicates that the interment took place before the last great period of glaciation, making this pre 25,000 BC.

In Dr Ronald Hutton's book *The Pagan Religions of the Ancient British Isles*, he informs us that those buried during the Stone Age seemed to be arranged in a crouched foetus position, aligned in a north / south direction, a fact that has caused much speculation as to the reason behind this. Some have suggested that the individual was returned to the earth in the same position as that in which they came into the world in order that they might be reborn. In addition to this, some Palaeolithic burials as far apart as Russia and Wales sprinkled the body with red ochre, which again has caused many ideas to be put forward as to the reason behind it, including that it was perhaps symbolic of a baby emerging from the womb, or that the mourners were trying to restore the colour to the deceased cheeks.

During the Bronze Age, cremations became the popular method of body disposal, as evidenced from fields of funerary urns, whilst the mid Iron Age once again saw the return of the traditional burials, albeit on a far grander scale than was formerly seen. Dr Hutton tells us that the people living around the Yorkshire Wolds began to construct huge cemeteries within rectangular ditches and once again the bodies were arranged in the foetus position and laid out in a north-south direction.

In the late Iron Age, much contact through trade was made with Roman Gaul, whose influence dramatically affected burial rituals and cremation re-emerged as the most popular way of disposing of bodies.

During the time of the Saxons however, burial once again waxed in popularity along with the accompaniment of numerous grave goods, as evidenced at Sutton Hoo. Saxon burials saw the deceased placed in wood, lead or stone coffins, with a coin placed in their mouths with which to pay the ferryman to ensure a safe passage to the afterlife.

The early Christians saw the passing of the dead as a joyous event and as such, traditionally wore white at their funerals. They continued the tradition of burial as opposed to cremation for their belief was that bodies should be kept intact in anticipation of Christ's second coming. In contrast to Pagan burials however, a Christian body would be buried in an east-west direction, in order that the deceased would be able to witness the coming of Christ who, it was assumed, would appear from the east. Grave goods and food did not form part of a Christian burial, for presumably it was believed that neither of these would be required in heaven.

The arrival of the Normans however in 1066, saw a dramatic change in the way in which death was approached and it was from this point on that the mood of a funeral became sombre and fearful, with an emphasis on the Day of Judgment, sin and punishment.

During the five centuries that followed burial was, for many quite a temporary affair and although they were initially buried, their bones were dug up after a few years when the flesh had decomposed and placed in a charnel house, many of which can still be found alongside large churches and cathedrals. This was an efficient use of both land and materials as coffins were not needed as permanent receptacles but only as a method of transport.

During the 17th century, private graves became popular, but with a sharp increase in population, shortage of space became an issue and it was at this time that cemeteries were created.

Today, a funeral is often approached with almost clinical precision from the arrival of a funeral director to the choosing of a highly polished coffin, from the wearing of obligatory black to the depressing sombre atmosphere that descends upon the household. All of this however is a Victorian invention and one which thankfully many of the Irish have managed to avoid, for although they mourn the death of the deceased, they also celebrate the life and the Irish wake still holds firm.

Once again during the 20th century, cremation gained in popularity and up until the 1990's accounted for seventy five percent of body disposal methods. In 1994 however, the first woodland burial site in the world was opened at the Municipal Cemetery in Carlisle, which allowed bodies to be buried in coffins of wood, cardboard or wicker. Loved ones were encouraged to become more involved in the whole process and although headstones were not allowed, the planting of trees and shrubs was welcomed, with which to mark the grave and encourage wildlife.

This is perhaps a return to the old ways; returning the body to the earth from whence it came, improving the environment for the living, providing a place of peace for loved ones to remember and a beautiful setting for the released soul to find freedom.

In Celebration of Fungi

To choose just one creature, plant or tree from the thousands that roam or grow in the earth is almost impossible, however, in keeping with the chapters that have gone before, a humble earthy specimen has been chosen in the form of fungi.

Fungi, in their many forms, can often be overlooked and yet, without their presence, the earth would literally choke in its own waste and so it is to mushrooms, toadstools, moulds and yeasts that homage is paid.

Since time immemorial, man has found fungi of all kinds endlessly fascinating, for no other group of organisms are so diverse in their use or appearance.

As if by magic, they seemingly appear overnight in the darkest corners of silent woodland, enigmatic, ethereal and almost other worldly, they are a testament to their often enchanting names such as; Witches Butter, Fairies Bonnets, Scarlet Elf Cap and Dryads Saddle.

The use of mushrooms for a variety of purposes dates back thousands of years and Egyptian hieroglyphs disclose the fact that the Pharaohs believed them to be the plant of immortality. In fact, so prized was the flavour of mushrooms by the Pharaohs that they were declared 'too good' for the common people to eat and only royalty were allowed to consume them.

The later Romans also held the mushroom in high esteem and referred to it as *'cibus deorum'* or the 'food of the Gods', eventually naming one particular species, *'Amanita Caesarea'* or 'Caesar's mushroom'. Subsequently many other mushrooms were also given affectionate names in order to follow this royal or saintly trend, namely; 'King Alfred's Cramp Balls', 'St George's Mushroom' and 'Adonis Mycenae'.

Fungi are however, paradoxical by nature, which only adds to their enigmatic quality. For in their many guises as mushrooms, lichen, yeasts and moulds they are capable of both giving to mankind and taking away. A true representative no doubt of the Goddess in her many guises.

The study of fungi, or mycology as it is known, is a complex subject, although broadly speaking they can be divided into two categories; those that can be seen with the naked eye, known as '*macrofungi*' and those which are invisible to the naked eye known as '*microfungi*'.

Approximately a quarter of British macrofungi, known as '*mycorrhiza*', form a symbiotic relationship with a variety of trees, providing them with a protective sheath around their roots, called an '*ectomycorrhiza*'. This sheath prevents the roots from drying out and supplies the tree with vital nutrients and water. In return the tree provides sugars and starch, which are absorbed by the fungi to ensure its survival. Some species of macrofungi, however, known as '*parasites*', are unable to enter into a symbiotic relationship and use trees solely for their own benefit as hosts upon which to live.

The parasites referred to as '*obligates*', manage to live on trees without killing them, however parasites known as '*opportunists*' actually kill their host. Ironically this is not as unfortunate as it appears, for once the opportunists have succeeded in their mission, they evolve into fungi known as '*saprophytes*' which then feed on the dead tree, recycling the decaying matter into substances that are both useful to themselves and other life forms. Without saprophytes, woodland would eventually suffocate in its own waste.

As a food, certain species of macrofungi are both delicious and nutritious, providing a very enjoyable source of protein to both carnivores and vegetarians alike. The famous writer of epigrams, Martial once said:

It is easy to despise gold and silver, but exceedingly difficult to refuse a plate of mushrooms.

On the other side of the coin, many types of fungi

actually destroy food, such as *'penicillum digitatum'*, which forms the green powdery coating on rotting oranges and *'monilina fructigena'*, that turns rotting apples brown.

The medicinal properties of mushrooms have been known for thousands of years. Hippocrates in the 5th century BC mentions the use of mushrooms in the preparation of certain medicines, whilst in Asia the shitake mushroom, has been highly prized for over two thousand years as a fungus that promotes longevity.

For centuries, *'ganoderma lucidum'* (a bracket fungus) has been used as a vital ingredient in the elusive elixirs of life and is now being investigated as a cancer inhibitor.

Perhaps the most notorious of medicinal fungi however was that discovered by Alexander Fleming in 1928, when he brought penicillin to the world stage, courtesy of the fungi called *'penicillium notatum'*, which immediately changed the face of modern medicine.

Caution should always be exercised however when collecting or especially eating fungi of any kind and the sinister names of certain fungi such as the 'death cap' or 'destroying angel' give us a flavour of our fate should we eat the wrong one. Ingestion can lead to severe illness at best and even death in the worst case scenario, illustrating that as with all aspects of Mother Nature She can be exceptionally benevolent, yet have no qualms about reminding us of our fragility.

Dionysus

Her heart beats the drum of anticipation,
Nervous hands twist the linen napkin.
Every movement spells possibility,
A swish of the door, a heel on the floor.

Mrs Darley's Pagan Elements

In the blink of an eye he enters,
Her thoughts dissolve into a hot shower of desire.
Dark, rich, unrivalled, he comes to her table.
His scent envelops, intoxicating, consuming.
Across the table she reaches for him.
He finds her lips. Passion consumes.
Dionysus is dead.

Mythical Creatures of the Earth

Many people love the idea of sharing the earth with 'the little people' or fairy and, over millennia, many tales and myths have built up from around the world of tiny beings who occasionally make themselves known to us, often with rather dire consequences. In many of the Celtic lands these beliefs still hold strong with the sidhe forming an important part of Irish mythology and the piskey taking its place in the hearts of the Cornish.

The Piskey and the Small People

The Cornish piskey is a tiny creature, no bigger than a mouse who wears a white waistcoat, green stockings and a brown coat and breeches. His shoes are shiny and buckled with a gleaming dew drop, whilst his head is covered with a wig of grey lichen that protrudes beneath his bright red cap. He is said to chatter incessantly and uses snails as his preferred method of transport.

Some say the piskey came over with the saints from Ireland, from where their prankish teasing nature derives, whilst others believe they are the souls of virtuous Pagans from ancient times. Certain trains of thought suggest that they were perhaps once the Pagan Gods, giant like in stature, but when considered a threat to the Christian church, were sprinkled with holy water and thus shrank in both importance and size.

Like humankind, the piskey can be both naughty and nice, for he is said to help the elderly and thresh the corn but, by the same token, is capable of bewitching the unsuspecting, leaving them to wander helplessly in a strange landscape until they fall into an exhausted sleep.

In a similar vein, the Cornish 'small people' also tend the elderly and the sick, bringing them flowers and singing songs and many a fisherman has witnessed seeing these beautiful fairies from their boats as they come in close to the cliffs, down the far west of the county close to Land's End.

The small people are described as beautiful tiny creatures, elegantly dressed in lace and velvet with shimmering jewels of diamonds encased in silver. The pale faced ladies are said to have curled hair which sits beneath their pointed hats, whilst the dark faced men folk are often dressed as soldiers sporting tricorn hats trimmed with silver bells.

Some people have been lucky enough to witness the small peoples' presence from close quarters but have unknowingly trespassed upon fairy ground when doing so and, as a result, have been spirited away to the fairy realms. The case of the legendary William Noy a resident of St Buryan in Cornwall in the early part of the 19th century tells of his journey to the land of the fairy.

One dark night, as William was making his way home, he became hopelessly lost and did not return to his bed. His family, sick with worry searched for him day and night, until finally, on the third day, they found him asleep in the shelter of a tumble down building covered by thick brambles. When his family awoke him, he seemed to have lost all sense of time and place, although he did recognise his family and friends and asked questions as to how he came to be in the shelter.

267

Eventually, upon being taken home he began to reconstruct the events of the previous night.

He recalled crossing Selena Moor and remembered allowing his horse free reign to gallop across the open moorland. Within a short while however, they both became totally lost and found themselves in a dark forest. Upon looking through the trees, William became aware of candle light shimmering in the distance and the sound of beautiful music, but to his surprise his horse refused to venture any further and so he tethered the horse to a tree and proceeded on foot.

Eventually William came to a clearing in the trees where he saw an old house, in front of which stood a girl dressed in white, playing the fiddle, whilst before her on the grass, danced hundreds of tiny people. William decided he would like to join the party, but the fiddle player shook her head and drew him aside. It was at that moment that William looked into the eyes of his long lost love, Grace Hutchens, who had, so he thought, died three years previously. Feeling overjoyed, he moved to kiss her, but she quickly pulled away, warning him that he must not touch anything he saw, for everything was enchanted. Grace went on to tell him of that fateful evening three years ago when, while crossing Selena Moor, she too became hopelessly lost and found herself in the same forest and the same clearing as William, however, having no one to warn her that this was the land of the fairy, she plucked a plum from a tree and bit into it. Once in her mouth the sweet juice turned sour and she fainted. Upon her awakening she was surrounded by hundreds of small people who were celebrating the fact that they now had someone to care for them and their fairy babies.

William suddenly decided that the land of the fairy

held very little appeal and so, remembering that a garment turned inside out would break a spell of enchantment he took his glove, reversed it and threw it into the fairy crowd. At once everything changed; the house became a ruin and the grass become thick with brambles. Looking around for his beloved Grace he was distraught to see that she had not come with him and immediately he fell to the ground and slipped into a deep sleep.

From that day until the day he died William searched endlessly for Grace but never found her. Finally his body was buried beside what everyone thought was hers in Buryan church yard, or perhaps he once again returned to his love, Grace and the land of the fairy, but this time wished never to return.

The Spriggans

Spriggans are considered to be the least benevolent of Cornish fairies. They have been described as rather ugly with large wizened faces upon tiny shoulders and have a tendency to hiss, spit and grin maliciously at those with whom they have contact.

Their job however, is one of protection with particular jurisdiction over cliff tops, cairns, quoits and burial mounds which they supposedly haunt, safeguarding the treasures of the old Pagan folk that lie beneath.

Spriggans are attributed with the ability to raise storms and whirlwinds in order to terrify the lone traveller and have the ultimate power to ruin a farmer's harvest by summoning storms of rain and hail to flatten the corn.

Perhaps their most hideous crime however is their liking for human babies, which they are thought to steal from their cradles, replacing them with one of their own wizened off spring, often referred to as a 'changeling'.

Dryads

The word 'Dryad' is a collective term for a variety of beautiful female nymphs, whose jurisdiction is said to cover copses, trees, groves, woodland and mountain forests.

The word 'dryad comes from the Greek, 'dryades' meaning 'of the tree or oak' and each type of dryad has their own particular domain as illustrated below in Table 2.4 below.

Dryad	Dominion
Meliai	Ash trees, born of Gaea when impregnated by the blood of the castrated Ouranos
Oreiades	Mountain conifers
Hamadryades	Oak and poplar trees, riverside trees and ancient groves. (They are born with the tree and die at its demise)
Maliades, Meliades, Epimelides	Fruit trees and sheep ('melas' in Greek means apple and sheep)
Daphnaie	Laurel Trees (very rare nymph)
Nymphai Aigeiroi	Black Poplar
Ampeloi	Grape Vine
Karyai	Hazelnut
Kraneiai	Cherry Tree
Moreai	Mulberry
Pteali	Elm
Sykei	Fig
Alseides	Sacred Groves
Aulonides	The Glens
Napaiai	The Vales

Table 2.4

Elves

Elves are the magical beings of Norse myth, more beautiful than humans and, who have a liking for dancing beneath the light of the moon. Elves were generally said to be divided into two groups; the *'Ljosalfar'* or 'light elves' who were benevolent sky dwelling creatures, whilst the *'Dopkalfar'* or 'dark elves' were more sinister in nature and lived in the woods or underground. The Dopkalfar however were said to be able to fashion weapons of magic from the raw materials of the earth.

Gnomes and Goblins

Gnomes are serious creatures whose domain is the earth. They often offer practical help around the home to those who ask respectfully, although they can be stubborn and inflexible if offended in any way. The word gnome comes from the Greek *'gnoma'*, meaning knowledge.

The King of the gnomes is called Ghob, which is where the word 'goblin' derives. Goblins are similar creatures to the gnome and both are often portrayed as being somewhat mischievous or harmful. This is however a common misunderstanding for they are particularly fond of children to whom their naughtiness appeals.

Gnomes and Goblins are thought to be fascinated by silver coins and if you wish to ask a favour of them, bury a silver coin and make your request. They are particularly good at helping us mere mortals with:

- Mental stress
- Psychic attack
- Practical matters
- Grounding
- Material concerns
- Luck

They are also thought to protect the garden, hence the appearance of many a gnome or goblin statue amongst the flora and fauna. If you wish to attract these earth elementals into your garden then certain items situated in the northern most corner will help, including:

- Moss
- Lichen
- Wild flowers
- Herbs
- Trees
- Rocks and stones

The Magic and Alchemy of Earth

The great psychologist Carl Jung believed that just as the four elements exist on the material plane in the forms of air, fire, water and earth, so these energy types also exist in our inner world or subconscious and can be described as thinking, intuition, feeling and sensation, or in relation to the old humours can be likened to the temperaments of sanguine, choleric, melancholic or phlegmatic. He believed that in an individual who he would describe as 'unconscious', then one energy type would always dominate, but that in order to become balanced we must learn to develop each category even though we would always retain the main aspect of our personality.

Jung went on to divide the four categories into two groups, namely perception and judgement. Perception, he stated, tells us what is happening through intuition and sensation, whilst judgement takes us through the decision making process by thinking and feeling.

In terms of human existence, earth symbolizes the sensation aspect, the part of us which operates through the physical senses, of touch, hearing, smell, taste and sight. The earth element is grounded in the present and relays back to us what is happening now in the present moment. It is the function of factual memory that tells us in no uncertain terms how things are and how things used to be.

Jung believed that those with a dominant earth aspect to their personality are the realists and although they rarely live in their imagination, they do have the ability to see life as it is and are usually quite practical in their approach, having common sense in a crisis and the ability to take the ideas of others and turn them into reality in the material world.

Our language illustrates beautifully the many aspects of earth. We use one of earth's densest elements to describe something weighty and say it's 'as heavy as lead'. When someone or something is reliable we may use the term, 'steady or solid as a rock'. In describing something of great height we may say it was 'as high as a mountain' or when someone is pretty we may liken them to 'an English rose'.

In ancient Greek philosophy, earth is one of the four classical elements and is considered to be both cold and dry and, according to Aristotle, occupies a place between water and fire amongst the elemental spheres. Each element is also associated with one of the four humours, which in the case of earth is black bile and, like earth, is cold and dry. It is considered to reflect the melancholy personality and as such people of this nature can be moody, anxious, rigid, sober, pessimistic, reserved, unsociable and quiet.

The symbol used by Plato to depict water was the cube (formed from six square sides), making earth the clumsiest of the elements which causes it to crumble and break.

In alchemy the chemical element of salt was associated with earth and therefore its alchemical symbol became a downward pointing triangle bisected by a horizontal line.

In Hindu tradition, the Earth Goddess is referred to as Prithvi, derived from 'the Sanskrit *'prthivi'* the Hindu word for earth. As Prithvi Mata or Mother Earth she is partnered with Dvaus Pita, or father Sky and in the Rigveda the pair are depicted as two half shells.

Magical Earth
Ever since mankind has walked upon the earth he has attempted to harness and work in conjunction with her natural forces especially when making magic.

In earliest times the natural world was the domain of the wise woman and cunning man for they knew how to attract love, good fortune and health by working in conjunction with the seasons, the moon's cycles, and the elements of air, fire, water and earth.

The practice of ceremonial magic in its many forms also incorporates the element of earth into its teachings.

In Wiccan ritual the element of earth is placed in the cardinal direction of the north and is protected by the gnome as guardians of the northern quarter. This direction is associated with old age, death, night and winter and is symbolically represented with earthy colours, particularly brown and green, the pentagram or pentacle (five pointed star) the tarot suit of pentacles, land based animals, wood, stones and percussion instruments.

In the casting of a magic circle, the element of earth is often depicted with salt and is symbolic of life, growth, health and increase of all kinds. Salt is abundant upon the

274

earth whether it is sourced from the sea or from underground and the salt routes are some of the oldest tracks known to mankind.

The use of earth's gifts in making magic is used by everyone, albeit sometimes unknowingly. If you have ever drunk peppermint tea to calm an upset stomach, or rubbed a dock leaf on a nettle sting, then you will have resorted to the element of earth to restore balance to your body. With today's interest in natural medicines, aromatherapists and herbalists all seek to use nature's gifts in order to restore homeostasis to the mind and body.

Herbs and oils however, are not only used to bring about health of mind and body. For millennia, wise men and women have used herbs in sachets, burners and baths in order to attract certain things into the life of the seeker.

Table 2.5 below (going over to following page) provides a selection of the most popular. It is not recommended that these are taken internally however and should you wish to do so please contact a listed herbalist.

Please note: If you are using essential oils in the bath please do not use more than 6 drops diluted in a teaspoon of oil, milk or alcohol before entering. Do not use the following marked * as essential oils either in the bath or if you are pregnant.

Herb or essential oil	Confers
Alfalfa	Wealth and abundance
Aloe	Luck
Basil*	Love and wealth
Benzoin	Purification
Cedarwood*	Healing and protection
Cinnamon*	Spiritual gifts, healing powers, love
Clover	Protection, fidelity, success
Dock	Healing, fertility
Hops	Peaceful sleep
Lemon balm	Love success healing

Rosemary*	Banishes negativity and nightmares
Witch hazel	Mends broken hearts
Yarrow*	Courage and psychic powers

Table 2.5

Trees too play their part in the creating of magic as each bestows its own gifts. Table 2.6 below offers a little insight as to the magical qualities of certain trees especially if you have them in your garden or close to your home.

Tree	Confers
Apple	Fertility, health and love
Ash	Travel, strength and healing
Beech	Knowledge
Birch	Health, wisdom, new beginnings
Cherry	Divination skills
Chestnut	Abundance
Elm	Peaceful sleep
Fir	New beginnings
Hawthorn	Courage, purification
Hazel	Wisdom, luck, knowledge, inspiration
Holly	Protection
Oak	Knowledge, power, confidence, potency
Rowan	Protection, psychic powers, healing
Willow	Intuition, healing, understanding
Yew	Endurance

Table 2.6

Flowers also have their role to play in the magical realms and many spells are created using flowers or their essences.

Simple divination techniques have always been employed by adults and children alike for who hasn't plucked the petals of a daisy, chanting, 'he loves me, he loves me not', or blow the seed head of dandelions in order to tell the time. Table 2.7 below offers a little insight into the influences of individual flowers.

Flower	Confers
Azalea	Caution
Bluebell	Fidelity, modesty, truth
Buttercup	Wealth, self esteem
Carnation	Strength, family ties
Chrysanthemum	Protection, peace of mind
Crocus	Renewed hope
Daffodil	Love, fidelity, self esteem
Dandelion	Increasing psychic powers, divination
Freesia	Trust
Geranium	Fertility
Jasmine	Passion, prophetic dreams
Orchid	Spirituality, blessings
Passion Flower	Friendship, peaceful sleep
Rose	Love, protection

Table 2.7

Earth is a very protective element for it nurtures and nourishes purifies and protects. In times gone by the elders of a village would scatter a handful of earth behind a departing loved one in the hope that this would protect them on their journey or in their task.

Earth magic is very much concerned with the physical realm. It is used to improve health on all levels, to increase abundance in material terms including money, career or property and to confer protection upon both people and objects

Mrs Darley Tale: The Antique Shop
It was one of those white days of summer, hot and sultry, when you know the sun is there but can't quite see it. The drive from Cornwall to Wiltshire along the never ending A303 had been sticky and uncomfortable and I, for one, was eternally grateful to park the car at the side of the road and step out into the fresh air.

277

Mrs Darley's Pagan Elements

'It looks at though it's up that way,' Rose said pointing ahead as we all donned our walking boots.

'Well there certainly seems to be plenty of people heading that way,' replied Phyllis, 'shall we try it?'

We all murmured our consent and five minutes later we were leaving the grass verge and heading off into the adjacent cornfield.

'Goodness,' gasped Rose after a steep uphill climb within the tractor tracks of the thigh high cornfield. 'Are we there yet? I'm ready for a lie down in this heat.'

'There, look,' said Phyllis pointing to her left, 'this is it, we're here.'

'May I make a suggestion, dears?' asked Mrs Darley. 'I think we should all go our own way, form our own opinions and savour our own experience. If you're agreeable then we'll meet back here in 45 minutes.'

I for one was more than grateful to have the opportunity to soak up the atmosphere of my first crop circle alone and immediately went to a quieter part to inspect its formation.

It was difficult to work out from the ground, exactly what shape the formation took, suffice to say that it was both huge and complex enough for me to doubt the involvement of mankind's hand. The flattened corn was simply bent, not broken and every edge was sharp and precise, totally free from human error.

I decided to close my eyes and sit for a while in peace and solitude, noting as I sank down onto the corn, just how soft and springy it felt, unlike the hard spiky surface I had expected. I also became aware that the ordinary sounds of everyday life had become inaudible; no distant traffic noise, no voices, no buzzard cries, almost as though I was in a sound proofed space, a sacred circle that stood between the worlds.

It was only when I stood up in readiness to meet with the others that I began to notice the beginning of a headache, which gradually increased in severity as the day progressed, despite the administering of several pain killers.

Upon regrouping, we all agreed to keep our experiences to ourselves until we found somewhere to have lunch in nearby Avebury, a mystical place of ancient history and strange phenomenon.

Arriving in the village of Avebury via the impressive two-and-a-half mile row of standing stones known as 'West Kennet Avenue', we parked the car and made our way to the nearest hostelry in order to partake of welcome refreshments.

'So,' said Mrs Darley once the food was ordered and we were all settled, 'what did you think of the crop circle?'

'Well,' began Rose, 'I don't know whether it was my imagination, but I kept hearing a strange clicking sound, just as though someone was snapping their fingers right by my ear.'

'Oh dear,' laughed Phyllis, 'I'm glad I didn't hear anything like that, in fact I thought the whole thing felt very peaceful and I found the formation of it fascinating, not a piece out corn out of place.'

Mrs Darley nodded, 'and what about you, dear?' she asked turning to me.

I recounted my feelings and observations but omitted to mention my increasingly nauseating headache for fear of being thought overdramatic.

'And what did you feel?' Phyllis asked Mrs Darley.

'I felt that it was the Goddess offering yet another piece of the mysterious puzzle of life for us to muse over,' Mrs Darley replied in her usual ambiguous way.

Mrs Darley's Pagan Elements

With lunch over, I wanted to get out once again into the fresh air and discover more about the fascinating place in which I found myself. From the window of the pub I had noticed a little antique and gift shop nestling along side a tiny church on the opposite side of the road and, after arranging to meet everyone later for afternoon tea, I set off to explore.

Avebury, I discovered, is the site of a large henge which houses three stone circles. It is one of the finest and largest Neolithic monuments in the world dating back to around 3,000 BC, and is thoroughly deserving of its acclaim as a World Heritage Site.

Leaving my exploration of the stones until later, I made my way over to the little antique shop and thankfully stepped into the cool interior, where a little bell rang to announce my arrival although the shop continued to remain empty.

I began to browse the rather sparse collection of antiques but soon found my interest captured by a dusty glass case full of Roman artefacts and Neolithic flints.

'Ah,' said a voice behind my left shoulder, 'I see my lady is interested in the ancient as opposed to merely the antique.'

I spun round, startled by this sudden intrusion, especially as I considered myself to be alone in the shop.

Standing in front of me was an elderly man with the deepest blue eyes I can remember and a smile that lit up his rather weather-beaten face.

'Sorry, my lady,' he said bowing, 'I didn't mean to startle you. Forgive me'.

I smiled, 'Of course,' I said somewhat amused by his rather peculiar yet quaint mannerisms, 'I didn't hear you come in that's all.'

'And what brings you to this mysterious place?' he

asked. 'Are you on holiday?'

I shook my head, 'No, we're just here for the day. In fact the real purpose of our visit was to see one of your famous crop circles.'

'Ah,' he murmured, 'and what did you think?'

'It was strange, otherworldly somehow and,' I said somewhat surprised to hear my own admission, 'I seem to have developed a rather severe headache.'

'That will be the effects of magnetic stimulation on your brain,' he said in a matter of fact way.

'Oh,' I replied, somewhat taken aback and a little concerned about the fact that my brain may have been affected.

'No need to look so worried,' he smiled. 'I and many more of a like mind consider crop circles to be made by an electromagnetic force within the earth.

Each of us as living creatures also has an energy field that vibrates at a specific rate according to our mental and physical health and our spiritual development. I'm sure you'll agree, my lady, that some people you feel attracted to and comfortable with, whilst others almost repel, just like a magnet, and we use phrases like, "I don't feel as though we're in tune", or "He's on my wavelength".'

I nodded feeling quite excited about the fact that everything he was saying made sense.

'So,' he continued, 'it is quite understandable that when we come into contact with an electromagnetic force of the strength and magnitude necessary to create a crop circle we are, in some instances, going to feel a little strange.

For you the energy is perhaps too strong and therefore you have developed a headache, for some it is more severe and they are physically sick or may become cognitively impaired for a while. On the other hand,

281

others experience physical healing or a general feeling of elation. Everyone is different in every way and therefore our experiences are varied even when we face the same phenomenon.'

'That's fascinating,' I said, 'I've never been given an explanation like that before.'

'Then that is obviously why you were drawn to the shop,' he smiled. 'The knowledge of the ancients is open to everyone, it's simply a case of knowing how to access a portal through which it becomes available.'

I looked at him, somewhat puzzled, 'I don't understand what you mean,' I said. 'I simply noticed the shop whilst I was having lunch and decided to come inside to have a look.'

'I'm sure you did,' he said whilst taking my arm and leading me towards the open door. 'Now watch how you go, my lady, for the modern world is full of illusion as those of us who walk the ancient track are only too aware.'

Still feeling mesmerised by what I had heard, I stepped down onto the street, where I bumped straight into Mrs Darley.

'Oh,' she said, 'that was quick, you've only just gone in.'

I looked at her feeling rather puzzled, 'No,' I said 'I've been in there ages, I went in as soon as I left the pub.'

'I know, my dear, I followed you, I was going to join you, but no sooner you were in you were out again, isn't there anything worth seeing?'

I shook my head, which felt both painful and confused, 'No,' I said, 'I've seen all I need to see.'

Astrological Earth signs

The twelve signs of the Zodiac are each governed by one of four categories, namely those of air, fire, water and earth, and of the three signs which fall within each group, one is cardinal, i.e. initiatory; one is fixed, i.e. controlling; and one is mutable, i.e. restless.

The three signs that fall under the influence of the element of earth are the deep thinking signs of Taurus, Virgo and Capricorn and although each has their specific traits, they do have certain similarities. All three have a deep seated need for security, although the type of security required varies according to the particular sign involved as illustrated in the brief character outlines below.

Taurus

Taurus is the fixed earth sign and as such people born under this sign tend to illustrate their need for security on the most basic level, through the acquisition of money and tangible assets.

With regards to personality, Taureans are ambitious, determined, persevering, magnetic, patient, affectionate, courteous and honest. At times however the Taurean can be rather odd, stubborn and emotional and once their mind is made up it can be rather difficult to persuade them to change it but that said they are cheerful, optimistic and tenacious.

Financially, Taureans have a good earning capacity but their downfall is their ability to spend money far too freely. They can however achieve financial freedom if they are disciplined enough to save and invest in early life rather than speculate on dodgy deals.

Travel is something that the Taurean is very fond of and they will normally satisfy this urge throughout life on a regular basis.

A happy home life is necessary in order that success can be both achieved and enjoyed and Taureans particularly like entertaining in the comfort of their own home.

In affairs of the heart, those born under this earthy sign may have many love affairs, due to the fact that many have a rather magnetic personality, although few bring true happiness.

The Taurean is highly emotional and often seduced by culture, social standing and wealth but they do enjoy giving gifts to others. A mate should be selected with care, for the wrong choice will bring out frustration and anger whilst the right match will bring great happiness and contentment.

Career-wise: teaching, acting, music, artistic pursuits, writing, law, medicine or governmental work could all prove suitable.

Spiritually, Taureans are often attracted to nature based paths and possess both intuition and foresight.

In religious views, sensitivity and broadmindedness both play an important role to the Taurean and, as a result they will always study a spiritual path in depth in order to make a fair judgment before accepting or condemning it.

The greatest handicap for a Taurean is their impatience concerning the need to constantly be in an environment of beauty, harmony and change but once they accept that this cannot be a feature of everyday life and learn to accept what they have, then they will be able to feel happy successful and secure.

Virgo
Virgo is the mutable earth sign and as such those born under this sign also yearn for security although this time

they search for ways of making their life or organisation efficient, therefore allowing them to feel both safe and secure.

Virgoans are efficient, progressive, shrewd, methodical, refined and intellectual. They are usually discriminating and have an analytical mind although they can be rather nervous, restless and quite undemonstrative.

That said, they are endowed with more artistic and constructive talents than the average person and have a real talent for attending to detail.

Financially, money could be made in artistic pursuits or carrying out a job where attention to detail is paramount. Solid investments in land and property should outweigh speculative deals.

Travel plays an important role in a Virgo's life, especially if it involves research for work or pleasure in the realms of music, art or literature.

On the home front, Virgoan men often have unsettled home lives until middle age, whilst the ladies of the sign are ideal homemakers and enjoy creating harmonious surroundings.

In marriage or partnerships it is important for a Virgo not to expect too much of their partner, or to focus on traits that may not match their own high ideals. Usually, however, Virgoans are very discriminating when it comes to choosing friends or partners and are often attracted to intellectual types.

Career-wise, those born under the sign of Virgo are extremely tenacious and once set upon a path it will take a lot of setbacks in order to make them give up. The male Virgo excels at art, music, architecture, medicine, law and mechanics, whilst the ladies are more suited to nursing, writing, teaching, illustrating, journalism or demonstrating products and services.

Those born under this earthy sign often follow an orthodox religious path, whilst also being tolerant of the beliefs of others.

The greatest hindrances in life to the Virgo born are self-consciousness and worry, usually down to the fact that lack of money can make them feel inferior. Once this tendency has been overcome however, then a prosperous and happy life can be enjoyed.

Capricorn

Capricorn is the cardinal earth sign and therefore seeks the security or social order of the whole world. They are talented, industrious, courageous, truthful and forceful, although they can show a quick temper, which they sometimes find difficult to control.

Alongside this, plain speaking and a tendency to find fault with others can lead to a lack of support from friends and colleagues. That said people always know where they stand with a Capricorn.

In financial matters, those born under this sign potentially have good earning capacity, although this is sometimes prohibited by a lack of opportunity. Success comes from partnerships and working for or with large organisations. Money plays a very important part in their lives.

The Capricorn person is reasonably fond of travel although is not destined to travel widely throughout life.

Home has to be just so and if it is not maintained to certain standards then some born under this sign will spend a large part of their time elsewhere, perhaps working away.

In love, this sign is often accused of being indifferent, haughty and undemonstrative, whilst this is often not what they wish to portray.

Most Capricorns have at least one big romance during their lives. With regards to friends many Capricorns are often taken advantage of because of their good nature.

In career matters, administration, music, radio, car industry, insurance, agriculture and construction are indicated as good choices, although Capricorns often feel they have to try twice as hard as everyone else to make it to the top.

Spiritually, although many born under this sign have great intuition, they seldom tune into this gift and often find themselves following a path which may appear rather odd to those around them, yet to which they themselves stick rigidly.

Capricorn's greatest handicap is their tendency to worry which often causes them to descend into a melancholy mood. These lowering moods could be a stumbling block along the road to success if not consciously worked at.

Life
A thought,
Transformed by emotion,
Activated by passion,
Bears flesh
To carry
The sanctity of life.

Connecting with the Earth Element
Jung tells us that those who feel an affinity with the earth element are the practical souls, those who take action, get things done and who can be of use in a crisis. These are the people who use their hands to make and mend.

I am surrounded by people who fit into this category. Both of my parents were highly skilled, my father as an engineer and gardener and my mother as a tailor and flower arranger, whilst my paternal grandfather was a painter and my maternal grandmother a cook. My husband, amongst many other things, is a talented stained glass artist, whilst I stand and wonder where my earth element is buried.

I was always the child at school who was last to be chosen for the sports team, due to my lack of physical capabilities when it came to keeping my eye on the ball. My sense of perspective in art somehow disappeared over the horizon, my ability to sew a seam in a straight line never quite materialised and yet, I have nothing but admiration for people who effortlessly connect to this wonderfully practical earthy element.

As my life has, however, progressed I have, on occasions, found myself placed in positions where I have been forced to connect with this alien side of my nature. Mrs Darley was instrumental in making me see how far removed I had become from being 'earthy' and in order to counteract this, she encouraged me to make things, to participate in rituals, to enjoy the fruits of Mother Nature and to bring my head out of the clouds in order that I may occasionally visit the real world.

Still I found connecting to the practical side of my nature quite difficult and would, if I had a choice veer to my safety net of thought. When I decided to train in aromatherapy, following Mrs Darley's introduction to the subject, I tried to find a course which only taught the subject of essential oils without the practical skill of massage but unfortunately for me, the two went hand in hand. Therefore with much consternation I literally got to grips with massaging oily bodies, and eventually, much to my surprise, not only thoroughly enjoyed it but went on to teach the same skills to others around the world.

In sharp contrast to these practical aversions, I have always loved the natural world, the wild moors, secret forests, mysterious caves and majestic mountains. I am also drawn to earth's mysteries, Her ley lines, burial mounds, standing stones and crop circles and places that echo with spirits of the past.

Take a few moments to consider your own connection to the earth, do you enjoy making things, mending things or getting your hand dirty? Are you a carpenter, a plasterer, a builder, a gardener, a tailor, a potter? Do you frequently use your senses in touching, smelling, looking, listening or tasting? Are you drawn to earth's mysterious places or enjoy spending time in nature? If not then perhaps these are things which you can incorporate more into your daily life in order to connect with the elementals and Deities of earth.

Carole's Tale: Flora

I placed the envelope in Mrs Darley's outstretched hand and turned to walk away.

'And where do you think you're going?' she asked.

'Home,' I replied innocently.

'Oh no,' she said firmly taking my arm, 'you don't escape that easily. You can come in, have a glass of wine and read it to me.'

I shook my head, 'Oh I couldn't, I....'

Mrs Darley raised her fingers to her lips, in a gesture which said, 'stop' and said, 'Surely you know me well enough by now to realise that I'm not going to accept these feeble protestations?'

I nodded.

'Good. Then come in and make my afternoon by reading me a story.'

And so I began.

Mrs Darley's Pagan Elements

Flora: Tim's Story:

'Parking the van at the end of the lane one crisp spring morning, Tim collected a letter addressed to "Gerald S Avon, Esq" at "The Old Mill" and began to walk along the un-adopted track.

The soft rolling hills of Lunscombe rose skyward to his left, whilst to his right a neat hedgerow framed the lane, interrupted after a few hundred yards by a small wooden gate. Looking across, Tim noticed someone bending over one of the flowerbeds and called to her.

"Beautiful morning!"

A rather startled, yet strangely attractive young woman straightened and turned to face him. She smiled briefly but within an instant disappeared around the side of the cottage. Puzzled, Tim shrugged and continued his walk down to the Old Mill at the end of the lane.

"Ah, so you're the new postie then?"

The voice, which reminded him of an old colonel, boomed out behind him as he bent down to push the post through the letterbox.

"Yes," he said straightening and offering his hand, "I'm Tim."

His hand was shaken by a large framed man, nearing seventy, with snow-white hair and a well-waxed moustache.

"Well Tim, you've chosen a lovely post round. Old Colin was here for 25 years and would never have given it up if illness hadn't struck. Ah well, his loss is your gain eh?" And with these words he patted Tim on the shoulder and walked into the house.

A few days later Tim once again had occasion to walk along the un-adopted track with some letters for "Gerald S Avon, Esq", but as he approached the little gate in the

290

hedgerow, he was delighted to see the young woman he had spoken to a few days earlier tying up some wayward roses by the cottage door.

"Hello again," he called to her.

She turned and smiled, nodding in response. Undeterred he tried again, "You always seem to have good weather in Lunscombe."

This time she laughed, the sound of which reminded him of liquid silver but still she did not speak. Determined to engage her in conversation he made a third attempt.

"Sadly I never seem to have any letters to deliver to you."

She looked at him, with what he considered to be a look of disappointment before gathering her secateurs and disappearing indoors. Tim sighed, resigning himself to the fact that she wanted to be left alone and turned once again towards the Old Mill.

As he arrived, he saw Mr Avon balancing rather precariously on a set of stepladders, clearing out his guttering of winter debris.

"That looks dangerous," Tim called as he walked down the path.

Mr Avon turned and wobbled a little, hanging onto the down pipe to steady himself.

"Look, why don't you let me do that," offered Tim, "I've finished my round now and it won't take long."

Momentarily he thought Mr Avon was going to protest, but as the ladder shuddered for a second time, the older man gratefully accepted Tim's offer.

Half an hour later, Tim found himself rewarded with coffee and biscuits as he and Mr Avon sat together beneath the old chestnut tree.

"So, Tim," Mr Avon said pouring the coffee, "are you

291

going to be with us for the next 25 years like old Colin?"

"Oh, I don't know," Tim laughed, "I only took the job of postman as a temporary measure when I left university with a classics degree ten years ago but, I'm still here! Albeit with a van now, so who knows, I might well still be here in 25 years time!

Talking of the post, here are your letters," he said reaching into his postbag. "Oh, dear, I seem to have one here for someone else, I don't know how that happened."

"Who's it for?" asked Mr Avon.

"Flora," said Tim looking at the envelope somewhat puzzled, "It just says Flora. Oh, just a minute, Flora's Cottage, that's the little house I pass on my way down here isn't it? Never mind, I'll pop it in on my way back."

Tim placed the letter on the table feeling strangely elated at the thought of having an excuse to call at the house up the lane.

"There's no need," said Mr Avon picking up the letter and placing it in the breast pocket of his jacket "I'll drop it in later."

"No!" Tim said sharply, holding out his hand, "It's my job, and besides, I want to deliver it."

Mr Avon looked away in silence.

"Mr Avon?" Enquired Tim, "the letter, can I have the letter?"

Mr Avon turned around to face him, his demeanour somewhat changed.

"If you'll take my advice you won't get involved," he said, "and isn't it about time you had that van back?"

Tim drained his coffee cup and was torn between pursuing the matter further and trusting that Mr Avon would deliver the letter as promised. Deciding however, that discretion was the better part of valour, Tim stood, murmured his thanks and took his leave.

Early spring frosts gradually gave way to warm April days and the topic of conversation throughout Lunscombe turned to the forthcoming May Day celebrations, an event that Tim was determined to attend.

On May Day morning the mist rose early, evaporating into the heavens as the sun bathed in the first breath of summer. Tim too, rose early and delivered his post as always to the residents of Lunscombe, ending with a letter or two for Mr Avon.

Parking his van in its customary spot at the top of the lane, he began the familiar walk down the un-adopted track and, as always, looked to his right as he passed Flora's cottage.

It was then that he saw her. But saw her, as he never had before. Gone were her secateurs and twine, gone were her gardening gloves and worn trousers, gone were her shy ways and timid smile.

Flora was dancing, but dancing in a way he had never seen. She danced as though her very life depended upon it and yet it was more than that. Her dance was erotic, as if performed to entice a lover. Tim watched, captivated as a pale peridot diaphanous gown floated over her otherwise naked form.

Then, she saw him. But rather than running away, she smiled and beckoned him enter the garden.

Tim stepped into the tranquil oasis as if in a trance and, with his inhibitions left gasping at the gate, allowed himself to be swept into Flora's arms.

Her floral perfume wove its way into his senses and the warmth of her body against his ensured that he became enchanted, bewitched, lost.

Late spring turned to summer and as the sleepy village of Lunscombe baked beneath the sun's heat, Tim's obsession with Flora danced around his head and clouded his judgment, fuelled by the fact that she would neither see nor speak to him. He begged unashamedly at her door and bombarded her letterbox with a thousand pleas until finally, realising the futility of his actions, he began to drown in a sea of despair.

One golden morning towards the end of October, when the whisper of autumn could be heard in the falling leaves, he pulled a heavily padded letter out of his postbag in the back of the van and traced the name with his fingertip, "Flora."

He began to walk down Old Mill Lane, his heart fluttering in his chest and then, he saw her, bending over the flowerbed adjacent to the cottage.

"Flora!"

She struggled to straighten and turned to face him, hastily pushing strands of wispy silver hair back into place.

"Oh," he said disappointed, "I'm sorry, I thought you were someone else, I was looking for Flora I have a letter for her."

"You've found her." The old woman said.

"No," he said, "no, earlier this summer... I met her... here ... a young lady ...."

"I am Flora."

Tim looked into her eyes and for a moment felt his world spin, for this was in deed Flora, the unmistakable emerald eyes that so captivated him on May Day morning, looked back at him with such overwhelming sadness that it etched its way into his soul.

"I don't understand," he whispered delivering the parcel into Flora's outstretched hand.

"Ah," she said not offering any explanation but looking down at the envelope, "It is time."

Mr Avon was brushing up fallen leaves from the porch

A Celebration of Air, Fire, Water, Earth and Divine Spirit

when Tim ran down his driveway and almost collapsed at his feet.

"My dear boy, what on earth has happened? Come in, come in and sit down, let me get you a drink."

Within seconds Tim was sitting on an old settle in the hallway and, with trembling hands, gratefully took the glass of brandy offered by Mr Avon.

"It's Flora isn't it?"

Tim nodded. 'But how do you know... how do you know its Flora ... and who is she? Who is she?"

"Ah, Tim, I'd have thought a smart young man like you with a degree in classics would have been able to work that one out!"

"What do you mean?"

"Think back to your Roman mythology."

Tim rolled her name around his tongue, "Flora ... Flora ... Roman Goddess of the Flower...."

Mr Avon nodded.

"No," Tim shook his head. "It can't be ... this is madness ... you're telling me that Flora is the reincarnation of a Roman Goddess?"

Once again Mr Avon nodded.

"But how do you know?"

"Because I've made it my life's work to discover who she is."

"Why?"

Mr Avon sighed, "Because, Tim, fifty years ago, I too fell in love with Flora."

Tim stared at him, "You?"

Mr Avon smiled, "Yes, even me. I was young once you know!"

"But fifty years ago? I don't understand."

"Tim, Flora mirrors nature and, as such, germinates, blooms and falls to the reapers scythe, each season. But

295

every spring, she rises again, just as young and just as beautiful as last year, looking for a new lover, someone strong and virile to ensure the continuation of next year's crop."

Tim put his head in his hands, "This is bizarre, I just can't get my head around what you've just said but, if it is true, why didn't you warn me?"

"Oh, Tim, you would never have believed me and the only reason you're listening to me now is because of your own experience!

Mind you, I did try that day I took the letter addressed to her. I thought that if I delivered it then maybe you wouldn't become involved, that you would in some way be saved, but who am I, a mere mortal, to interfere in the will of the Gods?"

"So why did you choose to live here, so close to her, if you knew there was no future in it?" Tim asked.

"Because like you I was bewitched, I just wanted to be near her. I've never recovered from my... interlude and, foolishly, I thought I was different, I thought that she would return to me again, if only for a season. But, to no avail, for Flora's attentions are fleeting, a once in a lifetime experience."

Tim held his head in his hands, "My God, I feel such a fool."

"Ah well you're in good company, why do you think Colin, your predecessor, stayed with the same post round for twenty five years until he was no longer able to continue?"

"Him too?" Tim asked.

"Him too," Mr Avon confirmed.

The two men sat for a while in companionable silence, each reliving the moment they stepped into Flora's world.

"I know this may be of little comfort, Tim," said Mr Avon finally breaking the silence, "but if you do decide to stay on this post round, you will at least see Flora again next spring."

Tim looked at him, "But she'll never again invite me into her garden?"

Mr Avon shook his head, "No, Tim, she won't."'

Flora's Story:

'One day in early February when the sun shone through ice frosted windows the hard earth in the large clay pot in the tiny greenhouse began to crack and slowly, slowly, inch-by-inch, a new life was born.

Flora blinked in the early morning light and brushed the rich dark earth from her naked form. She caught sight of her reflection in the glass and was pleased with what she saw.

It looked as though this season's crop was without blight. She took the soft diaphanous gown of palest peridot from the hook behind the door and, throwing it around her shoulders, made her way into the cottage.

Gaining in strength over the next few days, Flora looked out into the garden and decided to begin with the maintenance jobs of mending the gate, weeding the path, tidying the beds and removing the algae from the greenhouse.

By early March the garden was filled with the yellow of spring and whilst tending the beds one crisp frosty morning, Flora was startled by a strange voice.

"Beautiful morning."

She turned and saw that the voice belonged to a pleasant young man who held a letter in his hand.

Her heart skipped a beat. Not yet surely? It was far

too early, but not wishing to be impolite she smiled at him but quickly made her way around the side of the cottage towards the back door.

A few days later, whilst tying up the wayward camellia around the front door, the same voice interrupted her work.

"Hello again."

She turned and smiled, also adding a little nod this time, noticing that the young postman held some letters in his hand.

"You always seem to have good weather in Lunscombe."

Flora laughed in response not wishing to be abrupt but knowing she could not afford to encourage him, after all, if he wasn't the one there would be little point. Seemingly undeterred by her lack of response, however, he tried again.

"Sadly I never seem to have any letters to deliver to you."

For a moment she felt a wave of disappointment, she felt sure that one of the letters he held would be for her and that it would contain the news she had been hoping for. Knowing however that she must await her instructions, she picked up her twine and secateurs and went indoors.

Just as dusk was falling later that day, Flora heard a dull thud on the mat in the hall and with a certain amount of excitement, brought a small brown envelope back into the kitchen. She opened it with trembling fingers and, after quickly scanning the page, smiled in satisfaction, for the letter contained the news she had been waiting for and, for a brief moment, she allowed herself to bathe in the pure human pleasure of eager anticipation.

Flora breathed in the intoxicating scent of May Day

morning as she walked out into her beautiful garden, wearing only the diaphanous peridot gown over her naked form.

Here she waited until she heard the postman's footsteps approaching along the lane then she began, her body moving seductively beneath the warming sun.

Flora danced. Danced to entrance, danced to bind, danced for her very life. She knew he was watching her and she danced until his yearning became tangible.

At last she beckoned to him and as he melted into her, she knew he was lost and his fate sealed.

His subsequent heartfelt pleas to see her tore her apart, but she knew that nothing could come of it. His task was accomplished and next years crop assured.

The season of the maiden is fleeting and as summer turned to autumn, Flora noticed her once youthful form beginning to fade into the ebbing light.

One golden October morning, she ventured into the garden in order to tidy the flowerbeds before winter closed in. She was weeding amongst the chrysanthemums when she heard his voice.

"Flora!"

She struggled to straighten, hastily pushing the escaping strands of wispy silver hair back into place and, as she turned to face him, the look of disappointment on his face was almost too much to bear.

"Oh," he said, "I'm sorry, I thought you were someone else, I was looking for Flora. I have a letter for her."

"You've found her," Flora said.

He looked bewildered and confused, "No," he said, "no, earlier this summer... I met her... here ... a young lady...."

"I am Flora."

He looked into her eyes and his image blurred a little as she fought back the tears.

"I don't understand," he whispered delivering the parcel into Flora's outstretched hand.

Flora looked down at the envelope and knew that this was the last time she would have any contact with him. "Ah," she said with a heavy heart, "It is time."

Flora sat that evening in her diaphanous peridot gown and stared at the envelope that held her fate. With a heavy heart, she placed the guard around the fire, checked that the doors and windows were secure and made her way into the greenhouse.

Here she carefully filled a large clay pot with rich dark soil and set it to one side, then with a sigh she leaned on the wooden bench and opened the padded envelope.

"Flora, Your season is ended, your work complete. The dark mother calls. It is time…."

Flora threw the letter in the little black bin outside the door and shook the remaining heavy item from the padded envelope.

Sitting down on an upturned plant pot she picked up the new secateurs and, with a resounding crunch, watched the newly grown sixth finger of her left hand fall onto the bench. Fighting the wave of nausea that followed, Flora picked up her finger and planted it carefully in the prepared clay pot, covering it liberally with earth. Her task complete, she removed her diaphanous peridot gown and hung it on the hook behind the door.

She opened the door of the little greenhouse with what strength she had left and, little by little, sank slowly into the rich, dark, earth.'

I sat and fumbled nervously with the sheets of paper,

shuffling them aimlessly into no particular order.

'Have you finished?' asked Mrs Darley.

'Yes, why?' I asked, 'Do you think the ending should be different, perhaps I could....'

She put her finger to her lips.

'I meant have you finished shuffling your papers?'

I smiled, placing them down on the table and waited for her verdict like an expectant school child.

'I know you're waiting for my comments,' she said. 'But what I think is quite irrelevant. It's what you think that matters.'

I nodded, knowing that she was right but feeling somewhat deflated at her lack of encouragement.

'But,' she smiled, leaning forward in order to fill my glass, 'For the record, my dear, you'd be a fool to stop now.'

Conclusion

Earth is the element that we perceive to be dependable and unchanging, something we think will always be here for us and yet, this is merely a myth that we have created.

Change is the only constant. It is the one aspect of existence of which we can be certain and the Earth is no exception. Our planet has and always will, until its eventual demise, continue to ebb and flow beneath our feet.

Earth is a living entity and as such is subject to both movement and moods. Within recent years however, our climate, seas, atmosphere and material resources have dramatically changed due to many varied factors, a selection of which include; CO_2 emissions, pollution, forestry destruction and the use of increased technology.

As part of humankind we cannot continue to bury our head in the sand, for much of what we are now experiencing stems from our lack of care in the treatment of the benevolent Mother upon which we live.

It stands to reason that if we treat the Earth with love and respect, then not only will She care for us in return, but we will also help to preserve this beautiful home for future generations.

Perhaps it is time to stop being selfish children and have a care for our precious parent.

Cariad
Cariad, Cariad
The earth's call comes,
Cariad listen to
Her beating drum.

In tree lined groves,
On barren moors,
In darkened caves
The earth's call comes.

Her vulva wakes,
Yields to the sun,
Cariad listen to
Her beating drum.

Chapter 5

Ether

Ether
Enveloping, surrounding,
Protecting, grounding.
Ethereal essence,
Divine presence.

Introduction

According to ancient and medieval science, ether or aether, which derives from the Greek word *'aither'*, meaning 'pure fresh air', or 'clear sky', refers to the material that fills the region of the universe above the terrestrial sphere. In Greek mythology it was considered to be the pure essence which the Gods breathed and in which they dwelt.

Aristotle included ether in the system of classical elements as the 'fifth element', or the *'quintessence'*, which was neither hot or cold, wet or dry and was a constant presence that did not change but simply moved in circles, away from and back to its source.

This sacred substance pervades everything we can imagine whether mineral, plant or animal. Each charged during its existence or life span with varying degrees of this divine energy and, once its life force is gone, the energy dissipates in a circular motion. Paracelcus called this the *'Archaeus'*, meaning 'the oldest principle' and described it as being of a magnetic nature, a substance which, although not enclosed in a body, radiates within and around it like a luminous sphere.

In 1608 Benedictus Figulus included in his compendium, 'Pandora magnalium naturalium', a verse by an unknown writer, which was translated into English in 1893 by A E Waite in his work, *The Golden and Blessed Casket of Nature's Marvels*. The following is an extract:

Wilt thou, by God's grace alone
Obtain the Stone of the Philosophers?
If so, seek it not in vegetables or animals,
In sulphur, quicksilver, and minerals;
Vitriol, alum, and salt are of no value;
Lead, tin, iron and copper profit nothing;
Silver and gold have no efficacy...
It is enclosed in our salt spring,
In the tree of the Moon and of the Sun.
I call it the Flower of Honey,
The Flower known to the Wise.
In fine, the Flower and Honey
Are the Sulphur and Quicksilver of the Wise,
Even water and earth,
With the whitish seed of all metals.
The water is volatile, the earth fixed;
One can effect nothing without the other...
The gods also have bestowed it upon man
As a singularly great gift,
Designed to assuage and comfort him...
Who will vouchsafe to enlighten our understanding,
That we may separate the dry from the moist.
Thus water is produced from earth,
The volatile from the fixed,
The animated spirit on the earth.

Water and earth, two visible elements,
Have, by God's grace and care,
Fire and air concealed within them.
They are also purely impregnated
With the fifth invisible nature...

Thus ether is an enigma, a paradox. It is invisible yet can be perceived, it cannot be felt yet it can be sensed, it is divine in nature yet it is not the Divine. It is the spark that pervades all and it is for each one of us to ponder upon and discover its meaning for ourselves, hence resting in our own truth.

Mrs Darley Tale: Ethereal knowledge

I was in Tintagel when the snow began to fall one late afternoon in mid February; I hurried to finish my appointment as I was anxious to be on the road before darkness fell.

Driving out of the village, I wound my way around the country lanes until I finally came to the A39 and knew I had to make a decision between taking the main road or, risking the shorter route, across the remote and unforgiving Davidstow Moor.

Even on a sunny day, the emptiness of this part of Bodmin Moor always made me a little uneasy. The flat moorland which surrounded the single track road rose up dramatically in the far distance towards the highest points of Cornwall's landscape, those of Rough Tor and Brown Willy, whilst marshes and bogs lay in wait for those who ventured away from the main paths.

The shorter distance, however, tempted me and, as darkness closed in, I found myself rattling across the cattle grid that heralded the gateway to the moorland road.

Mrs Darley's Pagan Elements

The snow, which was a rare occurrence in Cornwall, hurled itself into the headlights, clawing at the car as I drove along. A lone sheep stepped out onto the road just ahead of me and I slithered to an ungainly halt, well aware of the ditch that bordered the narrow strip of tarmac.

The wheels began to spin as I moved forward and, as the car stalled, I suddenly experienced a wave of panic at the thought of being stuck in the middle of the moor. My imagination also decided to add to my increasingly anxious state as it reminded me of unworldly tales associated with this part of the moor and for once I wished that Mrs Darley's story telling had not been quite so vivid.

The tale of Charlotte Dymond hovered at the edge of my mind and as the snow flurried and swirled around me, I could almost see her ghost dancing through the flakes.

Back in 1844 Charlotte Dymond had become the lover of Matthew Weeks and both were in service together at Penhale Farm on the outskirts of Davidstow Moor, which was then owned by a sixty-one-year old widow called Phillipa Peters.

Matthew was besotted with Charlotte and, although he was not the most handsome of men, he had inherited a little money which made him better dressed than many men of his social standing. Their relationship however was threatened by a rival for Charlotte's affections, one Thomas Prout, the nephew of Mrs Peters.

One day in late March, Thomas told Matthew that soon he would be moving to Penhale and that Matthew would then be deprived of Charlotte, a fact that Matthew did not take to too kindly.

On Sunday 14 April 1844, the servants, following their usual weekly routine, changed their clothes and around 4pm Charlotte and Matthew went out together. Upon leaving the farm, Charlotte indicated that Matthew would be back in time to milk the cows but that she would not.

Early that evening, a relative of Mrs Peters called at the farm and mentioned in passing that earlier that afternoon he had seen Matthew with a young woman walking on the moor. He had recognised Matthew from his limp, but could not say who the woman was. It was a rule that all servants had to be in by 9.30pm and although Matthew returned that evening, Charlotte did not.

The following day, Charlotte was still missing and Mrs Peters noticed that Matthew's stockings, which had been clean on Sunday, were muddy up to the knees.

As the week progressed suspicion grew and so Mrs Peters and her daughter searched Matthew's room. The only items they found however were two handkerchiefs and a newspaper cutting. Matthew was questioned by his employer, but denied all knowledge of Charlotte's whereabouts. One week later, Matthew dressed in his clean Sunday clothes and left Penhale Farm never to return.

Upon inspecting the dirty clothes Matthew had left behind, not only did Mrs Peters see the muddy stockings but also noticed that his shirt collar was torn and splattered with blood. This evidence prompted a police search of the moor, which finally revealed the body of a woman alongside Roughtor Ford. The body in question was that of Charlotte Dymond, whose throat had been cut from left to right, inflicting a wound so deep that it had pierced her vertebrae.

The search for Matthew Weeks began in earnest and, although he was not to be found at his parent's house at Larrick, he was finally arrested at his sister's home in

Plymouth, from where he had intended to escape to the Channel Islands.

On the 2 August 1844, Matthew Weeks was tried at Bodmin Assizes and found guilty of murder. He was hanged on 12 August the same year and his body buried in the coal yard adjacent to the prison.

Since that time, Charlotte's ghost had been reportedly seen by many who had ventured out across the wild and barren landscape of Roughtor Moor including the many soldiers who had inhabited the area around the time of the Second World War.

I shuddered as I re-started the engine and it was with great relief that I eventually rumbled over the cattle grid which signalled the end of the open moor. Within forty minutes I saw the familiar outline of the cottages and with a grateful sigh pulled onto my allotted parking space.

'Hello, dear.' I jumped as Mrs Darley's voice added to my already jangling nerves.

I lifted my head into the blizzard and saw Mrs Darley leaning over the half stable door.

'Hello,' I called, 'I'm so pleased to be back home tonight in this weather.'

'I'm glad to see you back, my dear, I think the snow is settling in for the night, I doubt you'll get to work in the morning, still never mind. Sleep well, my dear, goodnight.'

The following morning I opened one eye as the alarm went off and knew instantly that the snow had indeed continued throughout the night, for the room was flooded with an unfamiliar white light, accompanied by a tangible silence, both trademarks of a substantial snowfall.

Upon looking out, my suspicions were confirmed and, after making my obligatory phone call into work, I decided to spend the day tidying out some long overdue cupboards.

Around midday the phone rang, immediately putting an end to my cupboard tidying as Mrs Darley asked me to join her next door for homemade chicken soup.

Once we had settled down at the table with a bowl of steaming soup and a chunk of herb bread, the subject inevitably turned to the weather and I commented on how lovely it was to experience snow in Cornwall. I also admitted however to feeling rather anxious as I crossed Davidstow Moor the previous evening.

'Why was that, dear?' Mrs Darley asked.

I smiled. 'Sometimes I think your story telling is a little too vivid and my imagination begins to play tricks. I could quite easily have convinced myself that the ghost of Charlotte Dymond was walking through the snow on the moor last night.'

'Ah,' said Mrs Darley, 'yet another encounter with the fifth element.'

'Is this the mysterious element you once told me I had to discover for myself?' I asked.

Mrs Darley nodded, 'The fifth element is that which surrounds every living thing, that which houses the seat of the spirit, that which holds the blueprint of the physical body before birth and that which is last to dissipate after death.'

I looked at her aghast. 'I don't understand,' I said.

'Ether, dear. Ether!'

I shook my head, 'I'm still lost.'

'We are, you see, far more than this physical body, for we are surrounded by an energy field, which extends far beyond our physical form.'

As she spoke, the faint glimmer of familiarity skimmed my mind, for somewhere in the not too distant past I had heard the term 'energy field' before.

Seemingly out of no where, the memory of our day out in Avebury suddenly ran through my head as I remembered my strange encounter with the mysterious man in the antique shop and the explanation he gave concerning energy fields for the appearance of crop circles and my subsequent headache.

'So,' Mrs Darley continued, 'every living thing has an energy field, or an aura as it is sometimes known.'

'So why can't we see it?' I asked.

'Some people can,' she replied, 'in fact we all can if we try. Like most things it just takes practice but that is where the majority of humankind comes unstuck, for although we love the results that practice brings, we dislike its boring and repetitive nature. However, we must remember that the quality of the fruit is always determined by the quality of the labour.'

'Practice! How?' I asked, for now I was intrigued.

Mrs Darley sighed, 'Now that's an afternoon's conversation in itself, but I promise it is a subject to which we will return.'

I nodded, feeling somewhat disappointed but accepting that her promise would have to suffice.

'However,' she continued, 'a simpler answer to your question of "why can't we see it?" is simply because of its rate of vibration. You see, ether vibrates so quickly that it cannot normally be perceived by the naked eye.

Just think for a moment of the elements. Earth as a substance is dense, tangible and its molecular structure vibrates slower than any of the other elements, therefore we can touch it, feel it, mould it, shape it. Water on the other hand vibrates slightly quicker, yes, we can still touch it and feel it, yet it is liquid, it flows from our grasp, we are unable to mould it and can only be held within a container. Then we come to fire, which is faster still in its vibration. It flickers and dances, we can both see and feel it and yet we cannot hold it. Air of course is totally without shape or form and vibrates so quickly that although we can feel it, we cannot see it and are only able to perceive its effects upon the world around us, through the movement of trees or the whipping up of the sea. Then, my dear, there is ether, a substance whose vibration is faster than the wind.'

She paused for a moment and I stepped in. 'Presumably then, as far as ether goes, we are unable to hold it, touch it, feel it or see it?'

Mrs Darley smiled, 'I see where your thinking is taking you but, like the wind, ether too can be felt, for it is simply an energetic extension of who we are. All of us, whether we care to admit it or not, are capable of picking up on other people's energy. Quite often when someone walks into the room the whole atmosphere changes, sometimes for the better, occasionally for the worse and the factor that makes the difference is the imprint of their energy.

You see, our etheric field has many roles. It protects, it predicts, it records, it responds and, as mentioned previously, it houses the spirit. It is, my dear, a very valuable extension of who we are and one which we will discuss in greater detail at some point in the future.'

I could feel the emergence of a hundred questions and chose to ask the one which forced itself to the forefront of my mind.

'You said it houses the spirit?'

Mrs Darley nodded.

'Is that the same as the soul?'

'Ah,' she smiled, 'Now that is something which has long been a question of debate. For me the answer is *no*,

311

for others it may be *yes*, although I consider both to be divine in nature. As with anything in this world, my dear, you have to search for your own truth.

In most orthodox religions the belief is that the all powerful creator made us, yet we are not worthy to consider ourselves as having any part of Him or Her within us, i.e. we are not in any way, shape or form divine.

Some occultist beliefs, however, vary slightly in that although we appreciate that we are not the Divine, we do believe that we carry a spark of divinity within us, a spark which journeys through many lifetimes, and ultimately reunites with the source. Now that to me is the soul.

I believe that when the soul incarnates into the physical body, the flame of life is lit and that is what I consider to be the spirit. To me, spirit is the essence of life that sits within the etheric body. It ignites at our birth and evaporates at our death, which brings me back to the subject that first launched this discussion ... that of Charlotte Dymond's ghost.'

So intrigued was I by what I had heard, that I had completely forgotten about Charlotte and the anxiety she had caused me the previous evening.

'You see,' Mrs Darley continued, 'although the etheric body normally dissipates gradually at death, I believe that when someone meets with a violent or unhappy end, their etheric imprint, their life essence if you like, somehow remains upon the earth plain and continues to be replayed to those who are sensitive enough to perceive these higher vibrations of energy.

The same thing happens when someone in spirit wishes to contact us with a message and it is more often than not merely their energy imprint that re-emerges....

312

Remember Mariella?'

I nodded as I sat in silence for a few moments with the memory of little Mariella dancing through my mind as I allowed this fascinating new information to whirl around my head,

'So Charlotte still walks because she is not at peace,' I said, almost to myself, 'I find that strange, given that her murderer was brought to justice.'

'Who says Matthew Weeks was actually her murderer?' Mrs Darley asked. 'Have you perhaps considered the fact that Charlotte still walks because her real murderer was never caught?'

'But the evidence…,' I began.

'Was purely circumstantial,' said Mrs Darley. 'Remember, there was no forensic science then, the case was built merely on hearsay and spurious sightings. Matthew Weeks probably ran away because he could see the conspiracy building against him and he was, understandably, a frightened young man.

It is so easy, my dear, to become caught up in the ideas and thought trains of those whom we perceive to be more knowledgeable than ourselves but, as I mentioned earlier, we must all search for our own truth in all aspects of life. You see, it is only by reaching our own conclusions and living in a way that feels right for us as individuals that we ever truly achieve the maxim that is written over the entrance of the temple at Delphi. Quite simply; "Know thyself".'

'I wonder if any of us really do?' I asked.

Mrs Darley smiled, 'Now that,' she said, 'is the true quest of the spirit.'

****

313

Mrs Darley's Pagan Elements

Eternity

Burn my remains in the fires of our fathers,
Enfold my ash in the arms of the earth,
Carry my soul on the sweet breath of heaven,
Throw wide the door which leads to my birth.

Wash away mourning with tears of your sorrow
For the spirit of me has long flown away,
But still my soul lives through the mist of illusion,
Remaining forever a heartbeat away.

Other Titles by Mirage Publishing

Paperback Non-fiction Books

A Prescription from The Love Doctor: How to find Love in 7 Easy Steps - Dr Joanne 'The Love Doctor' Coyle

Burnt: One Man's Inspiring Story of Survival - Ian Colquhoun

Cosmic Ordering Guide - Stephen Richards

Cosmic Ordering: Sex Energy - Stephen Richards

Cosmic Ordering: You Can be Successful - Stephen Richards

Die Laughing: War Humour from WW1 to Present Day - George Korankye

Hidden Secrets: Attract Everything You Want! – Carl Nagel

Internet Dating King's Diaries: Life, Dating and Love – Clive Worth

Life Without Lottie: How I survived my Daughter's Gap Year - Fiona Fridd

Mrs Darley's Moon Mysteries: A Celebration of Moon Lore and Magic – Carole Carlton

Mrs Darley's Pagan Whispers: A Celebration of Pagan Festivals, Sacred Days, Spirituality and Traditions of the Year – Carole Carlton

Rebel Diet: They Don't Want You to Have It! – Emma James

The Real Office: An Uncharacteristic Gesture of Magnanimity by Management Supremo Hilary Wilson-Savage - Hilary Wilson-Savage

The Tumbler: Kassa (Košice) – Auschwitz – Sweden - Israel - Azriel Feuerstein (Holocaust survivor)

Paperback fiction Books

I Can See Clearly Now The Rain Is Gone - George Korankye (This incorporates a factual event of the Dunblane massacre into a highly sensitive work of faction.)

E-Books
7 Day Focusing Plan - Stephen Richards
Beating Procrastination – Stephen Richards
Boost Your Self Esteem- Stephen Richards
Forgiveness and Love Conquers All: Releasing You from the Past - Stephen Richards
FREE 7 Day Confidence & Ego-boost Affirmations- Stephen Richards
Releasing You From Self-limiting Beliefs - Stephen Richards
Supercharge Your Self-confidence – Stephen Richards
Think Your Way To Success - Stephen Richards

Cosmic Ordering Series in *CD& MP3* format
Cosmic Ordering Connection - Stephen Richards
Cosmic Ordering: Chakra Clearing - Stephen Richards
Cosmic Ordering: Rapid Chakra Clearing – Stephen Richards
The Ultimate Cosmic Ordering Meditation– Stephen Richards
The Ultimate Cosmic Ordering Meditation - Stephen Richards

Releasing you from series in CD& MP3format
Releasing You From Fear CD& MP3 - Stephen Richards
Releasing You From Insomnia CD& MP3 - Stephen Richards

Releasing You From Social Anxiety CD& MP3 -
Stephen Richards

The Ultimate series in CD& MP3format
The Ultimate Confidence & Ego Boost CD& MP3 -
Stephen Richards
The Ultimate Self Hypnosis CD& MP3 - Stephen
Richards
The Ultimate Stop Smoking CD& MP3 - Stephen
Richards
The Ultimate Success in Love CD& MP3 - Stephen
Richards
The Ultimate Wealth Creation CD& MP3 - Stephen
Richards
The Ultimate Weight Loss CD& MP3 - Stephen
Richards

Mini-series Paperbacks
Coming soon, check Mirage Publishing site

See these titles at:

www.miragepublishing.com

&

www.cosmicordering.net

Submissions of Mind, Body & Spirit, Self Improvement
and
How To manuscripts welcomed from new authors.
www.miragepublishing.com